GLADSTONE

A Bicentenary Portrait

GLADSTONE

A Bicentenary Portrait

WILLIAM GLADSTONE

William Gladstone

for David & Emily, July 2012
with thanks

MICHAEL RUSSELL

© William Gladstone 2009

The right of Sir William Gladstone
to be identified as the author of this work
has been asserted by him in accordance with the
Copyright, Designs and Patents Act, 1988

First published in Great Britain 2009
by Michael Russell (Publishing) Ltd
Wilby Hall, Wilby, Norwich NR16 2JP

Page makeup in Sabon by Waveney Typesetters
Wymondham, Norfolk
Printed and bound in Great Britain
by the MPG Books Group
Bodmin and King's Lynn

ISBN 978-0-85955-317-9

Contents

Introduction

W. E. Gladstone masterminded Britain's transition from aristocratic to democratic government, and he conceived and pioneered the concept of a fair and even inclusive society. He was the first statesman to communicate with the masses, and people travelled for many miles in the hope merely of catching a glimpse of him. His portrait hung in countless cottage parlours in admiration for what he had achieved for those who lived in them. Of all our premiers, only Winston Churchill has rivalled him in fame and in public esteem. He was fearless of the vested interests whose wrath he called down upon his head, and tolerant of nonconformity not only in religion but in all walks of life. This volume is a tribute to his memory at the bicentenary of his birth, but it is a portrait which paints him, as he himself would have wished and expected, 'warts and all'.

I have addressed my book to the general reader, although I hope there may be something in it for those whose particular interest is history, especially of Victorian times. I have tried to show who Gladstone was, as well as something of what he did. Here and there I have shed a rather different light on him from Roy Jenkins, the most recent author of a one-volume biography, and Richard Shannon whose work extends to two substantial volumes. The illustrations are mostly of documents which have remained in Gladstone's home at Hawarden and which have not previously been open to the public eye. Some of them are trivial in terms of their historical importance, but a few of them are of some significance. I have also included a few pages from printed works, illustrative of his life and times.

Gladstone's life was so long and complicated – far more so than that of any other Victorian statesman – that it is not easy to write a short book which gets close to the man and at the same time shows him tackling the problems which most concerned him. I have used the method rather of the dramatist than the biographer. I have presented him in a series of scenes. I have described his upbringing in Liverpool, recognised in those days as the second richest city in the world, second only to London. The atmosphere of his home was ambitiously commercial and oppressively religious. I have described him at Eton, where he made some lifelong friendships; and at Christ Church, Oxford, where he obtained his double first in classics and mathematics as Peel had done twenty-five years earlier; and he later represented the University in Parliament, as Peel had done, until he was rejected (as Peel had been) for his unacceptable politics. I have shown him in his first forays in the House of Commons, and then as a minister under Peel, to whom he owed so much. Then comes the scene in which, by cunning tactics and careful preparation of his case, he surprised and defeated Disraeli and succeeded him as Chancellor of the Exchequer.

The later scenes show how he became The People's William and then The Grand Old Man. There are two chapters on his foreign policy, one of them on the emergent nation of Italy and the other on the Bulgarian Atrocities, the subject of his most famous pamphlet. Gladstone's last two ministries were much preoccupied with 'the primacy of Ireland' and here I have made an exception and instead of presenting a scene I have written a continuous narrative.

Gladstone left an immense personal archive, and this has enabled historians to understand the way in which his ideas developed and changed over the course of his long life. He did carry through life some assumptions – his awareness of the presence of God, his respect for British institutions, his instinct for the joy of life and the beauty of the human form, for instance – but his political, religious and aesthetic ideas changed with the passing years. His open-mindedness and rejection of prejudice led him to abandon many of his early notions. In this respect he moved slowly, and his thought continued to develop into old age. He was not a Liberal ('in the sense of Party', as he put it) until he reached the age of fifty. He is often described as a High Churchman, but he started as an evangelical and ended as a middle-of-the-road Anglican in the Catholic tradition. I have therefore added to the 'scenes' some chapters which can be described as 'themes', looking at the evolution of his ideas and looking too at his Scottishness, which was a stronger influence than his Liverpool childhood, and his growing respect and affection for Wales, where he lived for half his lifetime.

In the 1880s Gladstone built a muniment room adjacent to his 'Temple of Peace' at Hawarden specifically to contain his own papers. John Morley used them when he wrote his magnificent biography, published in three volumes in 1903 after many months of labour at

Hawarden. Morley was an atheist, and it was agreed that he would not deal with Gladstone's personal religious beliefs; and not surprisingly he missed some important issues. Nevertheless he admired and understood Gladstone, who had relied on him as his chief support in the Cabinet over his Irish policy. The qualities which served Morley well then, including clarity of thought and the ability to master the complexities of big political issues, served him well as a biographer. His Life is still essential reading.

Morley's selection of documents of political interest, including the hand-written agenda and minutes of almost all the Cabinet meetings during Gladstone's four ministries and a mass of memoranda and correspondence, were given by the family to the nation. They were catalogued by Arthur Tilney Bassett and housed in a room of their own at the British Museum – a unique privilege for an individual, though one they no longer enjoy in the modern British Library which has replaced it. The non-political papers were sorted by Bassett into about sixty boxes and they have been deposited at Gladstone's Library, St Deiniol's, in Hawarden, and catalogued by the County Record Office nearby – in the former rectory where Gladstone's brother-in-law, son and son-in-law resided as incumbents of the parish. Together with the 32,000 of Gladstone's own books, often heavily annotated in his hand, which form the core of this library, they throw light on his private life, his friendships, and on his literary, classical and theological interests. They attract scholars from many countries who may wish to discover what Gladstone thought of a particular book or author.

After his death there was much discussion as to a suitable destination for Gladstone's diaries, a personal and often intimate record of his daily life from the age of sixteen until his mid-eighties. He had not destroyed them, so presumably he intended that they should be preserved. But if so, should they be kept private or should they be published? It was decided after discussions in 1926 to give them to the Archbishop of Canterbury. That meant that they would be kept at Lambeth Palace Library, and that the Archbishop of the day would decide whether they should be published. Eventually, after the publication of Sir Philip Magnus's biography of Gladstone in 1955 had awakened new interest in his subject, it was decided, with the family's support, to publish them. The first volume appeared in 1968, the last in 1994. The introduction to Volume One by M. R. D. Foot, the first editor, tells the story and assesses the character of the diaries, which were not literary works but summaries, often laconic, of the way the author spent his time. Foot's successor, Colin Matthew, introduced many Cabinet and other memoranda and letters to enrich the later volumes.

There is, of course, a mass of printed material to support these manuscripts, including the thousands of pages of Gladstone's speeches, in and out of Parliament. Each of his longer speeches in the House of Commons takes up to seventy to eighty pages in a standard textbook (about the same as the number of columns in Hansard). Then there are his prolific published works. But it is from the manuscripts that one can best follow his thoughts from day to day and understand the nature of the man. I have described a few of his speeches and some of his published books in these sketches, whether as 'scenes' or 'themes', but I have relied mainly on his manuscripts to compose my portrait. I hope that it may encourage some of my readers to look further.

Chronology

1840 *Church Principles Considered in Their Results* published

1841 PEEL SUCCEEDS MELBOURNE AS PRIME MINISTER
Re-elected for Newark
Vice-President of the Board of Trade

1843 President of the Board of Trade

1844 Railways Act

1845 Resigns from Cabinet (January)
Colonial Secretary (December)
Retires from Newark seat

1846 RUSSELL SUCCEEDS PEEL AS PRIME MINISTER
Out of office

1847 Elected MP for Oxford University
Oak Farm financial crisis

1850 Death of Jessy aged five
In Naples
Death of Peel

1851 Hope and Manning become RCs
Writes 'open letters' on government of Naples

1852 DERBY PRIME MINISTER (FEBRUARY–DECEMBER), SUCCEEDED
BY ABERDEEN
Re-elected for Oxford University
Speaks on Disraeli's budget
Becomes Chancellor of the Exchequer

1853 Re-elected for Oxford University
First Budget

1854 Second Budget
Oxford University Bill
May: War Budget

1855 PALMERSTON SUCCEEDS ABERDEEN AS PRIME MINSTER
Out of office
Speeches on reform of Civil Service

1857 Protests against unequal treatment of men and women in Divorce Bill

1858 *Studies on Homer and the Homeric Age* published
Lord High Commissioner for the Ionian Islands
DERBY PRIME MINISTER (FEBRUARY 1858– JUNE 1859)

1859 PALMERSTON PRIME MINISTER
Re-elected for Oxford University (three times in 1859, twice unopposed)
Chancellor of the Exchequer
Rector of Edinburgh University

1860 Budget
Commercial Treaty with France

1861 Post Office Savings Bill
Budget

1862 Budget

1863 Budget

1864 Budget
Speech on reform causes sensation

1865 Budget
Defeated in Oxford University election
Becomes MP for South Lancashire
Death of Palmerston
RUSSELL PRIME MINISTER (OCTOBER 1865–JUNE 1866)

1866 Budget
Exchequer and Audit Act
THE 'DERBY–DISRAELI' MINISTRY (DERBY PRIME MINISTER JUNE 1866– FEBRUARY 1868, DISRAELI FEBRUARY–DECEMBER 1868)

1868 Resolutions for Irish Church Disestablishment
Elected MP for Greenwich
Defeated in S.W. Lancashire
BECOMES PRIME MINISTER (DECEMBER)

1869 Irish Church Disestablishment Act
Juventus Mundi published

1870 Irish Land Bill
Elementary Education Bill
Peace Preservation (Ireland) Bill
Secret Ballot Bill

1871 Abolition of purchase of Army commissions
University Tests Bill
Army Regulation Bill
Parochial Councils Bill
Licensing Bill

1872 Alabama arbitration award by International Court
Death of the Revd Henry Glynne

1873 Irish University Bill
Becomes Chancellor of the Exchequer

1874 Dissolution of Parliament
RESIGNS AS PRIME MINISTER, SUCCEEDED BY DISRAELI
Re-elected MP for Greenwich
Death of Sir Stephen Glynne
The Vatican Decrees published
Resigns as Liberal Leader

1875 Sells 11, Carlton House Terrace

1876 Buys 73, Harley Street (sold 1882)
Death of Lord Lyttelton
The Bulgarian Horrors published
Speech at Blackheath
Homeric Synchronism published
Disraeli becomes Earl of Beaconsfield

1877 Resolutions on Eastern Question
Inauguration of National Liberal Federation
Visits Ireland
Elected Rector of Glasgow University

1878   73, Harley Street windows smashed by mob
       Speaks against Disraeli's imperial policy

1879   Accepts Midlothian nomination
       First Midlothian campaign
       Gleanings of Past Years published

1880   Second Midlothian Campaign
       Elected MP for Midlothian (and for Leeds)
       BECOMES PRIME MINISTER AND CHANCELLOR OF THE
       EXCHEQUER
       Compensation for Disturbance Bill (Ireland)
       Budget
       (1st) Boer War begins
       Irish Land Bill planned

1881   Army defeated at Majuba
       Budget
       Second Irish Land Bill
       Death of Lord Beaconsfield (Disraeli)
       Parnell arrested

1882   Budget
       Kilmainham Treaty: Parnell released
       Phoenix Park murders
       Arrears Bill
       Coercion Bill
       Bombardment of Alexandria
       House of Commons rules introduced to counter obstruction
       Succeeded as Chancellor of Exchequer by Childers

1883   Severe insomnia
       Visits Cannes
       Baltic cruise in *Pembroke Castle*
       Reform Bill prepared

1884   Gordon sent to evacuate Sudan (January)
       Reform Bill passes Commons, defeated in Lords
       Reintroduced and passed as Redistribution Bill
       Wolseley sent to rescue Gordon (September)

1885 Death of Gordon at Khartoum (February)
Afghanistan crisis
Government resigns on defeat of Budget
SALISBURY PRIME MINISTER (JUNE 1885– FEBRUARY 1886)
Baltic cruise in *Sunbeam*
Negotiations with Parnell
Re-elected MP for Midlothian
'Hawarden Kite'– conversion to Home Rule

1886 PRIME MINISTER (FEBRUARY–AUGUST)
First Home Rule Bill and third Land Bill
Chamberlain and Trevelyan resign
Home Rule Bill defeated in Commons
General Election: Tory majority
RESIGNS AS PRIME MINISTER, SUCCEEDED BY SALISBURY

1887 Welsh tour and Swansea visit

1889 West Country tour
Golden wedding
In Paris for French Revolution Centenary

1890 O'Shea divorce, resignation of Parnell

1891 Death of eldest son W. H. Gladstone

1892 Re-elected for Midlothian
Autobiographical studies
PRIME MINISTER FOR FOURTH TIME
Romanes Lecture at Oxford

1893 Second Home Rule Bill passed in Commons, defeated in Lords
Navy 'scare'

1894 RESIGNS AS PRIME MINISTER, SUCCEEDED BY ROSEBERY
Cataract operation
1895 Cruise in *Tantallon Castle*: Kiel Canal

1896 Publications on Bishop Butler
Speech on Armenia
ROSEBERY SUCCEEDED AS PRIME MINISTER BY SALISBURY

1898 Dies at Hawarden (19 May)
       Lying in state (26–7 May)
       State funeral and burial in Westminster Abbey (28 May)

1900 Death of Catherine Gladstone

I

Liverpool

Exactly who first said that Gladstone was 'Oxford on the surface but Liverpool underneath' is unknown, but words to that effect were repeated from time to time during his early political career. One can see what was meant, and although the northern vowels never entirely left him, the truth was subtly different from what was intended. The influence was not that of Liverpool, but of Scotland: indeed he was once (at least) referred to as 'a lowlander handcuffed to a highlander' and those who know Scotland (or have read one of Gladstone's literary heroes, Walter Scott) will understand the truth of that phrase too.

Gladstone's parents were in fact a lowlander and a highlander. His mother, Anne, a Robertson from Dingwall, brought what Gladstone called the 'narrow evangelical discipline' to the family. His father, John, son of a prosperous Leith corn merchant, brought the thoroughness of a successful trader.

The Gladstones are first recorded in Lanarkshire in the thirteenth century – one of them was knighted on the field of Crecy – and in Lanarkshire many of them remained for centuries, most of them around Biggar and Liberton, proprietors or tenants of farms including the Glead Stanes, the origin of the name, with the boulders on the hill where the kites or 'gleads' perched, the scavengers of the Middle Ages. W. E. Gladstone's grandfather, trading corn in Leith, the port of Edinburgh, was working the Baltic and the north German cities. But the Baltic was not big enough for his eldest son, who migrated to Liverpool to trade the Atlantic, and indeed the oceans of the world, to feed South Lancashire's burgeoning population during the Industrial Revolution. He succeeded largely because of his thoroughness, riding many hundreds of miles each summer judging the English harvest, and with spies in Cornwall reporting the ships entering the Channel. It was John Gladstone's method that he should know everything knowable about his market and certainly that he should know more than any of his rivals. In a bad year, as he once said, 'If our competitors survive we must reap a profit.' It was a particular strength of his youngest son,

William Ewart, that he always endeavoured to know whatever there was to know about the subject under debate in the Cabinet or the House of Commons.

John became one of the merchant princes of Liverpool as it grew into the second richest city in the world. The investment of his energy and his cash into many ventures, beginning with corn from the United States (he and his partners sent the very first convoy after the War of Independence) and ending with railways in the 1840s, are a commentary on the economic history of his times. He built his first substantial house in Rodney Street, named in honour of that Admiral's victory in 1782 over the French fleet at the Battle of the Saintes in the West Indies, an important event in Liverpool's trade in sugar. It was in Rodney Street that his fourth and youngest son William was born in 1809. It was from there that in 1812 John Gladstone persuaded Canning to represent the city in Parliament by offering to pay his election expenses.

John's success in promoting Canning as a member for Liverpool transformed his position from being one of a group of leading merchants into the leading light in the city, a view which would not admittedly have been shared by William Roscoe and his supporters whose candidate was Brougham. Canning and Brougham were the two most scintillating orators of their day, drawing the attention of the whole country to the election in which, in comparison with the less politically realistic Roscoe, Gladstone's organisation was ruthlessly efficient. Canning's success won him a role in the Commons as the leading advocate of the commercial needs not only of Liverpool but also of Manchester and the other great manufacturing and trading cities of England. Canning's supporters included both disillusioned Whigs and Tories who were more adventurous and reformist than the Liverpool Corporation: it was Canning occupying this middle ground who enabled electors in these two traditions to forget their differences and provide Liverpool with a balanced political position for fifteen important years.

On several evenings during the election of 1812 Canning addressed an excited crowd from an upper window in Gladstone's house in Rodney Street. When the result was declared he and the other elected member, General Gascoyne, were chaired and carried round the town. That evening, little Willy, almost three years old, was brought into the drawing room, stood upon a chair, and pronounced the words 'Ladies and Gentlemen', his first public speech. Some years later, while staying with the Gladstones, it was Canning who spotted William's precocious intelligence and persuaded John to send him to Eton, where as a loyal Liverpudlian he would defend his native town in schoolboy rivalries; and he was aware of a sense of homecoming when in 1865, rejected by Oxford, he arrived in Lancashire 'unmuzzled'.

John Gladstone soon wanted something grander than the house in Rodney Street, and built a mansion in the Palladian style on the sands to the north of the city, naming it Seaforth House in honour of his wife's home ground. Seaforth House and its estate later became the patrimony of the youngest of John's four sons, William. By the middle of his life all had disappeared under streets and houses, except St Thomas's Church, built at John's expense. The Fasque estate which John acquired in Scotland after his retirement from Liverpool went to the eldest son, Tom, and the second, Robertson, inherited the Liverpool business. The third, John, became a captain in the Royal Navy and died quite young.

About 1865 Tom Gladstone and William fell out: 'Uncle Tom, grubous and grim' as Catherine said. Robertson became one of Gladstone's most trusted correspondents and advisers (although there had been a glitch in their friendship when Robertson married a Unitarian). Now, when under stress, Gladstone would frequently write to or visit his brother in Liverpool, who invariably supported him with shrewd and generally reassuring comments. Robertson was a successful businessman and an esteemed citizen, twice becoming mayor. But he was not an entrepreneur, and as the world changed around him, neither he nor his six tall, eccentric bachelor sons had the inclination to come to terms with new commercial opportunities.

Robertson built a fine house, Court Hey, north of the city, and drove to the office in Union Court in a buggy drawn by eight sheep, wearing a specially built low top hat in a forlorn endeavour to disguise his immense size. He acquired for Court Hey the stone railway sleepers on which the Rocket had won the Rainhill trials, on that terrible day, never forgotten by the family, when Huskisson, MP for Liverpool and Home Secretary, had been run down by the train and fatally injured. Lining the drive, they are the only surviving feature of Court Hey deriving from the Gladstone ownership. Commercial activity in Liverpool by members of the family gradually petered out before the Second World War.

The Gladstone dock was built in the 1930s (named after Robert or Robertson, not William) to accommodate the largest ocean liners, but the investment paid its national dividend when it became the head-quarters of the Royal Navy during the Battle of the Atlantic. The swarm of dock labourers and the weaving horse-drawn carts and motor lorries, which could be observed from the overhead railway running from the Pierhead to the northernmost docks, declined gradually in the postwar era as massive cranes and gantries began to handle containers. All these docks are now a ghost-town and it is said that 400 workers can handle more cargo than 40,000 could in days gone by. They work at the Seaforth Dock. Few people realise that it was John Gladstone who initiated the name of Seaforth after his wife's clan when, having grown out of the house in Rodney Street, he built his mansion to the north of the city.

But it is not in commerce that the sole residual Gladstonian influence in Liverpool remains. In 1893 Gladstone bought the advowson of Liverpool Parish, enabling him to present – that is to say to select – a man of sound churchmanship as the rector of Liverpool, incumbent of the much loved 'St Nick's', and his successor still owns the advowson today. It was not known whether there was any other bidder. In 1898 the sale of advowsons was made illegal by Act of Parliament. By the rules of H. M. Revenue they therefore have no value and are thus not subject to inheritance tax. Perhaps this residual Gladstonian influence will survive.

2
Eton

Gladstone went to Eton in September 1821, just before his twelfth birthday, and stayed until December 1827. It was a rough and ready place, with disputes settled by fights and with its education confined to the classics, some mathematics, and French. There was a Chapel service daily, but no attempt at religious instruction.

In July 1825 Gladstone began to keep a diary, which he continued until failing eyesight prevented him in 1896. This, together with his letters home and the autobiographical essays he wrote in the 1890s, gives a vivid account of his life at school. The autobiographical notes include a description of Dr Keate, the formidable head master, who maintained discipline by the force of his personality and by flogging: 'To him nature had accorded a stature of only about five feet, or say five feet one; but by costume, voice, manner (including a little swagger) and character he made himself in every way the capital figure on the Eton stage and his departure marked, I imagine, the departure of the old race of English public school masters.' Another of the autobiographical notes is on Gladstone's Eton friend, Arthur Hallam. Hallam's 'cultivated domestic education' and 'immense moral superiority' rubbed off on Gladstone who could not recollect 'a sense of ever having learned anything, until I went to Eton'. Gladstone and Hallam regularly breakfasted together 'week about in his room and mine' and it was from Hallam's tutor, Dr Hawtrey, not his own, 'that I first owed the reception of a spark ...' After Eton Gladstone went to Oxford and Hallam to Cambridge, where Tennyson became his closest friend. He died young: 'In Memoriam' is Tennyson's tribute to him.

In spite of the wide and learned account of his reading in his diary, Gladstone said that an Eton classical education was 'without merit'. Nevertheless he wrote in old age (to A. C. Benson) that 'in one point it was admirable. I mean its rigid, inflexible and relentless accuracy. ... In my day a boy might if he chose learn something, or might if he chose learn nothing, but that one thing he could not do was to learn anything inaccurately.'

In the Eton Society (later called 'Pop'), which had its own rooms and strictly no connection with any of the masters, boys educated themselves. There was a fifty-year rule preventing debates on current politics, although there were various ways of getting round it, including 'private debates' – for instance on Pitt and Fox (5 October 1826). Old boys remained members and could continue to attend. They included no less than eight MPs. Gladstone was elected in 1825. The next year he became a friend of James Milnes-Gaskell who interested him in history and in politics and who was elected to the Society with one blackball, which Gladstone suspected was Selwyn's.

Here is a diary entry:

> 28 October 1826: Holiday ... read about 100 Lines of Electra; some Herodotus; some Cicero; Spectator; and did two propositions. Walk with Doyle; read papers. Question [i.e subject for debate in the Society] Hannibal or Epaminondas, who greatest character? Moved to read 'finest' for 'greatest', ill received: so I went behind chair; cd not vote the question being put so. Did a very foolish thing, and very unaccountable; interrupted Pickering when talking about Blackwood, for wh he had just moved, because the motion had not been seconded! Play in evening: rather poor acting – Love a la mode [by Macklin, 1759, a farce]. Fellows not knowing their parts. Breakfasted with Lady McGrigor.

At first Gladstone wrote out his speeches in full, but then came the stage when he began to add to them whilst speaking, and eventually he recorded with some satisfaction his first speech made from mere notes. Members took turns recording the debates in *The Eton Miscellany*, often with a touch of contrived derision about their own performances.

Gladstone's recreations, however, were not solely intellectual. Although he very soon gave up football, he played some cricket, including some on Upper Club and, as he states, for the XXII (still the name of the 2nd XI at Eton). He joined the scramble to get out of Chapel quickly so as to get a 'Fives wall' (Eton fives began between the Chapel buttresses). Above all, he enjoyed sculling on the Thames, which he did almost daily during his later summers – paying 50/- (£2.50) for the hire of his boat for the season. This was a skiff, with room for a passenger (sometimes Hallam), although he often sculled on his own. Sometimes he recorded his times between landmarks, but he never seems to have entered the 'sweepstakes' as the races were called.

Some of Gladstone's friends left in July 1827, but he stayed for the Michaelmas half and wrote, on Sunday 2 December:

I sit down with a heavy heart, to write an account of my last Eton day, in all probability. Would that it had been a more tranquil one. May God make my feelings on leaving Eton – my feeling that the happiest period of my life is now past – produce the salutary effect of teaching me to aim at joys of a more permanent as well as a more exquisite nature – and to seek humbly, penitently, constantly, eagerly, after an eternal happiness which never fades or vanishes. But oh! If any thing mortal is sweet, my Eton years, excepting anxieties at home, have been so! God make me thankful for all I have enjoyed here. I am perhaps very foolishly full of melancholy ... .

Received Sacrament – finished Paleys Christian Evidence – read Bible – called on Durnford to bid goodbye – & on O Reilly. Continued packing – which after all I shall have hard work to get through. Wrote to A.M.G. & to Canning.

And on Monday:

– & 11 o clock Schools, my last at Eton. Finished packing & settled bills &c. Took leave of Keate & my Tutor after 12 – at Society room as an Honorary Member. Left my kind and excellent friends, my long known and long loved abode at three. Finished & gave up my Petrarch Verses on Laura. Reached London about 6 – tea at Hatchett's – went to Covent Garden – saw Kemble as Falstaff, Young as Hotspur, Ventris in Don Giovanni, which I do not like. Slept at Hatchett's.

Then on Wednesday 'left London by the Umpire – travelled all night' and on Thursday 'weather not very good. Arrived at Liverpool safe and well thank God, at 6.'

In spite of his strictures, both on the teaching and on the slackness of Chapel services and lack of religious instruction, Gladstone retained a lifelong affection for the place, and he retained a number of friendships. He sent all his four sons to the school, and visited them when he could, quite often combining this with a duty at Windsor Castle. He was aware of the benefits to be reaped from competition, and he persuaded his friend and contemporary, Lord Lincoln, who was to recommend him as a Parliamentary candidate for Newark, to ask his father the Duke of Newcastle to endow a prize for excellence in the classics. Gladstone and another distinguished Etonian classical scholar, his brother-in-law Lord Lyttelton, acted as examiners in 1840. To win the 'Newcastle' remains the crowning glory of an Eton career.

The Eton which Gladstone visited to give a lecture in 1878 was a very different institution from the school he attended half a century before. After some strident cries from individuals in the 1850s a Royal Commission was appointed in 1861 to make recommendations regarding nine of the best-known old public schools. The Commissioners were thorough, making many recommendations about the staff, the curriculum and the religious and pastoral care of the boys. But their main task was to remove the old Fellows, who had been appointed for life and who milked the college of its endowments, and to replace them by what was called a 'Governing Body' with specified functions relating to policy and management. Its members were to include representatives of various respectable institutions. After several modifications it was eventually constituted in 1871. The Commission's work was, of course, very much in line with the reform of the universities in which Gladstone had played so prominent a part.

In 1878 Gladstone was persuaded to lecture by George Nathaniel Curzon, who arranged for his contemporaries to ask prepared questions at the end, for fear that they would otherwise be too shy. The next year Gladstone returned and, after watching the cricket match on the Upper Shooting Fields, he spoke, at his own suggestion, on Homer. 'Are they interested in Homer?' he had asked. The reply must have been politely encouraging.

His last visit was in 1891, when again he spoke on Homer: 'The audience were very kind'. This was now the Eton of Dr Warre, a clergyman (of course), scholar and athlete, founder and commanding officer of the Eton Battalion of the Volunteers, seminal coach of the VIIIs which were to win so many victories at Henley; inventor of the termly examination undergone by every pupil and appositely known as 'Trials', organiser and administrator ('write on one side of the paper only, *videlicet* on that which is ruled'). The Chapel services were a far cry from those of Dr Keate with inaudible sermons from Fellows holding office for life. 'Eton Chapel 10.40 a.m., a moving sight.' But in 1894 Gladstone discovered to his horror, from Lady Lyell, whose son was 'a distinguished boy at the school', that the 'Pop' he had known in the 1820s had been transformed into a club 'of no very elevated order', its room abundantly supplied with sporting magazines and papers, with two pictures on the walls, one of Ladas, the other of his jockey; and that 'except in connection with the subjects just indicated it has no activity or function'. This was the Eton debating society founded in 1811, 'the mother and model I believe of all the debating societies of the schools and universities of the kingdom ... . It fostered no small portion of the intellectual life of the school.' He deplored above all that its records 'kept with devoted care' had not been transferred to the Literary Society. 'How the transformation of the Society was brought about, I do not fully know: but I believe it began with the admission to the old Eton Society, in honour and goodwill, of the captain of the eleven and the boats.'

3
Oxford

Gladstone went up to Christ Church, Oxford (*Aedes Christi*, 'The House') in October 1828. He spent his two-term gap after leaving Eton remedying some of the defects of his education there, mostly with a tutor in Cheshire.

Nowadays we must be astonished by both the depth and the range of his school education, although of course modern science was in its infancy and had hardly touched the lives of schoolboys or undergraduates. Gladstone had read extraordinarily widely in Latin and Greek literature, tackling subjects which are simply regarded as too difficult and abstruse nowadays, and not 'useful' enough. He worked with the minimum of tools, rather despising the idea of using a dictionary, having had to create (quite how is not perhaps clear) his own Greek vocabulary; and indeed the lexicon used by all his four sons at Eton still did no more for the pupil than translating the Greek words into Latin.

Classical studies had already given Gladstone and his contemporaries a broad knowledge of ancient literature and civilisation, in addition to making them experts in the mental gymnastics required for translating difficult authors and for composing verses in a variety of both Latin and Greek metres. And woe betide the pupil, as Gladstone remarked, who was not accurate in every letter, every syllable and of course every quantity. Inspired by their knowledge of the ancient world and their interest in modern politics and political history, the Eton boys who entered Oxford and Cambridge in the 1820s and 1830s had a far wider view of literature and history than their modern counterparts. Gentlemen were still expected to speak French fluently, and although the French master at Eton was inferior in the hierarchy to his classical colleagues, he had interested Gladstone in French literature, especially in Molière.

The amount of mathematics which Gladstone had imbibed before he reached Oxford has not been, and perhaps cannot be, researched. It was not extensive, but probably it was greater than has been generally suggested, and he strengthened it during his gap. He did a good deal of mathematics in his early terms at Oxford, then got his father's permission not to take it in 'Schools' (the final examinations), but in fact his efforts then revived, and were redoubled, and he obtained a first class. Technically the subject was 'Mathematics and Physics', and it could not be taken except by those who had already taken classics (known at Oxford then as now as Literae Humaniores).

Christ Church, like all Oxford colleges, was still 'unreformed', an eighteenth-century institution in character, strictly an Anglican monopoly with many rights and endowments originating in Tudor and Stuart times, and regulated accordingly. Many of its undergraduates, noblemen and gentlemen commoners, had no intention of taking a degree, and early in his career there Gladstone was attacked by a gang who considered him a prig. But he had many friends in the college, he started an essay society which came to be known as the 'WEG', and the academic life of the House had been transformed by the efforts of Dean Jackson, a process continued by Deans Smith and Gaisford. In Gladstone's final year five of the ten firsts awarded in the University went to Christ Church men. Gladstone felt after making comparisons with his Cambridge friends that Oxford suited him. It was less concerned with the finer points of scholarship than with the 'substance and spirit' of classical literature, with ancient history and with philosophy. Indeed, brilliant as his scholarship was, Gladstone failed to win the Ireland or the Craven Prizes and thus to 'knock the Salopians off their perch' as he had hoped. Rivalling Eton, Shrewsbury remained the leading classical school, just as Oriel was now rivalling Christ Church as an Oxford seat of learning.

There is no finer description of Gladstone's classical training than in G. M. Young's review of Garratt's book on *The Two Mr Gladstones*, including the following scene:

About the year 1830 a visitor to Christ Church, who had pushed open the door of the lecture room next to the hall staircase, would have seen assembled two head masters to be; three bishops; three Regius professors; three viceroys, Canning, Dalhousie and Elgin; Gladstone, Newcastle, and Cornewall Lewis. Lowe sometimes looked in, and Sidney Herbert regularly came across from Oriel. They sat there translating Aristotle's *Rhetoric* in turn at the feet of Mr Biscoe. He is little known to fame, but what villatic fowl ever hatched such a brood of eaglets? Among them was Martin Tupper, to whom we owe the roll of names.

Take now a young man of genius, trained at home in habits of friendly disputation and regular piety, always bracing himself to the evangelical standards of personal holiness; in all his social and intellectual relations of a most vivid and energetic disposition; subject him, in the most congenial surroundings, among contemporaries of the governing class, to a persistent discipline in scholarship, logic, and history; and above all, make him translate Aristotle aloud. What will be the result? To my recollection, Aristotle imposes himself on a young reader first by his determination to settle his meanings before he starts reasoning from them: and then by the resoluteness, often ungainly, often long-winded, often involved, with which he pursues his argument to the end: the parentheses, admissions, and qualifications into which he is always dropping being so many safeguards against interruption or misconception by the way. But our young man has also brought with him, from home or Eton, a gift or habit of words, vast, nebulous and resonant, recalling the Biscayan roll of the younger Pitt. Allow for that: and then tell me, have I not described the regular movement of Mr Gladstone's mind, on the platform, in Committee, or in those analytic and deductive memoranda which the poor Queen had to have translated before she could make head or tail of them?

Gladstone's reading is recorded in his diary, with laconic comments, as is his church attendance. There was a compulsory service every day in the Cathedral (Christ Church's college chapel), though it was conducted with no more enthusiasm than Chapel at Eton. But Gladstone noted – with dismay – the small number of communicants and although he could not have so identified himself he was part and parcel of the early stirrings of the Oxford Movement. With a few friends, all moving from an Evangelical towards a High Church position, he attended a reading party at Cuddesdon, near Oxford, in 1830, and began to think seriously of ordination. (He was dissuaded by his father on the grounds that his influence as a parish clergyman would be so narrow.)

Gladstone was a Tory – though, in the tradition of Canning, a Liberal Tory. Catholic Emancipation had been passed in 1829. The Whigs won

Gladstone as a young man: engraving by F. C. Lewis from a drawing by George Richmond

My brother Tom you know, has left Eton, & therefore I shall go back by myself for the future. About that I do not much care, excepting that my holidays will be a whole week shorter until I get into the fifth form.

We have now in the house, Mr Canning & his son, Mr Courtenay & his son, Lord W. Bentinck, Ld George Bentinck, H. R. Fox, Mr Hope, Mr Finlay & a Mr Chinnery, with about 5 servants — & 15 servants of our own, besides a man cook, & 8 of ourselves including Elizabeth. Altogether, in fact, we are not much short of 40 people in the house

A letter from Gladstone to his brother John, then a midshipman, in August 1822. He writes from Seaforth House, Liverpool, praising Canning and describing the large household. John, who retired from the Royal Navy as a captain, also became an MP. He died in 1863.

Mr Canning is uncommonly agreeable & amiable — I do not myself think that such another man for talent, experience, kindness, & firmness, of character exists in the United Kingdom. His son is about nine or ten, & is very clever, but very imprudent — He is to go to Eton next Christmas in a 2 years. He is now at school at Putney — his fourteen-year-ago son is about 16, very shy, & at Westminster.

This letter I know to be not interesting enough to wade through on receipt, & therefore I give you all the news, whilst I am glad to have any to give — You can you know read it & rather decipher it, at any leisure hours.

I am really very sorry that I have not the slightest shade of a chance of seeing you before your return from India.

4

Head Master.
Revd. Dr. KEATE.

———

Lower Master.
Revd. Mr. CARTER.

———

Assistant Masters.

Revd. Mr. YONGE.

Revd. Mr. KNAPP.

Revd. Mr. HAWTREY.

Revd. Mr. OKES.

Revd. Mr. CHAPMAN.

Revd. Mr. COLERIDGE.

Revd. Mr. WILDER.

Revd. Mr. GREEN.

Revd. Mr. DUPUIS.

Upper School.

L. School.

———

Extra Masters.
Mr. DUCLOS, FRENCH.
Mr. HEXTER, WRITING.
Mr. BOLAFFEY, ITALIAN & SPANISH.
Mr. W. EVANS, DRAWING.
Mr. H. ANGELO, FENCING.
Mr. VENUA, DANCING.

From the Eton School List for Summer 1825: the Staff

Yonge, *K. S.*	Battiscombe, *K. S.*
Martelli	Malcolm
Sanders, *K. S.*	Crutchley, *ma.*
Biddulph	Harvey, *K. S.*
Pickering, *mi.*	Baldwin, *K. S.*
Mr. Villiers	Jodrell
Morgan	Farr
Sparkes	Gladstone
Todd	Hallifax
Farquharson	Tucker, *ma.*
Hamilton, *ma.*	Broadhead, *ma.*
Antrobus	Corbet
Read, *ma.*	Nott
Pollard	Hoseason
Selwyn, *ma.*	Sir T. Boughey
Egerton	Sanford
Mr. Hervey	Hibbert, *ma. K. S.*
Hartopp, *ma.*	Lewis
Hand, *K. S.*	Baker
Voules, *K. S.*	Blackstone
Brooke, *K. S.*	Hallam

Eton, Summer 1825: part of the Upper V, including Gladstone, Selwyn and Hallam

SCRIPTORES GRÆCI:

SIVE

SELECTÆ

EX

SCRIPTORIBUS GRÆCIS;

viz.

HERODOTO,	PLATONE,
THUCYDIDE,	ISOCRATE,
XENOPHONTE,	LUCIANO.

CUM VERSIONE LATINA.

✦

IN USUM REGIÆ SCHOLÆ ETONENSIS.

✦

𝕰ditio 𝕬ltera 𝕽ecognita.

✦

ETONÆ:

Ex Officinâ E. WILLIAMS (nuper *Pote* et *Williams*):
Apud quem veneunt etiam, No. 10, *Red Lion Court, Fleet-Street,*
LONDINI.

———

1817.

Title page of the Greek Construe Book in use at Eton in Gladstone's time.
Like the Greek lexicon he also used, it translated the Greek into Latin.

Gladstone's doodles in his Homer (upper image enlarged)

The entire Eton Corps, consisting of four companies, was given the privilege of forming a guard of honour at the west door of Westminster Abbey for Gladstone's state funeral. From the *Eton College Chronicle* of 11 June 1898: 'The arrival of Mrs Gladstone in a private carriage, almost unnoticed at first, called forth the first salute. At last an expectant hush, broken only by the whirring of cinematograph cameras, told that the procession was in sight. Through a gap in the ranks of No. 2 Company, the long line passed into the Abbey, the Corps resting on arms reversed, and saluting again when the coffin itself appeared.'

the election of 1830 bent on Parliamentary reform. Gladstone became President of the Union and spoke against reform and in May 1831 he wrote to his father, in a letter now at Hawarden:

> One of the most formidable features in the present frightful circumstances of the country is, that we have so long been blessed, contrary to our deserts, with ease and peace and settled habits, that the upper classes in this country cannot bring themselves to believe that they are about to be wrested from them, and in consequence sit with hands folded and look on while the Revolution is in progress, instead of making strenuous exertions.

After taking his written papers in Schools, Gladstone and his contemporaries were subjected to formidable viva voce examinations. The story is well known that when one of the examiners said 'We will now leave that part of the subject' he replied 'No, sir, if you please we will not leave it yet.' What is not so well known, but is more to the point, is that before turning to theology the examiners tried to trip him up by a series of detailed questions on Herodotus, only to find that he used each question to air his knowledge more fully.

Fifteen years later Gladstone felt that as a member of Peel's government which repealed the Corn Laws he could no longer honourably seek the Duke of Newcastle's support in his Newark seat. He looked about for a new constituency and in 1847 secured a nomination for the University of Oxford, and became one of the University's two MPs. Oxford and Cambridge were exceptions to the rule that MPs were elected either to represent boroughs or as knights of the shire, the county members elected by the forty-shilling freeholders. Every master of arts of the University was entitled to vote, provided he was willing to travel to Oxford. This was not quite as exceptional as it might seem, for property owners could qualify in any county constituency where they owned land. Elections were therefore spread over about a fortnight so that plural voters could travel, although some were able to avoid this by finding men of the opposite persuasion with whom they could 'pair'.

Most of the Anglican beneficed clergy were Oxford or Cambridge MAs, particularly Oxonians, with the result that Oxford was something like a constituency of clergymen. Far more of the élite resources of the two universities were devoted to the task of educating the Anglican clergy than to any other profession or calling. Oxford University was roused in the 1830s by the birth-pangs of the Oxford Movement from the long latitudinarian slumber which had followed the slow decline of the old Jacobite Toryism. No institution in Britain had a stronger claim to the description 'unreformed', a characteristic enhanced by the petty quarrels of university politics.

The beginning of what became the Oxford Movement was later identified – by Gladstone amongst others – as Keble's Assize sermon on National Apostasy of 1833; but one can easily detect the early stirrings in Gladstone's diary as an undergraduate. A number (one cannot say a group) of the finest Christian minds and characters, including most notably Keble, Pusey, Newman and Froude, reawakened the ancient sacramental nature of worship and the claims of the Church of England to be the reformed Catholic Church with the traditions and authority of the Apostolic Succession, the authority granted to St Peter by Our Lord himself. The tracts they wrote, intended mainly as instructive pamphlets for the parish clergy, became the ammunition of vituperative Oxford controversy – 'the politics of the city state'.

The first round in a series of ferocious battles over doctrinal details was the Hampden affair in 1836 when the Puseyites, who objected to the appointment of the new Professor of Divinity, managed to get him excluded from the university's list of select preachers. Then came controversy over the Thirty-Nine Articles, one of several futile Tudor attempts to define the dogma of the English clergy, which ever since have been subscribed to by every priest, often encouraged to interpret them 'as was intended when they were published'. In Tract 90 Newman tried to prove that there was nothing in them contrary to Roman Catholic belief: his reward was to be treated by the University (that is, the heads of houses) as he had treated Hampden. Then Pusey was 'delated for heresy'. Then the Revd W. G. Ward, a young mathematics don at Balliol, something of a trouble-maker who was appointed editor of the Tractarian journal *The British Critic*, wrote that the Articles, though Protestant in intention, were capable of Roman Catholic interpretation, and that in subscribing to them he had not renounced any Roman doctrine. For his pains the University deprived him of his degree. He left and became a Roman Catholic layman. Newman, feeling unwanted, became a Roman Catholic in 1845.

Into this poisoned atmosphere Gladstone launched himself as MP in

1847, proclaiming his love of the University and his pride at being a successor of Peel. The Tractarian furore had persuaded many English voters that Oxford must be reformed. Oxford and Cambridge were condemned for living in a kingdom of their own and Oxford seemed to be arrogating to itself an authority which belonged only to the bishops. Gladstone was often labelled as a Tractarian but he was known to be liberal in his approach. Keble trusted him, even if he might disagree with him on this and that. Gladstone denied that he was a Tractarian, saying that he had not read the Tracts (but he had read some of them). He attacked Ward in an article in the *Quarterly Review*, but voted against the draconian penalty of deprivation. 'I must say I have committed myself to no party in the Church, and no party has a right to reckon me among its members,' he wrote.

In 1850 Lord John Russell, 'worked upon' as Morley puts it 'by a persevering minority', proposed a Royal Commission on University Reform, and the Commission reported in 1852. By 1854 its fairly generalised proposals had been widely canvassed, considered by the Government and embodied into a most elaborate Bill, with Gladstone, though Chancellor of the Exchequer, doing most of the work. He regarded this massive task as a welcome relief from the requirement for the Exchequer to finance the Crimean War. 'I fear', wrote Russell, 'that my mind is exclusively occupied by the war and the Reform Bill, and yours by the University reform.' Russell introduced the Bill, but acknowledged Gladstone's predominance, and it was Gladstone who worked it through its various stages in the House of Commons. It involved an immense amount of research into the Laudian University Statutes and the ancient legal rights and privileges of every college. Gladstone had to cope with a vast flow of correspondence, much of which has survived; but if he had surrendered the opportunity to steer the Bill, he would also have surrendered the influence to steer his constituency. 'As one of your burgesses', he said, 'I stand upon the line that divides Oxford from the outer world, and as a sentinel I cry out to tell you what I see from that position.'

Gladstone came to two important conclusions. A liberal school of thought expected the power of the colleges to be replaced by a new concept of the University. They wanted to see a departmental university, a 'Professoriate' rather than a collegiate institution. But Gladstone wanted to 'work with the materials we possess, improve our institutions through the agency they themselves supply, and give to reform the character of return and restoration'. This was the classic position of the nineteenth-century reformer, but Gladstone realised there was no alternative. The daunting complication of the legal rights of colleges and individuals made radical reform impracticable: every detail would be contested by clever lawyers and the task would never be concluded. Any attempt at wholesale abolition of existing rights and privileges, and replacement by a written University Constitution would have been rejected. The University, for better or for worse, has consequently remained until this day a federation of partially reformed (as Mrs Thatcher discovered) colleges. In order to cope with the mass of detail Gladstone hit upon the idea of an executive commission with statutory powers – 'sub-legislation' as he called it: a first step, presumably, along the dire path towards statutory ministerial orders; but it solved his problem.

From the formidable task of consultation, mostly on paper, emerged eventually the Bill, Gladstone directing its composition and mercilessly keeping his draftsmen up to the mark. Its objectives were to provide the colleges with representative 'governing bodies', a new label which was the target of a good deal of scorn – a model soon to be applied also to the public schools. Massive ancient endowments were to be awakened and applied, on the basis of competition, to the fulfilment of definite functions, and to the reorganisation of professorships. Privileges awarded subject to ancient conditions and restrictions were to be abolished. The Dean of Christ Church said the Bill was inexpedient, unjust and tyrannical; Pusey said the University was ruined and overthrown; but Jowett said that the Bill must be acceptable to any reasonable reformer and he wrote to Gladstone saying 'It is to yourself and Lord John that the University will be indebted for the greatest boon that it has ever received.' Gladstone introduced the second reading in a masterly speech. 'To behold one's old enemies slaughtered before one's face with the most irresistible weapons was quite intoxicating' wrote Arthur Stanley, who had been heavily involved in the drafting: 'one great charm of his speaking is its exceeding good-humour. There is great vehemence but no bitterness.' This is a verdict which applies to many of Gladstone's telling Parliamentary pronouncements. He said, too, that he regarded the intervention of Parliament in university affairs with reluctance, and emphasised the Bill's objective to enable rather than to drive reform.

The Government achieved all that it considered possible. The process of reform was slow and incomplete. The various tests confining offices and functions to Anglicans were only gradually removed; and positive steps actually to facilitate the entry of dissenters were, in effect, indefinitely postponed. Gladstone, too, was over-sanguine in his aim that the reformed use of endowments would open the colleges to candidates without private incomes. But the long drawn-out series of measures designed to reform the Civil Service and open it to competitive examination were a by-product of the correspondence in which Gladstone was involved, leading to the Northcote-Trevelyan Report. Surviving amongst Gladstone's papers is a memorandum describing the opposition of 'the existing corps of civil servants' because 'the introduction of well-educated active men will force them to bestir themselves ... they cannot hope to get their own ill-educated sons appointed under the new system. The old established political families habitually batten on to the public patronage – their sons legitimate and illegitimate, their relatives and dependents of every degree, are provided for by the score.' Only the Indian Civil Service was immediately reformed: the Foreign Office was eventually the last bastion to fall. Disraeli went through the motions of opposing the Bill in such a good-natured way that his irony is hardly detectable in the written reports of his speeches, and he did not divide the House on the second reading. He remarked that it was nonsense to refer to the superiority of German professors over British ones: it was simply that once the revolution of 1848 had been crushed the best brains in Germany had no openings in politics.

Gladstone had said that he stood on the line which divided Oxford from the outside world and told the University what he saw from that position. But his constituents did not always like what he told them and in 1865 they unseated him. Palmerston had hoped that he would remain there where he would be to some degree muzzled. Gladstone used Palmerston's phrase when he was elected the same month for South Lancashire – 'I come among you unmuzzled.' But he retained a lifelong affection for the University. In 1875 he attended the gaudy at Christ Church: 'It was an occasion of real interest.' In Christ Church hall hangs the striking 1885 portrait by Millais. A first portrait by Watts was rejected in 1878 after criticism at the gaudy – returned to Watts's gallery where Mary Gladstone described 'a weak, peevish old man'. Next, Sir William Blake Richmond had a go. It was not a success, 'shewn in the Grosvenor Gallery and condemned'. Then Millais painted a fine portrait intended for Christ Church in 1884, but Lord Rosebery gazumped the college (of which he, too, was a member) by persuading Millais to sell it to him personally; whence it eventually found its way in to School Hall at Eton. So Millais had to paint another, and this is the one in Christ Church hall. Millais had previously, in 1878, painted a three-quarter length, a pair with one of Disraeli. Now in the National Portrait Gallery, it portrays a benign old man, with no force of character, as (more suitably) does Millais' last effort of 1889, presented by women of England, Scotland, Wales and Ireland for the Golden Wedding, and hanging now at Hawarden in the Temple of Peace. Millais' Christ Church portrait, with the scarlet DCL robe and the piercing eye, sits well in its magnificent surroundings, although it does not quite come up to the more profound study by Frank Holl at Hawarden, personifying Gladstone's dictum, pronounced in a speech at another University: 'Thought is the citadel.'

In April 1878 Gladstone spoke at the official opening of Keble College in a three-day visit to Oxford packed with activities and conversations, and again visited the college and stayed with Warden Talbot ten years later. His youngest son Herbert had been an under-graduate there, and had achieved a first in Modern History. In 1890 he stayed for a week at All Souls, now the Grand Old Man, a venerable honorary fellow of the college, much of his conversation being recorded in C. R. L. Fletcher's *Mr Gladstone at Oxford, 1890* and – in 1933 – by Sir Charles Oman in *Things I Have Seen*. The college was predomi-nantly Tory or Unionist, but he was greeted by the younger fellows with attentive curiosity and respect. Two years later he made his last visit to Oxford to give the inaugural Romanes Lecture in the Sheldonian in October. There had been some hesitations and a willingness to post-pone the date; after all he had become Prime Minister for the fourth time in August. But clearly he wanted to take this last chance to show, to himself as to others, that he was more than a politician. The modest title was 'An Academic Sketch', but he had done much reading on medieval universities. He was in good voice and the only interruption was in the form of cheering by the crowd outside.

4
Two Speeches: 1833 and 1838

After coming down from Oxford, Gladstone, with his eldest brother Tom, travelled extensively in Europe on a reduced version of the eighteenth-century Grand Tour. At Milan he was surprised to receive a letter from his Eton and Christ Church friend Lord Lincoln, offering on behalf of his father, the Duke of Newcastle, his influence in the borough of Newark, should Gladstone agree to become an MP. The Duke was the descendant of the greatest of all the landowning parliamentary patrons of the eighteenth century. Newark was not a 'pocket' borough, a decayed town with a handful (or less) of voters, nor was it a 'rotten' borough which could be bought by the bribes (or threats) of its richest landowner; but the Duke's influence there was considerable, and he had been impressed by Gladstone's speech against reform in the Oxford Union. Like almost all pre-reform constituencies, it returned two MPs. Gladstone came top of the poll with 887 votes.

Several books say that Gladstone's maiden speech in the House of Commons was in defence of slavery, and one respected author has even reported that his father was a 'Liverpool slave-trader'. The truth is different. John Gladstone had invested in sugar plantations in the West Indies and South America worked by slave labour and he was therefore a slave-owner. The slave trade had been abolished in 1807, so a plantation dependent on slave labour was a wasting asset. Sugar was a necessity: British imports and international trade were assured. Whatever the condition of the labourers might be, if slavery itself were abolished there would be some form of compensation for the owners.

The calculation of the value of an investment was thus fraught with risk and complication.

It was generally agreed that slavery in British colonies must be abolished, but it was recognised that it could not be done overnight, and the debate was about the details of the timetable and the status, and indeed the protection, of former slaves. There were merits and demerits in the fine points of any proposal, and nobody believed that the process could be achieved without a hitch. Feelings ran high. Debates were not free of acrimonious accusations, one of which was made by an MP, Lord Howick, in intemperate terms, about an estate owned by John Gladstone. Tom and William were both MPs, and they could not remain silent, but it was two days before William could catch the Speaker's eye.

The maiden speech was not, then, given on an occasion or a subject of the speaker's own choosing. Under slavery, William said, there had inevitably been cases of cruelty, and this was 'a substantial reason why the British legislature and public should set themselves in good earnest to provide for its extinction'. This speech still had some characteristics of an Eton Society or Oxford Union performance – provocative here and there, and with a purple passage towards the end; but it refuted Howick's accusations rhetorically and it dealt with the condition of the slaves thoroughly, lucidly and calmly. The House, in accordance with custom, heard the maiden speaker courteously. Lord Stanley, the 'Rupert of Debate', later Prime Minister as Earl of Derby, and an opponent of Gladstone's view, personally praised the speech (though in a slightly double-edged manner). A few days later, at the Harrow Speech Day, where Gladstone had gone with his friend and future brother-in-law Stephen Glynne, 'Sir R. Peel came up to me most kindly and praised the affair of Monday night.' The King wrote to Viscount Althorp rejoicing that a young member had come forward 'in so promising a manner as Lord Althorp states'. That was not a bad line-up of fans for a beginner: Derby, Peel, Spencer and the Sailor King.

Peel at once recognised Gladstone's usefulness and in December 1834 he made him a junior Lord of the Treasury, just before his twenty-sixth birthday. Even more remarkably, a month later after a general election Peel made him Under-Secretary for War and the Colonies under Lord Aberdeen. He thus became the minister responsible in the House of Commons for a major department of state. 'I do not know six offices', said Peel, 'which are at this moment of greater importance.' A few months later the Government was defeated and Peel was succeeded by Lord Melbourne.

It was not until 1838 that Gladstone fully made his mark as an orator in the House of Commons. This was for him an eventful year – the year of the Maynooth grant, of his first book, *The State in Its Relations with the Church*, of speeches on Canada and a landmark speech on the colonisation of New Zealand. His speech of 30 March on the West Indies plantations is mentioned neither by Jenkins, nor by Matthew, nor by Shannon. Yet it was the first of Gladstone's speeches to be printed and published as such, and it was the foretaste of his greatest feats in the Commons. He astonished the House by his masterly and unrivalled knowledge of its subject; he set out a mass of complicated detail clearly and logically, and he handled an apparently unexciting subject in a manner that gripped the attention of the House. It lasted two hours, from 11 until 1 am.

The speech was essentially a defence of the interim system of apprenticeship by which Parliament had replaced slavery in the West Indies, and a 'remonstrance' against unfounded criticism of that system. There had been much debate as to whether the time limits should be shortened, or indeed the whole system abolished. Needless to say, there had been abuses, and accusations that the state of apprenticeship was worse than slavery, especially but not only in Jamaica. Speeches were full of emotion. Parliament had monitored the system through a Negro Apprentices Committee, of which Gladstone was a member. It had now set up a committee to investigate the complaints about Jamaica, of which he was also a member. He was therefore in a good position to know the facts without having to make private researches; but he knew the facts in remarkable detail, far more thoroughly than anybody else. The case which he made, 'handling' as Morley says 'detail upon detail without an instant of tediousness, and holding the attention of listeners sustained and unbroken', was unanswerable. Those who had made false or faulty accusations were simply floored. True, it was essentially a defence rather than a proposition, but it made a dramatic impression. It placed Gladstone firmly amongst the leading men in the House of Commons and it foretold the shape of things to come.

5

Gladstone and Peel: Politics, Railways and Finance

Sir Robert Peel, Prime Minister from 1834 to 1835 and from 1841 to 1846, was the outstanding British statesman of his age, unequalled by any of his contemporaries in intellectual brilliance, in integrity, force of personality, strength of character and political skill. No other Victorian Prime Minister, except Gladstone himself, so managed and dominated his Cabinet or influenced the whole flavour of British politics. A conservative in the tradition which Gladstone inherited, Peel was eventually persuaded by famine in Ireland to repeal the tax on imported grain (the Corn Laws), thus removing the financial bulwark of the Tory Party, in 1846, splitting his party. Peel died in 1850 but the Peelites remained a substantial force in politics for many years.

Gladstone was Peel's protégé and Peel was Gladstone's mentor. But there was another side to that coin: Peel wanted Gladstone's services for their usefulness; and it was for that reason that he summoned up a great deal of patience to tolerate and soften the hard edges of the young man's principles and prejudices, and even occasionally to praise Gladstone's successes. He was, as Gladstone said, 'very sparing of laudation'. He was reserved and unbending in personality and in politics. Queen Victoria described him as a 'cold, hard man'. Yet Gladstone's relationship with Peel was far from cold and hard. It was said that Peel had learnt his reserve during his long stint as Chief Secretary for Ireland when he was endlessly pestered for patronage or support: experience taught that the only prudent response to importunity was silence. But between Gladstone and Peel there grew strong bonds of affection, witness the touching final scene when Peel was in deep trouble and Gladstone agreed to rejoin the Cabinet and support the repeal of the Corn Laws. The two men clasped hands.

It was because of Gladstone's thoroughness and his qualities as a speaker that Peel made him a junior Lord of the Treasury at the age of twenty-five and the Government's minister in the House of Commons for the Department of War and the Colonies at the age of twenty-six. In 1843 Peel brought Gladstone into his Cabinet as President of the Board of Trade. Gladstone by then was known to get through as much work as four ordinary men and, since he could work for sixteen hours a day, to do the work of eight. He listened patiently to delegations from particular trades because this was the best way of acquiring detailed, specialised and practical knowledge, and in one session of Parliament he spoke no less than 129 times, as one customs duty after another was reviewed.

Gladstone learnt many lessons from Peel. On one occasion, perhaps surprisingly, he asked Peel: 'Shall I be short and concise?' 'No,' said Peel, 'be long and diffuse. It is all important in the House of Commons to state your case in many different ways, so as to produce an effect on men of many ways of thinking.'

Above all, Peel taught Gladstone that politics is the art of the possible. Members of a government must be willing not to stand apart on one particular issue, however strongly they feel. Gladstone disapproved strongly of the wars against China fought to prevent China from suppressing the opium trade. He spoke strongly and effectively on this subject in 1840. When Peel asked him to join his Government, Gladstone was unhappy to do so unless a proposal was dropped to obtain compensation from China for the opium she had confiscated. Peel pointed out (with consummate tact) that in view of what had already been done, his Government 'would not be wholly unfettered. ... He thought I had better leave the question suspended.' According to Gladstone, he also learnt from Peel how to make a point tactfully, although it may be said that in some respects Gladstone went too far: 'his arguments were in favour of free trade, and his parentheses were in favour of protection.'

Gladstone also learnt from Peel that logic does not always carry the day in politics. He provided an elaborate brief for Peel on the sugar duties. Peel lost it, and asked him to write it out again, which he did. It was not accepted by the Cabinet. Gladstone then supported it with more memoranda, each logically argued and generously supported by facts. But neither the facts nor the arguments received much attention. Logic mattered in politics, but it did not carry the day against the question of what was, and what was not, politically acceptable. Compromise was essential, and so often was delay. Never bring to the Prime Minister a difference of opinion between colleagues until every possible effort has been made to resolve it. On no account try to deal with a question before it is ripe: this indeed became one of Gladstone's key principles, 'right timing', on which he later so much prided himself. Gladstone also learnt from Peel that he must grow a thick skin, and keep his head when heckled during a speech. He became almost impervious to the taunts of his opponents.

In January 1845 Gladstone resigned from the Cabinet because he disagreed with Peel's proposal to increase the annual grant which the British Government made to Maynooth College, the Irish seminary for Catholic priests. At first sight it appears that Gladstone had certainly not learnt the lessons which his objection to the opium wars with China had taught him at the beginning of the Government's term: that passionately held views on a single issue must not divert a statesman from the issues of mainstream politics; and that what had been accepted in the past could not always be unscrambled. Gladstone had actually voted in favour of the original grant to Maynooth; it was an increase in that grant to which he was objecting. This seems to rule out the perhaps charitable view that Gladstone was imprisoned by his own past – by his book *The State in Its Relations with the Church* (1841), which argued against Government support for any religious denomination other than the established Church. But the issue was clearly not as simple as that. Having resigned because he could not support the proposal, he then voted in its favour. What are we to make of that?

This proposal to increase the grant was the most generous and selfless act of Peel's whole career. It is not difficult to see that in the face of famine he could take steps to reduce the price of bread, even against the interests of the main body of his supporters, the agricultural landlords of England. But for the Tory leader to increase a grant to the Irish Roman Catholics was indeed heroic. It stands in line with the whole of Gladstone's later political career: his 'robbery' of the endowments of the Anglican Church in Ireland because it was the church of a small minority, in order that the great majority, the Catholics, should not be penalised; his determination to end the English 'ascendancy' in Ireland; the breadth of his own churchmanship, not only in relation to Ireland but also to English and Welsh nonconformists. Was Gladstone's motivation that of a stern, unbending Tory? Matthew suggests that many Tories, churchmen, and even nonconformists 'looked to Gladstone as the natural leader of the opposition to Peel', and points to strong pressure on him to lead the opposition to the increase in the grant. In that case, once he had resigned in opposition to the grant, why did he vote in its favour? Perhaps, instead of attempting to unravel the Maynooth question, we may simply put ourselves in the shoes of Peel by looking at an entry in Gladstone's diary: 'The records of my official catastrophe need not be so prolix. On Tuesday January 28th Sir R. Peel sent for me and told me that he had offered my office to Sandon ... but was staggered on hearing that I had resigned because of Maynooth.'

Peel was the foremost financier of his generation, perhaps of the whole Victorian era, and his achievement in stabilising the currency removed or alleviated many of the problems which Gladstone would otherwise have had to cope with. He headed the Committee in 1819 which restored the gold standard, but he is best known for repealing the Corn Laws, which were seen by their opponents as a device for propping up the economic prosperity of landowners. But the problem was more complicated, and the Corn Law of 1815 was introduced to stabilise the price, as far as possible, of much the most important commodity in Britain, namely bread. The greatest difficulty was to decide what constituted a 'fair price'. Of the two most celebrated political economists of the time, Ricardo was the expert on rent, Malthus the authority on a fair price of corn, given that Britain must remain something like self-sufficient in food production except after a poor harvest. The price which the 1815 Act provided made landowners and farmers very unhappy. Imported corn mostly had to be paid for in gold, because the European countries which produced a surplus were not sophisticated enough to accept paper. Thus the need to reassert the balance of payments brought a rise in bank rate, making it more difficult to borrow money and decreasing wages and employment.

The operations of the Bank of England, and indeed those of the very numerous private banks all over Britain, had gradually been subjected, largely by intelligent guesswork and trial and error, to an agreed set of principles during the eighteenth century, but these were inadequate to handle economic problems after 1815 when, amongst many other circumstances, the old state system, with its elaborate controls and restrictions, was being dismantled in the face of new market forces. Amongst these controls were those of apprenticeships and wages; an upper limit of 5% on the interest which banks could charge not on an economic but on the moral basis of the laws against usury; the protection of many trades from foreign competition (including the Navigation Acts forbidding imports except in British ships);

and the reliance of the Government on indirect taxes in the form of duties for most of its income. The Industrial Revolution was transforming the shape of trade and industry, and increasing the scale of economic volatility – so that bad times brought mass unemployment, deprivation, and even starvation.

The Bank Charter Act of 1833 established a set of principles, but it did not do the trick. There were massive crazes of speculation abroad (especially in South America) and then at home in the construction of railways. The Bank Charter Act of 1844 did result in the return of a certain received wisdom as far as the Bank of England was concerned, but it did not stop rash lending by private banks before the collapse of the railway mania in 1847. Peel, having masterminded the return to the gold standard (abandoned during the Napoleonic Wars), enacted the limitation of bank note issues and a substantial reduction and simplification of indirect taxation, paid for by a temporary revival of income tax. All this was accompanied, to Gladstone's lasting admiration, by budgetary economy, and the whole economic process involved Gladstone in Peel's thinking. This was how he learnt his trade as a future Chancellor of the Exchequer. He also inherited a fairly stable currency and a banking system which tended to discourage surges of rash speculation.

One of Gladstone's most famous achievements was the 'cheap trains act' of 1844. The construction of our railways was the largest series of industrial enterprises that Britain – and indeed the world – had ever seen. Restrictions on the formation of joint-stock companies and share trading had been tightened after the South Sea Bubble in 1720, and the partial removal of these restrictions in 1825 came at just the right moment for the companies formed to construct railways. Somebody invented the quaint but not inappropriate phrase 'redundant capital', and many writers of history followed suit, to describe profits and savings for which there were few alternative investments to Government stock or to risky speculation overseas, where many fortunes were lost. In spite of the fact that liability was unlimited, the vast sums required for railways were easily raised, a unique phenomenon in Victorian Britain.

Gladstone was one of the last generation to travel by stage coach. He complained of the smoke in his eyes on his first railway journey from Euston to Crewe, and in old age he became a 'stage coach bore', with rather too many anecdotes of the old days. His first Bradshaw's railway timetable is still at St Deiniol's Library, vividly illustrating the problems of travelling when the time at Bristol was different from that at London – or Swindon. His Railways Act was best known for insisting that every company must provide good covered accommodation (for third class passengers) at one penny a mile. It also insisted that every company must run at least one train between all its stations every twenty-four hours – the 'Parliamentary Train'. This provision was almost forgotten by the 1890s – but not quite: Gladstone's son Stephen on one occasion insisted on a railway company providing free alternative road transport for him and his family in a horse-drawn coach.

The cheap train and the Parliamentary train were, however, not the main features of the Act, which was inspired by Gladstone's worry about the lack of competition between railways, as well as his insistence that the privileges they had been given to enable their construction should be reflected in the service they provided for the public. Criticisms were aired for many years, and repeated during the twentieth century, that railway building in Britain had been unplanned and haphazard. In fact, however, the system which emerged could – with a few exceptions – hardly have been bettered. The standard of surveying was superb: there were, of course, gradual improvements here and there as the nineteenth century wore on – new cuttings, embankments and tunnels. But these were no more than modifications. The criterion of efficient railway (and road) construction must be that there should be no competition: the deliberate duplication of railway lines is wasteful of resources, although alternative routes here and there will clearly encourage competition; and many of these routes Britain possessed, until Dr Beeching closed them in the 1960s. What Gladstone conceived was nationalisation of the tracks, so that private enterprise could run competitive trains on them. He therefore introduced legislation by which the Government could purchase lines twenty-one years after they had been built on the basis of a valuation calculated on their profits. When the time came in the 1860s to begin this process he was Palmerston's Chancellor of the Exchequer. He and the Prime Minister decided that it simply could not be pursued, for two reasons: one was the practical one – the huge cost involved; the other was more philosophical, the vision of a minimalist state which, where it intervened, should be merely an enabler.

The prime objective of the Act was, however, neither to provide for nationalisation in the name of competition, nor to provide cheap travel or a Parliamentary train. It was to assert the Government's right to intervene. It seemed important to assert this right sooner rather than later. But since it did not have in mind any particular scheme, the Act could have been repealed as easily as it had been enacted, and historians have therefore commented on the Act with a certain measure of disdain. When Attlee's Government planned to nationalise the railways in 1945, they considered themselves to be starting with a blank sheet. Gladstone was keen on railways and there is a splendid photograph of him in an open truck at Edgware Road Station in August 1862 during the construction of the Metropolitan Railway, the first line of the London Underground, when he was Chancellor of the Exchequer.

The Bank Charter Act of the same year as the Railways Act (1844) did succeed in putting a damper on credit to provide speculative capital, but all the railways, I think without exception, were joint-stock enterprises which were able to invite a large number of investors, big and small, to buy shares. In this they were, in scale if not in theory, almost unique. The origins of 'capital', whether we see them as medieval or of the early modern age, involved an association either of a few institutions or of a few individuals, and this continued to be the case until surprisingly late in the nineteenth century. The great trading companies founded by Royal Charter, notably the East India Company, were rare exceptions. Industrial capital was its own chief progenitor; profits were ploughed back by the enterprising individual who had no intention of losing control by inviting the public to buy shares. He was on the whole shrewd enough not to have to worry about unlimited liability. What is true of industry is also true of commerce: neither banks nor traders wished or needed to become joint-stock enterprises of the modern kind. Historians, up to about the 1970s, often referred to 'joint-stock' banks as a kind of label. But most of them were not joint-stock enterprises at all. As the century wore on they had to become bigger and bigger: hundreds of local banks disappeared, amalgamating with larger ones. But the process was very slow. Meantime, however, banks did occasionally collapse. Gladstone had to cope with the last of these events to happen on a major scale, the Overend-Gurney collapse in 1866, sometimes quoted by journalists in 2008 as 'the last time this happened'.

The so-called 'joint-stock banks', which eventually metamorphosed into the large clearing banks of modern times, seem to have provided for many of the requirements of the two largest users of capital, namely agriculture and housing. They also provided short-term credit for a host of small businesses and individuals, but they did not play a big part in providing capital for commerce or industry. When eventually commercial and industrial enterprises did need to raise large capital sums, this became the function of the merchant banks, a type originating in Germany and quite late arrivals on the scene in London apart from the Rothschilds and the Barings; firms such as Hambros, Lazards, Goschens, Morgans, Oppenheimers and others, whose leading lights quickly became the aristocracy of the City of London and were often chosen as the members of the Court of the Bank of England.

After 1879 the Bank of England bought or sold Government stock in order to increase or decrease money supply. This ironing out of the expansion or contraction of liquidity enabled the Bank to apply the gold standard more smoothly and kept the value of the pound steady, continuing to use Bank Rate to influence the international flow of capital through London, which had become the financial capital of the world: when money was short in London an increase in Bank Rate would bring it in from overseas and get business moving again.

This brief and simple summary of the financial scene which Gladstone knew does no justice to the kaleidoscopic nature of the City with its diverse specialised institutions: such as the discount houses which were instrumental in drawing in money from abroad, or the doyen of all insurers, Lloyd's, which never opted for limited liability but paid its claims as they arose, and which never became a joint-stock company, always consisting of individual names. Lloyd's collapsed in the 1990s, not because of its ancient constitution but for reasons similar to those which led to the collapse of banks and other financial institutions in 2008. Gladstone and his contemporaries, building on the measures devised by Peel, were able to rely on a comparatively stable value of money and a comparatively smooth flow of credit. In these circumstances the two pillars of Gladstone's fiscal policy, namely the removal of indirect taxation and rigid economy in Government expenditure (which was why he disliked income tax), played a vital part in the rapid growth of commerce and industry to which he referred in his budget speeches of the 1860s.

Until 1825 Parliamentary sanction was required for the formation of a joint-stock company. Thereafter various restrictions remained. These could be evaded by devices like equitable trusts, and Gladstone's Companies Act of 1862 removed them. This Act is well known as the one which introduced the limited liability company, a step of huge importance in the long run, although there was a previous but ineffective Companies Act in 1856, and numerous later Acts were required to perfect the system. However, as has been suggested, joint-stock companies in the modern sense were slow to develop, except in railways and then in similar services such as gas and water works. In 1883 93% of the quotations on the Stock Exchange were in Government stock or railway shares. Most of the other 7% were in public utilities. Less than 1% was in industrial shares. By 1885 only between 5% and 10% of industrial firms had become limited companies, though these were almost all big ones. This applies also to commercial firms, although harbours and docks were mostly joint stock enterprises. Thus neither banks nor the Stock Exchange contributed much to long-term investment in British commerce or industry. To a perhaps surprising degree Gladstone was contributing until the end of his life to the development of a financial system with which Peel would have been familiar.

Gladstone's achievement was based largely on a continuing development of the ideas of Adam Smith, Pitt and Peel. The rapidest-ever growth period of the British economy, during the mid-Victorian era, was in competition with the rest of the world. The firms which achieved it were more independent as entities than at any period before or since. There were no protective duties and few revenue-raising taxes. In his wholesale attack on restrictive indirect taxation, Gladstone as Chancellor showed, as Peel had suggested, that reduced rates could produce increased revenue. He avowedly applied the principle that if revenue was rising proportionately from a particular tax, then it could be afforded by those who paid it and it could be retained. Legislation was intended to be enabling legislation, and few restrictions were imposed except on humanitarian grounds. The value of money was kept fairly stable and interest rates were low. Firms did not have to look over their shoulders either to banks or to shareholders, let alone to the Government.

Only very late in Gladstone's political life did the sea-change begin to occur as mass-production required huge accumulations of capital and ownership became separated from the responsibility of management, with the complex weave of advantages and problems which that sea-change brought in its wake. Nevertheless the economic and financial world in which Gladstone played so celebrated a role was in many of its characteristics still recognisable until the 1920s.

The last chapter in the relationship between Peel and Gladstone concerns the repeal of the Corn Laws in 1846. Only about one-third of the Tory Party, including Gladstone, voted with Peel; the great majority remained Tories. They remained Tories not, as has often been suggested, because Disraeli appealed to their party loyalty with the false argument that the survival of the two-party system depends not on its flexibility but on rigidity. They refused to go with Peel because they believed that the Corn Laws with the sliding scale were necessary for the stability of the nation's food supply. They knew, too, that Ireland had been in most years an exporter of grain to England. This could have been stopped, or the law temporarily modified as Peel wished, but he was frustrated in his efforts.

Peel was aware that if the failure of the potato crop in 1845 were to be repeated in 1846 there would be widespread distress and probably deaths from starvation in Ireland. He tried introducing American maize, but to little effect. He asked Lyon Playfair to investigate the possibility of preventing the disease, or failing that of making use of diseased potatoes, but without success. He came to the conclusion that taxes which increased the cost of imported corn must be abolished, and he hoped to take the Tory Party with him. In common with the abolitionist campaigners, he was not much interested in British farming and farmers, forgetting the yeomanry and the freeholders and the need for a prosperous agriculture to fuel the technical advances which alone could increase the supply of home-grown food for the rapidly increasing population. His background was in manufacturing. His instinct was that landlords, not the farmers, would suffer, and he argued that this had to be accepted. He convinced Gladstone.

Gladstone's father had been a corn merchant. He had created the Liverpool Corn Exchange, thus providing a futures market in order to stabilise the price of bread for the burgeoning industrial population of Lancashire. Then he had become an agriculturalist in Scotland, intent on improving the methods of his tenants. As both merchant and farmer, he was as well positioned as anyone to advocate the need for Huskisson's sliding scale of corn duties (Huskisson had followed Canning as MP for Liverpool). This he did in cogent leaflets in the late 1830s. It was doubly difficult for his son to abandon the arguments both of his father and of the Tory Party in which he felt at home.

The detailed political story need not detain us. Peel's Cabinet fell apart and he resigned – only to be back as Premier a fortnight later. Gladstone was still out of Parliament, not having succeeded in finding

an alternative to his Newark seat. It was on Peel's return after his resignation that Gladstone agreed to take office. The moral and intellectual
arguments convinced him, but there were personal considerations too.
Disraeli and Bentinck had orchestrated the opposition: Gladstone did
not like that. He had a deeply affectionate regard for Peel, and agreed
to become Colonial Secretary. The Government did not last long. On
the same day as the Corn Bill passed its third reading Peel was defeated
on a coercion bill for Ireland and resigned. Gladstone was one of those
of Peel's colleagues who were shocked by the tone of his valedictory
address on the achievement of Cobden, who had referred to the landlords of England as 'plunderers and knaves'.

In his old age Gladstone wrote a note:

My relations with Liberalism (as incorporated in party)
Began in 1846
Took form in 1852
Checked in 1855
Sealed in 1859

He always took a long time to come to big decisions, yet when they
were taken they took people by surprise. Peel's tenure of office ended
within a matter of months of his agreement to join the Cabinet, but,
once decided, Gladstone's support for free trade was unshakeable. This
was an important step on the long trail from Canningite Liberal Toryism to Gladstonian Liberalism, but it was only a step. The late 1840s
and the 1850s were years of uncertainty: they represented an identity
crisis in Gladstone's political career.

6

Two Budgets:
December 1852 and April 1853

Derby's first Government succeeded Russell's in February 1852. The Prime Minister had a good deal of difficulty in assembling a Cabinet and invited the distinguished financier Thomas Baring to become Chancellor of the Exchequer. Baring refused and Derby had to persuade Disraeli, who was already Leader of the House. With the Premier in the Lords, this would normally have precluded the Leader from accepting so burdensome an office, and as is well known Disraeli pleaded that he know nothing of financial matters; only to receive the famous response: 'You know as much as Mr Canning did: they give you the figures.'

The key question to be settled by the Government was whether or not they were Free Traders. Until, and even perhaps after, this general question had been settled, it was not clear whether they could command a majority. But although the Government and the Opposition were now forced in to the open by the general question, the vote in the House of Commons still depended to some extent on particular interests, of which shipping (and the Navigation Acts), the landowners (over the Malt Tax), and the sugar interest were the largest.

The debates on Free Trade took place from 13 to 26 November, Government and Opposition trying to outwit each other tactically, with many private meetings of groups and long conversations between Gladstone and Aberdeen. Disraeli made his major speech on Tuesday 23rd. Gladstone replied on Friday 26th – actually in response to a speech by Cobden. 'I am glad', he wrote in his diary, 'I had not to say out what was in me about Disraeli's speech on Tuesday. Divided in 336:256 and in 458 to 53. So ends the great controversy of Free Trade. Nervous excitement kept me very wakeful: the first time (after speaking) for many years.' Both parties henceforward were avowed Free Traders.

This was a landmark in British politics. But the Budget reflecting it was still to come. Disraeli had, in fact, presented a six-month Budget soon after the Government took office. Technically therefore, this was not his first, although it is generally so regarded. After the Free Trade vote, Disraeli decided to present his Budget without delay, although he could have waited until March or April 1853. Events were to reveal that this was a mistake. He had in December no surplus to show from his proposals, a fact which he did not succeed in concealing. The theme of the Budget as presented on 3 December was compensation for those who would suffer by the end of protection. This was to be provided by the extension of Income Tax to earned (or 'precarious') incomes down to £50 p.a. In addition, the House Tax was to apply to houses down to £10 p.a. rateable value. These were unwise and politically dangerous proposals.

In the 1850s Budgets were presented to the House in Committee, and were then debated at length. They came in to force by a number of separate Acts. The rule that a member could only speak once in a debate did not apply in Committee. The debate began on 13 December. Gladstone rose at 1 am on the 17th, after Disraeli had summed up. Gladstone, although he had spoken briefly earlier in the debate, was determined to have the last word and the rules of Committees could not prevent him. He said that Disraeli's speech called for an immediate response – 'on the moment' – thus giving the impression that his speech was not a prepared one. He was heckled a good deal for the first quarter of an hour and the ends of some of his sentences were drowned in the noise and are lost for ever. But gradually, as he began mercilessly to strip Disraeli's proposals to pieces, members became spellbound. A thunderstorm raged meanwhile, adding further drama to the scene.

Gladstone began by attacking Disraeli's proposals for the House Tax, and their interaction with his proposals for Income Tax. He demonstrated that they had not been thought through and would damage certain classes unfairly, especially the yeomen, the small landowning farmers, whom Disraeli had promised to relieve. He then came to the Malt Tax. This was the only occasion in the speech when he went in to detail, pointing out that Disraeli's proposed relief actually amounted to three-eighths of a penny (from 5d to 4⅝d) for a quart of beer. There were 240 pence in the pound, so the saving was £0.3%: 'that is the reduction for which we are now called upon to surrender £2,500,000 of public revenue … .'

Next, Gladstone showed that Disraeli's calculation of the surplus, which Disraeli claimed was £400,000, was bogus, and he then embarked on his criticism of the Income Tax proposals. 'Has the right honourable gentleman … submitted to us a plan for the reconstruction of the income tax, or has he not? I say that a man who promises to vary the different rates of the income tax in different schedules, without having formed his plan for doing so, is guilty of a high offence against the public.' Gladstone deals with Schedule D, with some lecturing on the principles applied by Peel when he revived Pitt's Income Tax in 1842 to pay for his remissions in indirect taxation.

> What is the use of a Minister of the Crown … saying … we must recognise a difference between temporary and precarious incomes, and when challenged upon the absurdities and anomalies, inconsistencies and self-contradictions of his plan … says 'That is not my plan! I found it in the Schedules as they stand; but they are all to be reconstructed'?
>
> If I vote against the Government, I vote in support of those Conservative principles which I thank God are common in a great degree to all parties in the British House of Commons, but of which I thought it was the particular pride and glory of the Conservative party to be the champions and leaders. Are you not the party of 1842? [His point here is that when Peel had revived the Income Tax he had at least ensured that it produced a surplus.] Are you not the party who, in times of difficulty, chose to cover a deficit, and to provide a large surplus? And are you the same party to be united now in a time of prosperity, to convert a large surplus into a deficiency?

The speech ended 'a little before four o'clock in the morning'. Gladstone had convinced the House of the carelessness and profligacy of Disraeli in contrast to the mastery of finance and the proper use of direct taxation of Pitt, the originator, and Peel, the reviver, of Income Tax. The division was taken. The Government was defeated by nineteen votes. The cheering was 'deafening'. Thus Gladstone, in one fell swoop, in an apparently impromptu speech, slew the Government single-handedly. Before the month was out he himself was appointed Chancellor.

[55]

Almost exactly fifty years later, when John Morley published his *Life of Gladstone*, it became apparent that this speech was not quite as impromptu as it had seemed. Gladstone wrote almost daily to his wife when they were apart, and Morley had read the letters:

Dec. 3 I write from H of C at 4½ just expecting the budget. All seem to look for startling and dangerous proposals ... If there is anything outrageous, we may protest at once; but I do not expect any extended debate tonight.'

Dec. 6 ... A long sitting at Lord Aberdeen's about the budget ... The said budget will give rise to serious difficulties. The first day of serious debate will be Friday next ... .

Dec. 8 ... I have had a long sit with Lord Aberdeen today talking over possibilities. The government, I believe, talk confidently about the decision on the house-tax, but I should doubt whether they are right. Meantime I am convinced that Disraeli's is the least conservative budget I have ever known.

Dec. 14 It has been arranged that I am not to speak until the close of the debate ... ministers have become much less confident ... whether they will or not (I expect the latter, but my opinion is *naught*) they cannot carry this house-tax nor their budget. But the mischief of the proposals they have launched will not die with them.

Dec. 15 I write in great haste. Though it is Wednesday, I have been down to the House all day to unravel a device of Disraeli's about the manner in which the question is to be put, by which he means to catch votes ... the debate may close tomorrow night. I am sorry to say I have a long speech fermenting in me, and I feel as a loaf might in the oven. The government, it is thought, are likely to be beaten.

Dec. 16 I have been engaged in the House till close on post time. Disraeli trying to wriggle out of the question, and get it put upon words without meaning, to enable more to vote as they please ... . But he is beaten in this point, and we now have the right question before us ... . It is weary work sitting with a speech fermenting inside me.

Dec. 18 I have never gone through so exciting a passage of parliamentary life. The intense efforts which we made to obtain, and the government to escape, a definite issue, were like a fox chase, and prepared us all for excitement. I came home at seven, dined, read for a quarter of an hour, and actually contrived (only think) to sleep in the fur cloak for another quarter of an hour; got back to the House at nine. Disraeli rose at 10.20 [Dec.16], and from that moment, of course, I was on tenterhooks, except when his superlative acting and brilliant oratory from time to time absorbed me and made me quite *forget* that I had to follow him. He spoke until one. His speech as a whole was grand; I think the most powerful I ever heard from him. At the same time it was disgraced by shameless personalities and otherwise; I had therefore to begin by attacking him for these. There was a question whether it would not be too late, but when I heard his personalities I felt there was no choice but to go on. My great object was to show the conservative party how their leader was hoodwinking and bewildering them, and this I have the happiness of believing that in some degree I effected; for while among some there was great heat and a disposition to interrupt me when they could, I could *see* in the faces and demeanour of others quite other feelings expressed. But it was a most difficult operation, and altogether it might have been better effected. The House has not I think been so much excited for years. The power of his speech, and the importance of the issue, combined with the lateness of the hour, which always operates, were the causes. My brain was strung very high, and has not yet quite got back to calm, but I slept well last night. On Thursday night [*i.e.* Friday morning] after two hours of sleep, I awoke, and remembered a gross omission I had made, which worked upon me so that I could not rest any more. And still, of course, the time is an anxious one, and I wake with the consciousness of it, but I am very well and really not unquiet. When I came home from the House, I thought it would be good for me to be mortified. Next morning I opened the *Times*, which I thought *you* would buy, and *was* mortified when I saw it did not contain my speech but a mangled abbreviation. Such is human nature, at least mine. But in the *Times* of to-day you will see a very curious article descriptive of the last scene of the debate. It has evidently been written by a man who must have seen what occurred, or been informed by those who did see. He by no means says too much in praise of Disraeli's speech. I am told he is much stung by what I said. I am very sorry it fell to me to say it; God knows I have no wish to give him pain; and really with my deep sense of his gifts I would only pray they might be well used.

A further seventy years passed before Gladstone's diaries for the month of December 1852 were published. Only then did the extent of Gladstone's preparation become apparent. On November 12, 26 and 30 and December 1, 2, 3, 7, 8, 9, (probably) 10 and 16 he read every House of Commons debate on Income Tax from its origin under Pitt, the evidence of the Parliamentary Committee on the subject, and an advance copy of the latest expert pamphlet, Maitland's *Property and Income Tax, Schedule A and Schedule D.*

The significance of this history was not lost on a House of Commons of the 1850s, because Pitt's tax introduced during the French Revolutionary War had constituted the first ever comprehensive system of direct taxation in Britain, apart from the massive occasional capital levies imposed on landholders and bishops in the Middle Ages. Pitt's scheme was elaborate and complicated in its endeavour to be both fair and comprehensive although it was rough and ready in comparison with modern refinements; and it was Pitt who introduced the word 'income' into the English language in its current sense. It was Pitt's financial system which, a decade after his death, finally ensured that France should not dominate Europe. It was Pitt who had borrowed the money which paid for the Allied armies, creating the huge national debt which the Chancellors of the 1850s and '60s (and beyond) were having to service. The least interesting parts of Gladstone's Budget speech in 1860 concerned the Long Annuities of Pitt's time, which had to be repaid. Without the Income Tax the country could not have paid for Nelson's navy or, after Pitt's death, for Wellington's army.

The revival of the tax by Peel in 1842 had been subject to a full review of its complexities, and this is why Gladstone was able to persuade a majority in the Commons that Disraeli's proposals simply had not been thought through. As so often in Gladstone's Parliamentary life, it was thorough preparation leading to mastery of his subject which led to his success.

2 W. E. GLADSTONE – 18 APRIL 1853

Having become Chancellor of the Exchequer designate on 18 December 1852, after weeks of research on the history and principles of British taxation, and well experienced in the fiscal policy of his master, Peel, during the 1840s, Gladstone was well equipped to prepare in detail the Budget he was to present on 18 April 1853. He was forty-three years of age. This was his first Budget, but his speech was one of his greatest, laying down all the main principles which were to govern taxation in the mid-Victorian era: the production of a surplus, a balance between indirect and direct taxation, very careful consideration of the way indirect and direct taxation would interact, a fair burden on every class of taxpayer, a system which would encourage trade and industry, a system which would encourage and benefit hard work and entrepreneurial qualities and thus lead to the reduction of rates of taxation; and a massive effort at simplification where this would, by encouraging economic activity, actually increase the revenue from a tax.

The revenue was required for three purposes: to service the National Debt (the burden of the French wars), to pay for the Navy and Army, and thirdly – much the smallest – to pay the costs of Government. Welfare and education were assigned to voluntary efforts, or paid for by endowments. Compared with the modern state, the sums involved were small. But the value of money was stable, and returns per cent were also very small compared with the post-1945 era. The system of taxation, therefore, was not merely perceived as a vital organ of national prosperity: it actually was one. Public expectation of what a Government could or should do was modest, but small percentages of income taken in taxation could be very burdensome. The rising tide of prosperity in the 1850s and 1860s was due to much more than the manoeuvres of the Exchequer, but the world looked on the British political system with envy.

Notwithstanding the unrivalled understanding of taxation he had displayed in December, Gladstone's diary records work on his Budget on 64 of the 87 days (excluding Sundays) between 1 January and 11 April, nearly always late at night, before putting his plan to the Cabinet, where it was considered in detail. His diary tells the story:

Feb. 1 Worked on papers in evg. A most dense fog.

Feb. 3 This day we moved to our new abode in Downing Street. West Indies' Loan Meeting 2–3¼. Cabinet to 5½. Read Ranke's Ferdinand I. Sir C. Trevelyan on Consolidated Annuities.

Feb. 7 [11 letters; and minutes.] Saw Wine Duties Deputn – Stamp Duties Depn.. [6 meetings, including one on hops and two with the Bishop of London]. A party of 14 to dinner: our housewarming. Got 40 mins of walk & drive. Sat working till 2½ – in consequence got no sleep till near 8. Read Book 1 of the Prelude [by Wordsworth, published 1850].

Feb. 9 Dined at home: worked till 1 on Treas. Papers &c – wrote on Income Tax. I here note that I shall not during Lent, at any rate until the end attempt restraint in quantity of food.

Feb. 17 [13 letters; and minutes. Worked on an index of his books. 10 meetings.] Chicory Deputation. Hop Deputation. H. of C. 4½ to 7½. … Eight to dinner. Worked till past 2 am.

Feb. 18 Yesterday I had 15h work: today not much over 13.

Invited by his old and close friend and Cabinet colleague Sidney Herbert, he gave himself and Catherine from Tuesday to Saturday after Easter to visit Wilton, near Salisbury, seat of the Earls of Pembroke. After a day's work on Easter Monday 'Went with C. to the Lord Mayor's dinner – a lamentable hole in my evening 6½–12. Came home and worked until four on Budget Plans of Finance of all kinds – and on Customs Reform Minute.' After another day's work on Tuesday 'Left at 4½ for Wilton & arrived at nine: where we were received with the utmost warmth. Read Ed. Rev. [the *Edinburgh Review*, January 1853, a long article on Income Tax] – Thring on Colonies [an article in favour of self-government].' On Wednesday afternoon they 'drove up the hill & saw the lie of the country' before reading Rickards's Oxford lectures on Political Economy, Travers on Tea Duty and Bagot on Spirits in Bond. On Thursday they saw Stonehenge (after writing seven letters, reading the *New Quarterly Review* 'on Gold', writing on Income Tax, and a conversation with Herbert on the same): 'it is a noble & an awful relic, telling much, & telling too that it conceals more.' On Friday (after church, four letters, writing on Income Tax and reading pamphlets) they drove to Salisbury and saw the Cathedral. 'The exterior is on the whole a wonder of harmony and beauty, especially from the South ... wrote on Income Tax & Funds.'

On Saturday 2 April, after the usual letters, he wrote a memorandum on proposed reforms of Oxford, and another on Wine Duties, left Wilton at 7.30 am and reached Downing Street at 11.15. 'Arranged about entertainments: one of the petty but rigid necessities of my position.' He attended the Education Committee ('12½–2'), saw Cardwell (President of the Board of Trade, a trusted adviser on finance), then attended the Cabinet from three to six to present a part of his plan for the Budget: 'Got authority for my Exchequer Bond &c Resolutions. Fifteen to dinner.' Before bed he read the 1848 debate on Income Tax and Brown on railroad accidents.

On Friday 8 April, Saturday the 9th and Monday the 11th the Cabinet again considered his financial plan. The problem was that the Government's majority was small and fragile. The Premier admired the plan but said 'you must take care your proposals are not unpopular ones'. Palmerston said the plan was a great plan and admirably put together, but it opened too many points of attack: Disraeli was on the watch. 'Lord John Russell then fell in and said it appeared to him I had a task of great difficulty to perform ... he was disposed to abide by the plan as it stood.' Graham (himself a notable Chancellor) was strongly against lowering the line of exemption from Income Tax from £150 p.a. to £100 p.a., as Gladstone proposed.

Between them, the members of this very distinguished Cabinet had many objections and qualifications, and the next day they met again. 'Palmerston drawing the distinction between the goodness of the plan & the practicability of carrying it said he always thought Disraeli's Budget a very good plan, but then it could not be carried – and he thought we should be broken on this plan.'

Then Gladstone had a private discussion with Cardwell, who 'suggested a new view of it', which had the merit of great simplicity. But Aberdeen was against it: he reminded them that on forming his ministry he had declared that the especial mission of the Government would be to extend the commercial policy of Sir R. Peel. Cardwell's plan would forgo this. Then (on 14 April) the Government was defeated by thirty-one votes on a debate about the advertisement duty.

This was an odd situation because, the Budget proposals being secret, the Government could not make a proper response. The next day Lord John 'stated or hinted an opinion that we must contract the Budget, take in a reef or two in consequence of what had happened, for safety's sake'. But Gladstone pointed out that modifications had already been made, and in the end 'we parted well resolved & ... likely to stand or fall by the Budget.' That was on Friday night. Gladstone worked hard on Saturday and for once, very rarely for him, on Sunday. He went to church twice, read a sermon to his household in the evening and read Dante's *Paradiso*, 'but I was obliged to give several hours to my figures'.

On Monday (18 April) he wrote minutes and read Shakespeare (at night). 'This day was devoted to my working up my papers and figures for the evening. Then drove and walked with C. Went at 4½ to the House. Spoke 4¾ hours in detailing the financial measures: and my strength stood out well thank God. Many kind congratulations afterwards. At 11 o'clock the Herberts and Wortleys came home with us and had soup and Negus.'

The speech was his longest ever. It occupies seventy-two columns in Hansard and sixty-eight pages in Arthur Tilney Bassett's *Selected Speeches*. One has to allow for a packed House of Commons, with the back benches literally in the dark, half his audience behind him, and therefore a necessarily slow and laboured enunciation. Nevertheless it is not easy today to imagine listening with attention to such a marathon. It is well attested that Gladstone was clever at making figures interesting and even exciting, and it is surprising how interesting the speech is. Some passages are indeed laborious for the uninitiated: the complications of the value of Exchequer loans and annuities; and the difficulties in continuing a process of harmonisation between Irish taxation and that of England, Scotland and Wales, which were substantially the same, although not so as regards duties on whisky in Scotland (and income tax assessments on feu-duties). But for the most part Gladstone does not labour details, passing rapidly from one subject to another, covering the whole range; and where he does go into detail, he always holds one's attention.

One of the first things that strikes one is the calm, almost easygoing style. The sentences are elegantly and logically framed but modestly phrased. There may be didactic moments but there is no hectoring, no pomposity, no sarcasm, no verbosity, no purple passage. The

Committee (i.e. the House) is often offered the choice of decision on particular points, even if somewhat rhetorically, but where Gladstone is convinced there is no choice, he does not pretend otherwise. It is clear that he has carefully considered his objective: to convince the floating voters amongst MPs by logical argument, clear evidence, and sweet reasonableness.

Any attempt at a summary will rob a speech of its character, and of the magic touch which enabled Gladstone to retain the interest of his audience. Nevertheless, readers will wish to understand the ground he covered and the main measures which he introduced.

He begins with a survey of the total revenue required for the year and then deals comprehensively with Income Tax, giving a history of this 'mighty engine' of finance introduced by Pitt in 1793. Without it, he says, we could not have defeated the French and preserved our independence and our liberty; even with it, we are still left with a massive national debt. Abolished after the war, the tax was renewed by Peel in 1842 to enable him to complete – except for the Corn Laws – the abolition of protective duties. Gladstone now planned to abolish it after five more years – two at 8d and three at 5d in the £. He points out the difficulties, which he considers insuperable, of defining 'precarious' incomes for a reduced rate, and he points to the shortcomings of self-assessment, for instance that it led to fraud, that it used an unjust theoretical system for the valuation of assets, and that it used gross rather than net incomes from land. He deals with Schedule D in some detail; although he had said it was unjust to tax the gross profits of land, yet he thought it impractical to allow the merchants to deduct the cost of management: 'You must include the cost of clerks, sub-agents, ground-bailiffs, offices, stationery, receipts and so forth ... arrears of rent, abatements of rent ... how much shall we allow under these heads?' Then 'when we approach Schedule C, we begin to tread a very delicate ground: are public stocks or funds to be taxed?' He thinks Mr Pitt's answer was the best. Then he surveys the whole field of joint ownerships, and finally considers the taxation of trading companies and associations holding funded property. Eventually he comes to his proposal to lower the threshold from £150 to £100 a year, at the reduced rate of 5d, largely on the ground that people in this 'band' have benefited from the big remissions in indirect taxation. This he quantifies by four examples: a country tradesman with £120 p.a., a retired Liverpool tradesman (having six children)

[63]

with £120 p.a., a widow with an income of £135 and a clerk in a country town with £100 p.a. – and he shows that all these have benefited proportionately more than those with higher incomes from the reductions in indirect taxes.

He then gets on to Legacy Duty: which hitherto applied only to personal property: he extends it to land, so that landowners will have to pay (if one may borrow the words of a modern Chancellor) 'like everybody else'. (However, the civil servants made a monstrous error in over-estimating the proceeds. Largely because of this, and also because a great proportion of settled land was burdened with debts and obligations, this important proposal produced only a quarter of what was expected, with painful results to Gladstone's calculations. The problem came back to haunt him over his War Budget the following year.)

At last he came to indirect taxes, starting with palm oil (for soap). His reduction of duty, he thought, would encourage cultivation in West Africa, which would therefore have less need to resort to the slave trade! Then stamp duty, stamps on receipts, advertisement duty, tax on hackney carriages. Then the 'assessed' duties (i.e. those variable in relation to value) – on menservants and carriages; on horses – 'a vast variety of rates' (even though agricultural horses were exempt), which he proposed to replace with just horses and ponies. Then dogs: 'They are usually great favourites with their owners – not so much so with the rest of the community': there are two rates, 14s and 8s, and 'inasmuch as they lead to much difficulty and evasion, we propose to unite at a sum of 12s.' Then he came to customs duties – for it was in trade that 'the elasticity of the powers of the country has chiefly been shown'. He began with the big ones – wine (a complex problem) and tea (to encourage the emergence of China in Western trade); then food: apples, cheese, cocoa, nuts, eggs, oranges and lemons, butter, raisins – all these duties were reduced. Then, on 123 articles, the duty was abolished. Musical instruments were the most difficult, for 'we must introduce a number of complex descriptions to get rid of one very simple one'. Thus ended the grand plan to abolish, simplify or reduce the surviving ancient intricacies of indirect taxation – and after a final summary (and the only Latin tag in 4¾ hours) he drew to a close.

The Budget was a triumph. Far from rocking the Government's uncertain majority, it served to increase and stabilise it, and strengthened the

<u>Dictionaries & Books of Reference.</u>

Œschyli Lexicon a Linwood. 8vo. ~~8vo~~ . Lond. 1847 . . . 1

Ayscough . See Shakespeare . . . .

Arabic . Catafago's A. Dictionary . cr 8vo. Quaritch. Lond. 1858 . - 1

Bayle . Dictionnaire Historique et Critique . 3d
   Edition . 4 Vols. folio . with Articles Omis, and
   Communiqués. Rotterdam 1720 . . . . . . - 4.

Bartlett . Dictionary of American Words and
   Phrases . royal 8vo . Boston 1859 1

Beckmann . History of Inventions . 12mo. Lond. 1846 . . . 2

Buttmann . See Biblioth. Homerica .

Biographie Universelle Anc. et Moderne . 8vo Paris 1811 . . - 52

Benfey, Griechisches Wurzel Lexicon 8vo Berlin 1839 . . . - - 2

Calmet . Dictionary of the Bible : with Biblical
   Fragments by Taylor. 7th Ed. 4to London 1838 . . . - 5

Chambers. Cyclopædia of English Literature .
      Imp. 8vo. Edinburgh 1844 . . 2

Clinton . Fasti Hellenici . I. to Ol. LV.
   II . Ol. LV to Ol. CXXIV .   4 to .   3
   III . Ol. CXXIV to the Death of Augustus   Oxf. 1827..34

Chalmers Biographical Dictionary . In London.

A page from one of Gladstone's many catalogues of his books. Arranging and listing his library was a therapeutic exercise (chapter 8).

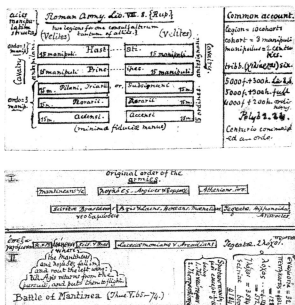

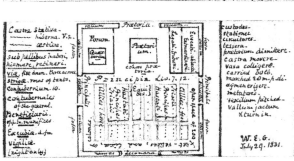

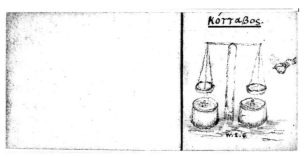

Gladstone's Oxford Finals revision cards (actual size)

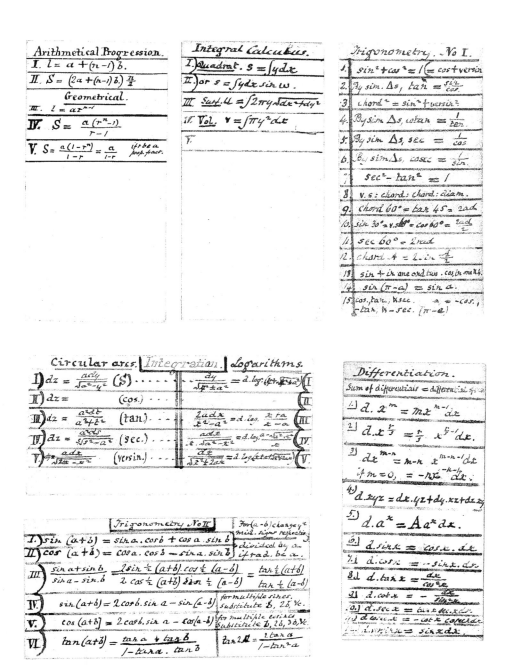

A further selection of Gladstone's Oxford revision cards

RATES OF INCOME TAX, 1853–98

From and to April 5th	On £100 to £150	On £150 and upwards
	Rate in the £	
1853 to 1854	5d	7d
1854 to 1855	10d	1s.2d
1855 to 1857	11½d	1s.4d
1857 to 1858	5d	7d
1858 to 1859	5d	5d
1859 to 1860	6½d	9d
1860 to 1861	7d	10d
1861 to 1863	6d	9d
1863 to 1864	7d	
1864 to 1865	6d	
1865 to 1866	4d	
1866 to 1867	4d	
1867 to 1868	5d	
1868 to 1869	6d	
1869 to 1870	5d	
1870 to 1871	4d	
1871 to 1872	6d	
1872 to 1873	‚4d	
1873 to 1874	3d	
1874 to 1876	2d	
1876 to 1878	3d	
1878 to 1880	5d	
1880 to 1881	6d	
1881 to 1882	5d	
1882 to 1883	6½d	
1883 to 1884	5d	
1884 to 1885	6d	
1885 to 1886	8d	
1886 to 1887	8d	
1887 to 1888	7d	
1888 to 1892	6d	
1892 to 1893	6d	
1893 to 1894	7d	
1894 to 1895	8d	
1895 to 1898	8d	

NOTES: Differential rates were abolished by Gladstone in 1863. Incomes under £100 were exempt and incomes between £100 and £400 received an abatement of £60, eg. an income of £160 paid tax on £100. The Nil band and/or the abatement were adjusted in 1871, 1878 and 1895. By 1894 the exempt sum had risen to £160 and refinements were introduced in bands up to £600.

AVERAGE PRICE OF CONSOLS FOR THE PAST HUNDRED AND SEVEN YEARS, WITH THE AMOUNT OF INTEREST PRODUCED.

1792	84¾	3	10	9	1819	71⅞	4	3	5	1846	95½	3	2	10	1873	92½	3	4	10
1793	75¾	3	19	2	1820	67⅞	4	8	4	1847	86⅜	3	9	5	1874	92½	3	4	10
1794	67½	4	8	10	1821	73¾	4	1	4	1848	85	3	10	7	1875	93¾	3	4	0
1795	65¾	4	11	3	1822	79⅛	3	15	10	1849	93¼	3	4	4	1876	95	3	3	2
1796	61⅞	4	16	11	1823	78⅞	3	16	1	1850	96⅝	3	2	1	1877	95⅜	3	3	0
1797	52	5	15	4	1824	90¾	3	6	1	1851	97¾	3	1	4	1878	95 3/16	3	3	10
1798	52⅝	5	14	0	1825	84⅝	3	10	11	1852	98⅞	3	0	8	1879	97½	3	1	6
1799	60¾	4	18	9	1826	79⅛	3	15	10	1853	95⅞	3	2	6	1880	98⅜	3	1	0
1800	63⅝	4	14	3	1827	83⅛	3	12	2	1854	90⅓	3	6	3	1881	100	3	0	0
1801	62⅛	4	16	7	1828	84⅝	3	10	11	1855	90	3	6	8	1882	100½	2	19	8
1802	72½	4	2	9	1829	89⅞	3	6	9	1856	90¾	3	6	1	1883	101 3/16	2	19	2
1803	61⅝	4	17	4	1830	85⅞	3	9	10	1857	90¾	3	6	1	1884	101	2	19	4
1804	56¼	5	6	8	1831	79¾	3	15	3	1858	96⅜	3	2	2	1885	99⅓	3	0	2
1805	59½	5	0	9	1832	83⅝	3	11	9	1859	92 11/16	3	4	8	1886	100⅘	2	19	8
1806	61½	4	17	7	1833	87¾	3	8	4	1860	94⅛	3	3	8	1887	101⅘	2	19	0
1807	61	4	18	9	1834	90¼	3	6	5	1851	91¾	3	5	4	Reduced to 2¾ per cent.				
1808	65⅞	4	11	1	1835	91	3	5	11	1862	93¼	3	4	4	1888	97 11/16	2	16	4½
1809	66⅞	4	9	8	1836	89⅜	3	7	1	1863	92⅝	3	4	9	1889	98	2	16	3
1810	67⅛	4	9	4	1837	90⅞	3	6	0	1854	90⅛	3	6	6	1890	96⅓	2	17	3
1811	64¼	4	13	4	1838	92⅞	3	4	7	1865	89½	3	7	0	1891	95¾	2	17	7½
1812	59	5	1	8	1839	91½	3	5	7	1866	87⅛	3	8	3	1892	96 11/16	2	17	6
1813	61	4	18	9	1840	89⅜	3	7	1	1867	93	3	4	6	1893	98½	2	15	10¼
1814	67	4	9	7	1841	88⅞	3	7	6	1868	93⅛	3	4	0	1894	101 1/16	2	14	5
1815	59¾	5	0	4	1842	91¾	3	5	4	1869	92⅞	3	4	7	1895	106⅛	2	11	9½
1816	62	4	16	9	1843	94⅝	3	3	5	1870	92½	3	4	10	1896	110¾	2	9	7¾
1817	73⅛	4	2	0	1844	98½	3	0	8	1871	92¾	3	4	8	1897	112 13/32	2	8	11⅗
1818	77½	3	17	4	1845	96¼	3	2	4	1872	92½	3	4	10	1898	110 15/16	2	9	6¾

BANK OF ENGLAND MINIMUM RATE OF DISCOUNT, 1884 TO 1898

MONTHS.	1884.	1885.	1886.	1887.	1888.	1889.	1890.	1891.	1892.	1893.	1894.	1895.	1896.	1897.	1898.
January	3	5	3⅝	5	3⅖	4 1/10	6	4¼	3⅓	2 9/19	3	2	2	3⅞	3
February	3⅓	5	2 4/7	4	2⅜	3	5 4/7	3	3	2½	2⅜	2	2	3⅛	3
March	3⅝	3 14/31	2	3½	2⅛	3	4½	3	3	2½	2	2	2	3	3
April	2½	3½	2	2⅔	2	2⅗	3⅖	3¼	2½	2½	2	2	2	2⅞	3 13/16
May	2½	2 23/31	2⅕	2	2⅗	2½	3	4½	2	3½	2	2	2	2¼	3⅞
June	2⅓	2	2⅗	2	2⅗	2½	3⅙	3⅔	2	3	2	2	2	2	3
July	2	2	2½	2	2½	2½	4	2½	2	2½	2	2	2	2	2½
August	2	2	2⅗	2⅛	2⅜	3	4⅖	2½	2	4	2	2	2	2	2½
September	2	2	3½	4	3⅝	4 1/10	4⅛	2⅜	2	4¼	2	2	2 7/15	2⅛	2⅝
October	2¾	2	3⅝	4	5	5	5	3	2⅖	3	2	2	3⅓	2⅝	3⅝
November	4¾	2 13/30	4	4	5	5	5⅛	4	3	3	2	2	4	3	4
December	5	3 14/31	4½	4	5	5	5 1/10	3⅔	3	3	2	2	4	3	4
Average......	2 19/20	3	3	3⅓	3½	3½	4½	3⅓	2½	3 1/20	2½	2	2½	2⅝	3¼

Consols (the Consolidated Fund of the United Kingdom), paying 3% until 1887, were devised by Pitt and used to pay for the French wars. The income from £100 invested is given in £.s.d. and was remarkably stable throughout Gladstone's political life. Bank Rate was rather more volatile, but was used with very considerable success to stabilise the economy (chapter 5).

It is equally used as a substantive and an adjective. Thus: 'what a ph you are!' 'Lord —— is become a ph.' Or 'ph talk,' 'ph company,' &c. Examples: * * * * * *ᵃ

SITTING TIGHT.
SITTING CROSSLEGGED.

These phrases are put together in illustration of the great difficulty of discriminating accurately between some of the expressions of this language. They do not mean quite the same, yet nearly so. They both mean sitting in expectation of some probable or anticipated event. Perhaps it may be said briefly, that to *sit tight* is to be in *eager* expectation, to *sit crosslegged* to be in *patient* expectation.

The former when the event is much desired, and imminent: but *may* fail.

ᵃ The examples here are omitted for obvious reasons. This and some other omissions are supplied in the original Manuscript, and the omitted passages may be learnt from the Author by any discreet enquirer.

The latter when it is pretty sure to happen, but may be delayed for some time. Etymological considerations may justify this view. To *sit tight* suggests the idea of a person who feels that some slight movement on his part might hinder the desired event, and is therefore careful to prevent it : while to *sit crosslegged* is the posture of composed and comfortable vigilance.

The latter also, from its passive character, may be especially used when it is an *evil* that is looked for.

Illustrations : A lady looking for an advantageous proposal for her daughter, *sits tight* for it.

Another lady, awaiting the deferred arrival of the dentist, *sits crosslegged* for it.

TOTTERTON.

This so far differs from *phantod*, that it is confined to the case of imbecility from second childhood, or premature old age. Otherwise a distinction cannot readily be perceived.

Two pages from *The Glynnese Glossary* compiled by George Lyttelton (chapter 8)

Rev. Dr. Pusey.

Could the Radcliffe actually joined to the Bodleian?

365. To transfer the books of the Bodleian on Physical Science to the Radcliffe, would also be to transfer the greater to the less. The Radcliffe, at present, does not seem to be arranged for a large library. It might, I suppose, be a question whether it could contain all the books, if they *were* transferred, and, still more, whether it would have room for future accessions. It would perhaps be practicable, by a covered way, actually to join the Radcliffe to the Bodleian, without any disfigurement. The greater part of the School Quadrangle is already occupied by the Bodleian, so that they could easily be united, if it were no dis-sight.

366. Dr. Greenhill mentions a Collection" of Persian, Arabic, and Sanscrit MSS. which might be exchanged with the Bodleian. As to the Persian and Sanscrit I am no judge. The Arabic I examined with a view to a Catalogue, when engaged in editing that of Dr. Nicoll. There were several collections of poetry which were not in the Bodleian; else there was nothing, I think, of any account.

A small library specially formed for Undergraduates, the most useful plan for them.

367. The value of such libraries as the Bodleian, or even the College libraries, to the Undergraduate is very much overrated. The Undergraduate Student does not, ordinarily, want books of research. The books which he uses most he ought to have of his own. It is almost essential for a student to be able to mark his books for himself. Other books which the poorer student might not be able to procure, as classics with fuller notes, books on antiquities, &c. could be much better provided for him by a student's library on the plan of Darling's Theological Library, on a smaller scale, or such as, I understand, the students belonging to "the Union" have formed for themselves. I understand that at Colleges where the Undergraduates are allowed to take books out of the College library, the privilege is used to a very slight extent.

Conclusion.

368. I have now, I fear, taxed your attention more than I could have wished; but the greatness of the main subject will, I am sure, excuse it in your eyes. If you in some respects should differ from what I have said, you do not become responsible for it by allowing me to express my meaning to you. But I know that you will think with me, in the main, that this

" P. 229.

Rev. Dr. Pusey.

is a great crisis for Oxford, and that upon what she does now, depends her future importance for good, or (God forbid it) for evil. You will think with me, that the problem of Oxford is not to furnish a mere stimulant for intellectual study, but so to impart knowledge and to discipline the mind, as to form (by God's grace) Christian men. She has to recover the ground which she has lost by letting the education of the country so slip out of her hands; to train the youth of the land so that they shall be "qualified to serve God," as we pray, "in Church and State," soundly, solidly, religiously. But this, I am convinced, may be better attained by steady progress, than by any sudden, hurried, sweeping, revolutionary changes.

369. A thoughtful person (afterwards the first Professor of Moral Philosophy) said to me in 1825, when much was spoken around us of "the march of intellect;" "People may say what they please, but no place has so solidly and steadily improved as Oxford." What was then dawning has since brightened, though very far from mid-day still.

370. It is right that Oxford should embrace all who will come to her to be educated in her way; it is right that she should enlarge her studies, by taking in, in their order and degree, those parts of study which can be combined with her system, and which may help to expand, cultivate, strengthen, consolidate, and, if rightly used, elevate the mind. It is well that she should help the student even to lay a solid foundation for his future special study. Only let it be really solid, and above all, under the control of a firm, unwavering faith, to the glory of God. It will yet be well with Oxford, if she forget not her own motto, "Dominus illuminatio mea."

Believe me,

My dear Mr. Vice-Chancellor,

Your's affectionately,

E. B. PUSEY.

The end of Pusey's lengthy response to the Royal Commission's Report on Oxford (chapter 3), with Gladstone's comments

Kyrie Eleison.

(Devised in Speech-Rhythm.)

W. E. GLADSTONE.

Lord, have mer - cy up - on us, and in - cline our hearts to keep this law.

Last time

Lord, have mer-cy up-on us, and write all these thy laws in our hearts, we be - seech thee. we be - seech thee.

[Clearly it should be softly sung, as nearly as possible to the rhythm of devoutly deliberate speech.]

This incorporates the whole of Mr. Gladstone's treble part and all that seemed clear and possible in his harmonic scheme. W. D.

London : NOVELLO AND COMPANY, LIMITED.

The Oxford Movement brought a reintroduction of Anglican chants (chapter 14), assiduously practised by Gladstone for the opening of St Andrew's, Fasque, in 1847 (chapter 13). He had a fine singing voice. No other composition by him is recorded.

ministry's credentials. On the 19th 'I received today innumerable marks of kindness: enough to make me ashamed.' The following evening 'Cabinet dinner at Lord Granville's. We discussed the budget – Advertisement Duty – meeting in Downing St. on Saty – & were very merry.' The purpose of the Saturday meeting was to decide what resolutions were necessary to get the Budget approved.

7
Political and Personal: 1846–59

For many years after 1846, when Peel split the Tory Party by resolving to repeal the Corn Laws, no Government was able to secure a firm majority. Contemporaries were as baffled as historians have been by the fluctuating groups which made up the House of Commons. General elections did not make it clear whether a Government could obtain a majority: for that, one had to wait for a vote in the new Parliament; and even then, as Gladstone noted in 1853, the strength of the Government was 'liable on occasions, which frequently arise, to heavy deductions'.

Gladstone himself was able, by the end of 1852, to refer (at least on paper) to the 'Conservative' and 'Liberal' Parties. Yet he could not quite bring himself to accept that he was no longer a Tory, and as he wrote in old age in his autobiographical notes 'It took a long time, with my slow-moving and tenacious character, for the Ethiopian to change his skin.' Throughout his life he was slow to make up his mind on fundamental questions – though formidable once he had taken the plunge. This was partly an inborn characteristic, nurtured by the assumptions of his younger years; and partly a fruit of the political lessons he learnt, especially from Peel and Aberdeen, about 'ripeness' and 'right-timing': the perception that a new idea takes many years to become generally acceptable. This was not, incidentally, one of the many lessons he learnt from his father: 'I am seldom long in making up my mind,' said John, 'though I have also sometimes had cause to regret having done so too quickly.'

Between 1846 and 1868, when Gladstone became Prime Minister, there were only two Governments which survived for any length of time, and in both of them Gladstone played a significant role. The first was a 'coalition' under Lord Aberdeen (1852–5) and the second depended on the fame and boldness of the only substantial 'name' on the political scene, that of Lord Palmerston (1859–65).

Aberdeen's Government was a 'ministry of all the talents', made up of men of exceptional brilliance but varying political views. Gladstone wrote a long and interesting memorandum (1852) on the conditions required to form what he called a 'mixed government.' Aberdeen, gentle, scholarly, high-minded and diplomatic, was probably the only statesman who could have formed and handled it. Gladstone had many long conversations with him as to the best way to approach a problem, admired him greatly and learnt much from him. As the Crimean War loomed, Aberdeen summoned Gladstone to seek his younger colleague's opinion: could the Premier, who hated war (as a young man he had seen the carnage at Leipzig on the day after the battle) and who could not bring himself to fight in defence of the Turkish Empire, honourably resign? Gladstone replied, but clearly without conviction, and without convincing Aberdeen, that the war would be against Russia, not in support of Turkey, and that it would be a defensive, not an offensive war. Gladstone himself hated war too, and now it was his task as Chancellor to provide the money for the Crimea. His Budget was unconstructive and controversial and it blew away his masterplan to abolish income tax. When he continued to hope that he could achieve this, even twenty years later, he was perhaps deceiving himself – as in 1854 when he claimed he was raising the war revenue from taxation rather than by borrowing and thus adding to the vast unfunded National Debt. Just as Britain was launching into war, the Chancellor whose duty it was to finance it pointed out that the cost of a war was a salutary limitation on a government's ability to wage one.

Gladstone prepared his Budget in March, as negotiations still dragged on. He doubled income tax (temporarily), increased the major indirect taxes and, persisting in his argument that he was not borrowing, arranged an issue of £6m of short-dated bonds, repayable over the next six years. In the end they were not redeemed but simply added to the Debt, but they led Gladstone into a long, bitter and fruitless argument in the Commons. What made matters worse was that the issue was not successful, and as the news came in daily Gladstone was confronted with awkward questions from Thomas Baring asking for precise figures. Simultaneously he involved himself in a dispute with the Bank of England over deficiency bills. The Bank's case was presented in Parliament by Thomas Hankey, a former member of the Court of Governors. Gladstone's long-term objective was to subject the Bank to tighter Treasury control, and he chose this difficult moment – during the production of a running wartime budget, supplemented in May and then again in July – to end the custom by which, to tide itself over for short periods, the Bank was permitted, subject to certain conditions, to hang on to money raised by the Treasury; thus obliging the Chancellor to borrow in order to achieve the same result.

Gladstone had a good case but he chose an awkward occasion to challenge a time-honoured custom while his piecemeal efforts to finance the war, and his contention that he was not borrowing, were already calling down criticism from the City and the public; and this in the face of formidable opposition not only from Hankey but also from Baring, who had refused the Exchequership the previous year, and by Disraeli, who had felt obliged to accept it. Disraeli, of course, was delighted at the prospect of getting his own back for the mauling he had received from Gladstone over his Budget of 1852. 'I shall have rough weather', Gladstone wrote in his diary when he realised that his Exchequer bonds had failed, 'but this tries what a man is made of.'

This, then, was by far his most difficult and controversial Budget, not only with the inevitable problem of attempting to finance a war and to do so in the face of the deficiencies of the previous year's revenue; but with his insistence that he was not borrowing when, to almost everybody, it was clear that he was; with the failure of his short-dated bonds; and then with the self-imposed dispute over deficiency bills. He was treated roughly in the Commons, he was criticised by the press and the public, and he has not been kindly judged by historians. Nevertheless, he came through with flying colours, and he did indeed show 'what a man is made of'. He received total backing from the Cabinet, and the style in which he handled awkward questions in the House commands admiration: always courteous, never rattled, and masterly in producing complicated figures without notice, or delivering 'an answer answerless'.

The Opposition dared not go as far as a vote of confidence, but Baring challenged the Exchequer bonds. The big debate took place on 8 and 9 May. Gladstone spoke for three and a half hours on the 8th: 'Every appearance favourable to our plan.' He then left the House at 10.45 pm and attended the second act of the Queen's concert, with songs by Donizetti and Schubert; 'and walked afterwards'.

During the following day's debate Disraeli was badly worsted by Russell and Gladstone after making a serious procedural error in his attack on the Malt Tax: 'Mr Disraeli made an astonishing error resp. the Malt Tax and gave us (1) a majority of 81 (2) the prestige of a substantive decision (3) the advantage of an opponent's act of bad faith, at one and the same blow.' Thus ended the long battle over the 1854 Budget, enabling Gladstone and the House of Commons to turn to the more congenial business of the reform of Oxford University.

Politically the battle was won. But the Bank still refused to accept Gladstone's contention over deficiency bills, and in the autumn they asked him to obtain the opinion of the Crown law officers. This he did, and he won. In spite of having chosen the ground, the Bank still did not accept defeat but consulted their own counsel, who advised them to put their case to the Prime Minister. This evoked one of the most dusty letters ever penned by Gladstone. In effect it closed the dispute.

It so happens that Gladstone's papers relating to the Budget of 1854 were fished out of the Octagon – the muniment room at Hawarden – by his son Henry in the 1920s and sent, with various others, to the London Museum. In 1939 they found their way into an air-raid-proof shelter and they did not see the light of day again until eventually they were returned to Hawarden as being of no further interest to the Museum's visitors. It is unlikely that any historian has seen them since 1903. Some of them are not easy to date precisely. His notes do, however, illustrate his method of marshalling facts and arguments for consumption by the Commons, and much if not most of the material will be identifiable by the reader in the light of the explanation I have given.

First in my selection come the speech notes of 21 March 1854, when Gladstone replied to 'Disraeli and others'. Next comes 'Revenue of the Past Year', dated 11 April 1854: in his diary 'Worked on figures for statement tonight. ... Saw Mr Hankey ... H of C 4½ to 10¾. Spoke 1h on presenting Balance Sheet'. Then come more figures of May 1854 on the 'State of the Unfunded Debt'. Finally, in relation to the decisive debate of 8 and 9 May 1854, are his notes for the long speech on Mr Baring's motion on 8 May, with attention to Disraeli's series of errors (though not the final and fatal error over Malt Tax, which occurred the following day). Disraeli's errors are contrasted with 'Mr Pitt (always successful)' – but with warning of Mr Fox ('Do not worship him in his errors').

With these papers is an interesting memorandum dictated on 21 July by Gladstone for Lord John Russell, attempting to estimate the cost of the Crimean expedition. Russell, as a former Premier with a very strong personality, was something of a wild card in Aberdeen's Cabinet: he was within a short period Foreign Secretary, then a minister without a portfolio, then Lord President of the Council before he resigned in January 1855. Nevertheless he was a formidable debater and a powerful ally in defence of Gladstone's Budget. Gladstone had 'taken in March the possible charge of £1.25m' for a force of 29,000 men. 'A certain sum, but it is very hard to say what, perhaps £200,000, will be required for ordnance stores and ammunition.' Then he mentions the cost of the French expedition to the Baltic and the outlay in supporting a Turkish corps.

The Government was blamed then, as it has been ever since, for the incompetent supply of the Crimean campaigns, but most of the fault lay with the Army itself, which had no central staff. If ministers had been told what was needed, they could have supplied it. More at fault was the Cabinet's inability to formulate strategy and to contribute the appropriate leadership and initiative.

In 1855, when Aberdeen's Cabinet fell apart, Lord Lansdowne tried to form a Government, and sent for Gladstone who, for subtle and unfathomable reasons, refused office. It was widely thought that this was why Lansdowne abandoned the attempt. Gladstone soon began to regret his decision and he later 'looked back on it with pain as a serious and even gross error of judgment'. And yet in 1859 he joined Palmerston, whose personality and politics he had continuously and eloquently decried for some three or four years, apparently without a qualm. 'Never', he said, 'had I an easier question to determine than when I was asked to join the Government.' His diary for that historic day, 13 June 1859, confirms that his decision was not too agonising: 'Wrote to Robn.G. – Rev Mr Gregory – Rev Dr Croly – Johnson L & co. Read Italian papers: tracts. Saw Lovell: doing well. Saw Sir J Lacaita – Mr Algernon Joy – Mr Bonham – Sidney Herbert; bis. Went to Lord P. by his desire at night: and accepted my old office.'

Thus, at last, Gladstone took the plunge. No longer would he allow the best years of his life to slip by for the sake of scruples which, within the whole scene of government, seem to us as they seemed to Gladstone's contemporaries to be over-subtle and even unimportant. He longed to get back to the work for which twenty-five years of political life had prepared him; and from his decision of 13 June 1859 sprang his great series of Budgets and his emergence as 'The People's William'.

During the long period of political uncertainty when no Government could achieve a stable majority, there was curiously enough general agreement, at least tacitly, about the two crucial issues of the time: first, that there must be a new Reform Act to take forward the process begun in 1832: secondly, that Britain was moving inexorably towards free trade. But as to the first, there was endless debate but no agreement as to the details; and as to the second, many members were still prisoners of the assumptions in which they had been nurtured. Nevertheless, even if the ship of state appears with hindsight to have been in the doldrums, the issues of the day were the subject of a continuous process of brilliant debate in the House of Commons, and the two-party system was demonstrating the flexibility – the manoeuvring of groups until a majority emerged – which has enabled it to survive for centuries.

Gladstone accepted in 1846 that following his part in the repeal of the Corn Laws he could no longer call on the Duke of Newcastle's patronage in Newark. He was out of the House of Commons from June 1846 to August 1847, when he was elected as one of the two members for the University of Oxford. In London in 1848, he acted as a special constable during the Chartist riots. His truncheon is still available at Hawarden in case of emergency. He became a Commissioner of the Great Exhibition of 1851 in the Crystal Palace in Hyde Park, working closely with the Prince Consort, being heavily involved in the subsequent development of the South Kensington site with the Albert Hall, the Victoria and Albert Museum, and subsequently the Natural History and Science Museums and Imperial College. He was already a trustee of the British Museum and the National Portrait Gallery and he was one of the founders of the London Library. In all these activities he was needless to say a conscientious and meticulous attender of meetings in London.

In the autumn of 1850 Gladstone and Catherine set off for Italy for the benefit of the eyesight of their daughter Mary, and he spent a good deal of time informing himself about the government of the Kingdom of Naples (that is to say, Sicily and all of southern Italy). What he discovered disturbed him, and spurred him, on his return to England, to expose the regime's failings in a manner so trenchant as to cause a sensation.

Gladstone thus remained relentlessly energetic in a variety of ways while his political career seemed to be on hold, but this was a period of intense religious and sexual challenges, as well as extreme anxiety and distress in his family. His eldest daughter, Agnes, underwent a long and nearly fatal attack of erysipelas, which he himself caught, suffering severe pain. His second daughter, Jessy, died at the age of five from meningitis in 1850. His sister Helen suffered a mental breakdown, the effects being aggravated and prolonged by her treatment, leading to a long and distressing saga.

During his second 'interregnum' – after the fall of Aberdeen's Government in 1855 and before he joined Palmerston's in 1859 – Gladstone's most notable activity was as the Lord High Commissioner of the Ionian Islands. The islands had been made a British Protectorate, so the question of their future became the Government's responsibility; and Gladstone agreed to go to Corfu, consider the question, and report. An account of his time there makes entertaining reading. His careful, elaborate and indecisive report eventually emerged, concluding that the time was not ripe to grant them self-rule, and that there were strong reasons not to join them with Greece, at least for the time being. Three years later Palmerston, without a qualm, handed them over as part of Greece.

During the late 1830s Gladstone had many discussions on religion with two of his closest friends, Hope and Manning, both of whom to his intense distress later became Roman Catholics. In 1838 he devised a plan for a 'third order', an association of clergy and laymen to meet and pray and to undertake good works. In 1844 this idea influenced the 'Engagement', a brotherhood of fifteen High Church (or 'Tractarian') Anglicans, several of whom had been associated with his Essay Society, the 'WEG', when undergraduates at Oxford. Most of the rules of the Engagement were concerned either with prayer and worship or with charitable work, and there is a family tradition, which does not appear to be reliably documented, that a group of the members drew lots to decide where their efforts should lie, it falling to Gladstone to concentrate his energies on the rescue of fallen women. This was an orthodox form of charitable endeavour. The Engagement had a house for destitutes in Soho, and a nunnery in Clewer, near Windsor, for orphans, foundlings and repentant prostitutes. It was called the House of Mercy but the discipline was severe, and although the orphans and foundlings had time to get used to it, it was on the whole a failure with prostitutes.

Prostitution was a massive and widely recognised social problem in nineteenth-century London. Of many estimates, widely differing, Mayhew's, of 80,000 women roaming the streets day and night, which he regarded as conservative, is probably as good as any. There were in all about fifty refuges in the capital for criminals, destitutes and 'those who are exposed to temptation', including thousands ostracised from society for giving birth to an illegitimate child. Gladstone worked methodically, approaching many women and assessing the chance of helping them. He often paid the £5 donation expected for admission to a refuge. He was open about his work – Catherine knew about it and helped him with the placings – and he brought down on himself a certain amount of derision and indeed condemnation. Friends and colleagues unsuccessfully tried to persuade him to stop, fearing for his reputation, and in the 1880s he did eventually accept that his activities could do serious harm to the Liberal cause. On the only occasion when he was threatened with blackmail he went straight to the police.

Gladstone's motives were impeccable and his efforts heroic. His sexual morality was severe, and before he died he made a 'Declaration' to his son and spiritual guide, Stephen, that he had never had sexual intercourse outside marriage. But in his rescue work he did sometimes fall short of his own high standards, to the extent of admitting his enjoyment of a conversation with a prostitute whom he found beautiful. Whenever this occurred he noted it in his diary. When his diaries were eventually published his private thoughts were revealed, and it became clear that he was conscious of this sinfulness. His penance – not uncommon in High Church circles at that time, and even well into the twentieth century – was to scourge himself, and in the diary there appeared a little symbol of a whip. It is not known whether the flagellation was merely symbolic or physically painful – probably the former.

The cases to which this applied were few in number, but not surprisingly to some who now judge him, especially in view of his avowed high moral and religious principles, they have diminished him as a person. Others will judge not, that they be not judged: they will apply their own sense of proportion. To others again, for a leading political figure to carry on this work at all seems eccentric, and the fact that it sometimes excited him sexually a small matter. Judgement lies very much in the mind of the observer.

Gladstone was a man of intense physical and mental vitality. His doctor, Andrew Clark, described his physique as 'perfect'. He was a little under six feet tall, strongly built with never an ounce of superfluous fat. His energy amazed his contemporaries. He could work long hours night after night, accomplishing as much as several ordinary men in every hour. He had a good memory and could muster a mass of factual evidence which he could then lay before his hearers in a captivating manner. He walked astonishing distances and used his axes energetically until he was past his eighty-second birthday. He had a very strong sexual drive: he made several attempts to get engaged before becoming betrothed to Catherine. The beauty of the human form delighted him. He was not ashamed to find beautiful women attractive, including the Duchess of Sutherland whose weekend 'salons' he so often attended, and Laura Thistlethwayte, the reformed courtesan turned Methodist preacher. He was intensely religious and he followed a strict moral code, but he was never a puritan. He relished good food and wine, and in spite of his formidable independence of mind he was very sociable. He was earnest and he did not often tell jokes, but his ripostes were mercurial and his speeches liberally spiced with wit. The attractive feature of Gladstone is that in spite of all his earnest intensity and his brilliant gifts he was human. His marriage was exceptionally happy and fulfilling. It was his zest for life that made him what he was.

The mid-life crisis passed. The political scruples of the Maynooth affair were calmed, the churchmanship of the Engagement lost its Anglo-Catholic tetchiness and developed as moderate, middle-of-the-road Anglicanism. The rescue work became less frequent, his reflections on it less intense. He was on the path, at fifty years of age, to the People's William and eventually the Grand Old Man.

8

Hawarden

In 1839 Gladstone married Catherine Glynne, and George, Lord Lyttelton of Hagley Hall, Worcester, married her sister Mary, in a double wedding in Hawarden parish church. Both marriages were very happy. The Gladstones had eight children (seven of whom survived to adulthood) and the Lytteltons twelve.

The brides had two brothers: Sir Stephen, the ninth baronet, and the Reverend Henry, rector of the parish which, of course, was in the gift of his brother, the lord of the manor. Gladstone had known Stephen at Eton and at Christ Church, Oxford.

The estate which Stephen had inherited had been in the family since 1653 and had been extended by a marriage to a neighbouring heiress in the eighteenth century. Stephen's great-grandfather, Sir John, had demolished the old timber Hall and replaced it with a fine Georgian squire's house in 1750. The estate lay just inside Wales, south of the Dee, about five miles from Chester. In a vain but expensive attempt to keep that city open as a seaport, the tidal river had been canalised for several miles, and John Glynne had been able to reclaim a large area of marsh which became fertile agricultural land. John's grandson could afford to extend and castellate the house in Regency fashion in 1809, changing its name from Hawarden House to Hawarden Castle. There was, indeed, the ruin of a fine Edwardian castle guarding the ancient road from Chester to Conway only a hundred yards away.

Stephen inherited the house and a valuable estate providing an income of more than £10,000 a year – enough to run a large establishment and live in luxury. The reclaimed farms, having been enclosed, could in due course be tithed, and the rector's living was astonishingly rich with about £3,000 a year. No wonder all the incumbents from then until 1904 (when the cost of paying the curates had reduced the rector's income almost to a negative sum) were members of the family. Alas, it would not be long before the rector's income was much bigger than the squire's.

Although he was conscientious in public duties, being a member of Parliament (at the cost of hugely expensive elections) and Lord Lieutenant of Flintshire, Stephen was not a man of business. His favourite occupation was to visit and record, sometimes with the help of a professional illustrator, parish churches in many English and some Welsh counties. The notes he made have retained their interest because they describe churches prior to Victorian 're-ordering' and restoration, which often changed them almost beyond recognition. Gladstone, who occasionally accompanied him, was an ardent exponent of 're-ordering' – notably the replacement of the wooden communion table by an altar of stone, and of all the elaborations and improvements which robbed the churches of their ancient and dignified simplicity. Many of Glynne's 'Church Notes' have been published by county history societies.

Stephen allowed an incompetent and indeed unscrupulous agent to invest large sums of money in a rash speculation in coal and iron on a small property he owned in Staffordshire, known as Oak Farm. His Gladstone brother-in-law joined in the investment, supported by his father's money. The outcome in 1847 was a total disaster for Stephen; and Gladstone, perhaps tacitly accepting some responsibility, devoted much of his time and energy for several years to attempting to save the Hawarden estate from the wreckage. He succeeded, but only under a heavy burden of mortgages which were not finally paid off until after 1918. There was no such thing then as a limited company. The unlimited liability facing Stephen may have had something to do with Gladstone's promoting the 1862 Companies Act. Stephen had to get along for the rest of his life on £700 a year, later increased to £2,000.

The prospect of selling or letting the house was considered, but eventually it was agreed that William and Catherine, with their family, should come and live there together with the bachelor squire, Gladstone having inherited a considerable fortune from his father. This unusual arrangement worked happily, with Stephen sitting at the head of his table and the 'great people', as he called them, below him. The only condition on which Gladstone insisted was that he should have his own library. He built a new tower at the north-west corner of the house: the library on its ground floor was to become his 'Temple of Peace'.

Fortuitously Gladstone was out of office between 1846 and 1852, the years of his untiring efforts to save the estate. Faithfully recorded in his diary, railway journeys, often at night, were followed by meetings with his agent and others at Chester and Hawarden. At one stage it was hoped that the coal lying under the estate might do the trick, and he cheerfully noted the first evening when coal from Rake Lane was burnt in the grates at the Castle, but it came to nothing. He used to say, incidentally, that his knowledge of finance – and economical housekeeping – gleaned from Hawarden had been the most important element in his training as Chancellor of the Exchequer. If he thought so, what right have we to comment?

Stephen Glynne was a bachelor and Henry's surviving children were girls. The prospect was, therefore, that one of Catherine's sons would inherit the estate. Henry's wife died. For a dreadful moment he contemplated marriage with his daughters' governess, which the Gladstones considered most unsuitable. It did not come about, and when Stephen died in 1874 the estate passed to William and Catherine's eldest son, Willy. Apart from the work he undertook, Gladstone also paid substantial sums of money to save it. (The way in which the ownership passed was slightly more complicated than this, but the details need not detain us.)

From 1852, therefore, Hawarden was the Gladstone family's home. The four Glynnes, Stephen and Henry, Catherine and Mary, had spent a supremely happy and comparatively independent childhood there. Their mother was an invalid (and they consequently spent many happy days also at 'Audley End, my dear grandfather's', as Catherine recorded). They had their own language, later codified by George Lyttelton in *The Glynnese Glossary*. Glynnese had many words of its own: 'phantod', 'totterton', 'wizzy', 'daundering', 'bowdler', 'creebly', 'twarly', 'crierson', 'grubous', 'groutle', 'rogut', 'bathing-feel', 'high fee', 'pintoed', 'croix', 'creebly', 'maukin', 'stomatic', for instance. It also gave many common words a special meaning, such as 'antic' (used only in the singular), 'break', 'rebound', 'fragment'. It had many phrases: 'to take like pork', 'like a grasshopper's uncle', 'tell it to a passing pigman', 'to sit like a hen' (to incubate an idea), 'to take rank', 'to run like a lamplighter', 'to let down one's leg'. There were special usages too, as for instance the verb to be, analysed by Lord Lyttelton as follows:

THE USE OF THE VERB TO BE

in a peculiar and very emphatic ellipse, should have been noted above, in near connection with the phrases 'than which', and 'beyond', which it much resembles. It particularly belongs to Lady Lyttelton, who uses it for the same sort of purpose as the above phrase 'than which'; as thus. On entering into a room at Hagley or at Hawarden during one of those great confluences of families which occur among the Glynnese, and finding 17 children there under the age of 12, and consequently all inkstands, books, carpets, furniture and ornaments in intimate inter-mixture and in every form of fracture and confusion, the experienced 'Mother of Millions' will find relief in the aphorism 'Well, children are'. It is evident that there is some notable incompleteness in this saying to be supplied, as 'something too intolerable for the power of the English language to express'. But it is always uttered as if it was not only a complete, but a singularly full and perfect statement, to which nothing could possibly be added.

Many visits were made to the Lytteltons at Hagley, but Mary died giving birth to their twelfth child, and thereafter her children spent more time at Hawarden with their 'Aunty Pussy'. The Lyttelton cricket team founded the club in the park: eight sons, the father and two uncles.

Gladstone spent endless time arranging his books in his new library: this, to him, was a therapeutic occupation. Within a year he had built a private path (with the gate from the garden into the park inscribed with his initials and the date, ever since known as the 'weg' gate) in order to walk alone, as he did every day when he was at home, to the parish church, for the service at 8 am. This was, he said, the only solitary time he spent each day. Walking often in the park and in the 'Booberry' wood, planted by John Glynne in 1747, he soon took up his famous recreation of felling over-mature trees around the house. His first lesson was in July 1858.

Clearly the hard, physical exercise and the skilled use of hand tools appealed to him. This was almost unique: a menial task to be shunned as a matter of principle. Some woodwork was undertaken by the rich as a hobby – mostly at a later date; but nobody who could avoid it would dream of using a spade or an axe. The only exception I have come across was Sir Walter Scott. But Scott does not appear to have used the axe until April 1826 when he was fifty-six: Tom Purdie 'led me into the wood as the blind King of Bohemia was led by his four knights into the thick of the battle at Agincourt or Cressy and then like the old King "I struck good strokes more than one" (a quotation from Froissart) which is manly exercise'. Thereafter Scott records in his Journal several occasions when he felled trees, mostly small ones to thin out an avenue or plantation, but Gladstone did not see the Journal until 1890 when he read Douglas's edition, in two volumes, 'from the original manuscript at Abbotsford'. It seems unlikely that Scott was Gladstone's role model.

Nothing is recorded of any motives deeper or obscurer than physical exercise and skilled use of tools. Perhaps it was only as time went on that there was some connection with 'the dignity of labour'. Gladstone certainly admired the use of the spade by the Lancashire men, unemployed during the American Civil War, to whom he gave employment to create the Beeston Drive in the wood. His destruction of the forest was quite often used in cartoons, or ridiculed by political opponents, notably in Randolph Churchill's attack on Gladstone's Budget as 'nothing but chips ... the forest weeps that Mr Gladstone may perspire'. Meanwhile axes were presented from all over the world – 'The Gladstone: Fine and Even Temper' from Chicago, for instance – and hundreds of day trippers delivered by excursion trains searched the grounds for chips to carry home as mementoes. (Later this got too much, and they were obtainable only by application to the estate office.)

In the winter evenings the whole party would gather round the blazing coal fire in the library. (The library, built by Stephen's father, was much bigger than the drawing room, though it contained slightly fewer books) and there was much reading aloud and recitation, singing and piano playing. Gladstone's favourite game was backgammon.

The Temple of Peace was more than a library: it was Gladstone's study and his office. Every book he read was recorded in his diary. He was an avid reader of novels, but theology and the classics were his serious studies, and he produced massive publications on Homer. He was a prolific author, writing many pamphlets and long articles for the periodical journals which were so important in the intellectual communication of the eighteenth and nineteenth centuries. Just in the five years 1875–80 he produced sixty-eight publications on all manner of subjects, from *Juventus Mundi* (546 pages), *The Bulgarian Horrors* (140,000 copies sold), and *Gleanings* (7 volumes), to articles on such diverse subjects as 'Probability as the Guide of Conduct', 'The Evangelical Movement', 'Montenegro', 'The Royal Supremacy',

'Piracy in Borneo', the Preface to Schliemann's *Mycenae*, and reviews of books on Macaulay, the Prince Consort, and on Lewis's *Essay on Authority*.

There was always political work and correspondence, even when he was out of office. He had no official secretaries then, so his children – especially Mary, Harry and Herbert – had to step in; and Helen too, until she went to Cambridge as the first Vice-Principal of Newnham College. At the moments of the greatest political excitement about 100 letters arrived at Hawarden every day. Harry describes how he sorted them and handed his father about one-fifth of the total, of which Gladstone read a selection and answered about ten each day, in the proportion of three holograph postcards to two letters in his own hand. Postcards were his own invention. The penny post of 1840 had been so successful that he proposed that 'uncovered' short messages should cost a halfpenny. The stamp was already printed on them, and the 'holograph' was simply a rubber stamp bearing his signature: it is an ingenious device, inverting the side bearing the signature by means of a spring when pressure is released, and thus re-inking itself on a pad each time is has been used. On Gladstone's birthday about 500 letters and parcels would arrive, with a swollen postbag for several days, both before and after; but even on a normal run of 100 a day, 80 received no answer of any kind.

Willy, the eldest son, whose interests were music, Eton fives and country life, was browbeaten in to becoming an MP and conscientiously represented Chester for twenty years. Stephen was ordained, became rector of Hawarden in 1874, and periodically agonised as to how he could get away; he moved to a small parish in Lincolnshire after thirty years, to be succeeded at Hawarden by Mary's husband, the Revd Harry Drew. Mary was the 'home daughter'. Intelligent and urbane, she entertained the guests, from Ruskin to Rosebery, at Hawarden and in Downing Street, and organised the household in her parents' old age. She got the best of both worlds by marrying one of her brother's curates, later first vicar of Buckley when it became independent of the old parish, and finally rector of Hawarden. By then there was a telephone: the Castle (Hawarden 1) rang the rectory (Hawarden 2) to ascertain from Mary the Great People's breakfast menu each day: boiled eggs or fried?

Agnes, the eldest child, was the only one to escape altogether. She married the Revd Edward Wickham, Headmaster of Wellington

College and later Dean of Lincoln. The 'two Hs', Harry and Herbert, the youngest children, grew up more independently than the rest, free to devise their own escapades at Hawarden. Herbert got his first at Oxford and was drawn into the political world, an important support in his father's old age. Harry was not considered university material and joined the old Gladstone Liverpool firm in India. He was sacked for trying to modernise its ways; the best thing, as he said, that ever happened to him. After that he joined another old Gladstone family firm, Gillanders Arbuthnot, in Calcutta, where he was able to exercise his own judgement. He made money in Caspian oil before the turn of the century (a small fish in a pool which included Rothschilds and Nobels) and returned to Britain a millionaire. Having no children, he later made princely donations to the National Library and the University of Wales.

Catherine, with their eight children, spent much time in the 1860s and '70s at Hawarden. Gladstone wrote to her almost every day they were not together. She was a perfect foil for his earnest intensity. Easygoing and careless of tiresome detail, mildly eccentric, not least in her Glynnese turn of phrase, she has not always been treated by historians as the shrewd and highly intelligent woman she was. She is well known for having tried unsuccessfully to persuade her husband to 'pet the Queen'; but she was also his most constant support in political encouragement and advice, and she found it harder eventually to give up political life in London than he did.

It was always Gladstone's endeavour to leave an estate for his children; but Willy died in 1891 and it fell to his son, another William, who appeared in Little Lord Fauntleroy dress with his grandfather in the portrait by Millais, presented for the golden wedding by 'English, Scottish, Welsh & Irish women'. Some letters of grandfatherly guidance to him on the responsibilities of a landowner have survived.

As Gladstone grew older and more celebrated, people strolled every day in the park in the hope of seeing him. He obliged by taking a turn or two on the terrace after luncheon. Great fêtes were organised by 'the two Hs' in the 1890s to complete the building of the elementary day schools in the parish and the enlarged Hawarden Institute for the recreation of working men. On these occasions and at the local flower shows Gladstone would make a non-political speech to a bowler-hatted and cloth-capped crowd, particularly encouraging them to grow their own fruit and vegetables. Tiptree Jam and Hawarden butter owe their fame to these occasions.

In the late 1880s Gladstone built an octagonal muniment room adjacent to the Temple of Peace to house the correspondence of a lifetime. Thereafter the foundation of his Library, St Deiniol's, was a major preoccupation of Gladstone's final years, and he endowed it with £40,000. His idea was that others should enjoy his books in inexpensive lodgings and congenial society. The library is open to people of all creeds or of none. It was first housed next to the parish church of St Deiniol, in a corrugated iron building (the 'tin tabernacle') lined with tongue-and-groove dark stained pine. Gladstone spent days and days taking books there (some in a wheelbarrow) and arranging them. The readers' hostel was established next door in the old grammar school. After his death a fine building to house the library, designed by the Cheshire architect John Douglas, in red sandstone, became his national memorial, and his family built the adjacent hostel for up to about forty residents. The library is the only Prime Minister's library in Britain, and as a residential library it is unusual if not unique. Most of the books are still on open shelves and thus available for browsers. Gladstone's own books, some 32,000 of them, are a particular attraction to scholars by reason of his marginal annotations. Books continue to be accessioned on quite a generous budget every year, ensuring that the library does not become merely a historical collection.

The parish church of Hawarden carries strong reminders of Gladstone's devotion, with seven windows by Burne-Jones, notably the 'sunset' window at the west end; an Armenian window; and a stupendous memorial to William and Catherine by Sir William Richmond. The trio of buildings at the highest point of the village is completed by the grand Georgian rectory (much added to after 1918 as a theological college) which houses the County Record Office.

Gladstone had first proposed retirement in 1874, exhausted by the rigours of his first premiership. In the end, as the only Prime Minister actually to take office at over the age of eighty, he could not expect many years at his beloved Hawarden between – as he put it – Parliament and the grave. His eyesight had always caused problems. As a schoolboy he had complained of the difficulty of reading in the coach, as he made his way home to Liverpool from Eton. By the mid-1890s reading and writing were becoming very difficult and in 1896 he gave up making daily entries in his diary for that reason. In 1898 he died at Hawarden and his body, clad in his Oxford DCL gown, lay in the Temple of Peace before being conveyed to London.

9
The Budgets of the 1860s

Palmerston was keen to land Gladstone in his Cabinet in 1859, and Gladstone, after four years out of office, was keen to resume what he now saw as his life's work. He would accept only the Chancellorship of the Exchequer, but he was anxious that the best years of his life should not continue to slip away in Opposition.

He had already laid down what he saw as the principles of Government finance in his triumphant Budget of 1853. He had carried them forward in 1854, but had then been obliged, within months, to introduce a War Budget to finance the army in the Crimea. His proposal to abolish Income Tax had been blown away. His expectations of the Legacy Duty had wildly exceeded the results. His calculations and predictions therefore had been sadly astray; but his principles were unshaken. He was now about to launch the series of seven Budgets culminating in the triumph of 1865–6 and the high tide of Victorian prosperity.

Palmerston's Cabinets were very different from those of Peel and Aberdeen, 'acephalous' despite the strong personality of the Premier. The strength of the Government depended considerably on the agreement of Russell (who had been Prime Minister from 1846 to 1852 with Palmerston for most of the time as his Foreign Secretary), to serve under Palmerston, reversing the roles. Although he was Foreign Secretary, Russell was regarded as almost a one-man band, an especially privileged member of the Cabinet, and was not prevented from cutting across the problems of the Budget while they were subject to fierce debate by introducing a Reform Bill, and even taking it to its second reading. Gladstone's problem was that the Lords had rejected the bill abolishing paper duties – part of the Budget agreed by the Cabinet – and the last thing he wanted was a cross-current of debate on a Reform Bill. Palmerston not only spoke against the paper bill – his own Government bill – in the Commons, but also told the Queen that if the Lords did reject it, 'they would perform a good public service'. Russell was elevated to an earldom in 1861, which prevented his interference in the Commons, but he was still a big voice in the Cabinet.

Gladstone wrote down seven major issues on each of which the Cabinet was divided – in different combinations. 'We are not Mr Burke's famous mosaic, but we are a mosaic in solution, a kaleidoscope. When the instrument turns, the separate pieces re-adjust themselves, and all come out in perfectly novel combinations.' Quite apart from this, Morley quotes a private secretary of Palmerston's describing how Gladstone and Palmerston 'misunderstood one another, and how evidently each mistrusted the other, though perfectly cordial and most friendly in their mutual intercourse'. As Disraeli put it, 'we need not maunder in the ante-chambers to discover differences in the Cabinet.'

When he became Chancellor in June 1859, Gladstone at once inherited the expenses of a river war in China and the possibility of war with France. In a provisional Budget, he increased income tax from 5d to 9d (that is to say, to just under 4p), the highest rate ever charged in time of peace.

In September Richard Cobden came to Hawarden and 'proposed to me, in a garden stroll, the French Treaty'. This meeting bore fruit as the great Commercial Treaty with France of 1860, whereby each country agreed to many removals and reductions of duties, obliging the Exchequer, incidentally, to find £2m from other sources. Politics in France under Napoleon III were in a strange state: the negotiations over the Treaty had to be kept secret from the Foreign Minister who, far from welcoming a Treaty, was bent on an aggressive policy in north Italy and the annexation of Savoy and Nice, even at the risk of war with Britain. This threat led Palmerston to insist on major fortifications along the South Coast (especially near Portsmouth). Gladstone spent a great deal of time and energy during the next couple of years opposing the massive proposed expenditure. With France facing both ways at once, he was reaping the fruit of the Treaty with one hand and fending off defence expenditure against a hostile power with the other.

The Budget of 1860, dependent on this Treaty, was planned exceptionally for February, but Gladstone became seriously ill, with congestion of the lungs. On the road to recovery on 10 February, he saw his secretaries and his doctor as usual, had to make changes in his figures, reached the House of Commons at 4.30 and spoke at 5 pm.

The speech began with an optimistic review of revenue against expenditure. 'The country', he said, 'is richer than it was in 1853 in a degree really astonishing.' Tea and sugar duties, which were widely expected to be reduced or abolished, were kept as they were; the revenue from them was increasing, proving that people could afford to pay. What mattered, he argued, was not directly the cheapness of goods for the labouring class, but the increase in national wealth through growth in trade and industry, bringing increased employment and higher wages.

There had been much bargaining, and Gladstone met many deputations with regard to the French Treaty but the test, he said, was whether the reductions of duties were beneficial in themselves, regardless of the Treaty; and although to some degree the reduction on French wine was a concession to a powerful French lobby, he convinced the Commons that in every case this argument was valid. In the event, the Treaty was of immense benefit to both nations, amongst the most striking example being the growth in exports of British iron to France. Incidentally, the Treaty reduced the British duty on timber to a nominal rate, increasing trade but dealing a fatal blow to British forestry and consequently almost a disaster in 1914–18. Gladstone called on a mass of statistics, but may have had shipbuilding largely in mind, ironically just at the time when iron was replacing wood.

The second salient feature of the Budget – and much the most controversial – was the removal of the excise duty on paper, which would cost the important sum of £1m p.a. This was a radical step, designed to usher in the era of cheap newspapers, and thus very much contrary to Gladstone's arguments in his 1853 Budget against democracy: democracy, he had said then, would lead to uncontrollable public expenditure. His argument now was that the paper duty, 'a uniform duty on a very variable article', added only a small fraction to the price of 'dear books, which are published for the wealthy'; but on 'books brought out in large quantities by enterprising publishers for the middle and lower classes, it is a very heavy and a very oppressive duty'. But it was above all towards cheap newspapers, transported, of course, by railroad, that he was looking, and his argument included the problems caused by the impressed stamp, which was mandatory on all 'newspapers'. The stamp recognised the 'exceptional status of newspapers', i.e. their potential to do harm, 'and again raises the question: What is a newspaper? The Post Office authorities find it impossible to draw a distinction ... .' So the Stamp Duty was removed.

Gladstone argued, too, that the ever-increasing versatility of paper meant that the duty handicapped many trades: artificial limbs, tele-scope makers, boot and shoe makers, cap manufacturers for the foun-dations of caps and hats, forming all the peaks and many of the tops which look like leather, china and porcelain, coach makers, comb makers, doll makers, shipbuilders, optical instruments, pictures and looking glasses, portmanteaux, Sheffield goods, and teapots all used paper. 'One manufacturer has made panels for doors, and looks forward to making carriages when the duty is taken off.' Only this morning he was informed that paper pipes are made, prepared with bitumen, and capable of standing a pressure of 300 lb of water to the inch. As with 'What is a newspaper?' he is asking 'What is paper?' and he suggests that when rhubarb has been used for making British cham-pagne (a product now prejudiced by the removal of duty on the French version), 'the residual fibre should then be made into paper'. In the same lighter vein – indeed the whole of this section of his speech produced a great deal of laughter – he points out that the Inland Revenue used so much paper that his proposal would save £20,000 of public money. He also deplores the fact that the duty has extinguished the small manufacturers and concentrated the industry in 'a few great hands'.

Every Budget involved the subsequent passage of a number of Acts of Parliament enforcing the various changes. The House of Lords rejected the abolition of the Paper Duty, presumably being more of the anti-democratic mind, which Gladstone himself had represented seven years earlier, than the Commons now were. The Upper House argued that this was not a matter of finance, but that it involved the repeal of an Act of Parliament. This argument has often been condemned as specious; but the abolition was, as Gladstone himself had shown only too clearly, not a financial but a political measure. The Lords were circumvented the following year by turning the whole Budget into one Finance Act, not several. This was one of the most important steps in the invention of the modern Budget and the predominant power of the Treasury in Government.

Having covered the French Treaty and the Paper Duties, the Chan-cellor now turned to other duties and proposed the abolition of all but 44 of the remaining 419. Fifteen were retained because they provided revenue – increasing revenue – without hindering growth. The other twenty-nine were retained on 'special grounds' – as, for instance, the impossibility of distinguishing eau de Cologne from brandy.

He sums up: there will be on the British tariff nothing whatever (except the small remaining charges on timber and corn) in the nature of protective or differential duties. The consumer will know that every shilling he pays will go to the Revenue and not to the producer. 'You will have a great extension and increase of trade, you will have a remission of the principal restraints on travellers, and a great reduction on the expenses of the Customs and Excise Departments.'

Concluding, after a summary, at 9 pm after a speech of three hours and fifty minutes, 'without great exhaustion; aided by a great stock of egg and wine', he got home at 11. 'This was the most arduous operation I have ever had in Parliament.'

Then the debate began, and at 2.30 am on 25 February, having contributed a speech of 1¼ hours, he achieved 'the immense majority' of 116. Disputes on important elements, especially the Paper Duties, were still to come, but the main lines were clear. This Budget has generally been considered as Gladstone's greatest.

The Budget of 1860 set the tone of what was to follow, except in the important matter of Income Tax which Gladstone had covered exhaustively in 1853. His objection to Income Tax was, simply, that it was an invitation to profligate spending and it must therefore be reserved for emergencies. Reductions in Income Tax were popular, but popularity was not Gladstone's objective. By 1864 he had reduced it to 6d (2.5p). The next year he said that its abolition was not possible 'in the present state of opinion' but he brought it down a further 2d to 4d (1.6p), not a heavy rate by modern standards. One wonders whether he was deceiving himself, or perhaps keeping up a pretence as a matter of principle. The very last time he promised to abolish it was in 1874 after resigning at the end of his first ministry. This, however, seems to have been an uncharacteristic attempt to catch votes in a desperate situation. Nevertheless, economy was his watchword, and a Chancellor 'is not worth his salt if he is not ready to save what are meant by candle ends and cheese-paring in the cause of the country'.

No sooner was the plea for heavy expenditure on the fortification of the South Coast receding, than the American Civil War brought the cotton industry in Lancashire to its knees. In spite of this, and of three poor harvests at home, the revenue was still in surplus. In 1863 Gladstone put forward his proposal not to exempt charities from taxation, on the grounds that exemption was a gift of public money which a Government had no right to give. Parliament was not convinced and the plan was abandoned. The growth in the nation's wealth was 'almost intoxicating'. Exports to France had nearly doubled. Foreign and colonial goods traded in British ships had climbed from £9.5m to £21.75m since 1859; all aided by 'the wise legislation' of Parliament.

Important innovations during these years were the Post Office Savings Bank in 1861, the Public Accounts Committee the same year, and the Companies Act which became law in 1862. In theory, adequate facilities for small savers were available from the multitude of small private banks; in fact, however, small savers were daunted by the people and the procedures, as any reader of Dickens will readily appreciate. But to thrifty members of the labouring class, the local post office was friendly and familiar.

The Public Accounts Committee inaugurated the system culminating in the Exchequer and Audit Act of 1866 which brought every Government department under public scrutiny. It eased the transition from a Civil Service governed largely by private patronage and individual whim to a permanent professional body recruited by competitive examination. It also brought Government in all departments more and more under Treasury control.

Something has already been said in chapter 5 about the development of companies. The Companies Act of 1862 was driven by the need to limit the liability of individuals in industrial and commercial enterprises. Hitherto a company in the modern sense had not existed, although firms often referred to themselves as 'Smith and Company'. The only ways of forming a corporate body were by Royal Charter (as with the East India Company) or by Act of Parliament (as with railways, which required rights of compulsory purchase). Anyone who is aware of the labyrinthine character of modern company law will realise that this was only one step down the road which enabled the vast sums of capital required by new inventions and mass production to be accumulated, which separated ownership from management and from responsibility and which ended the old paternalism of the individual owner. There were still limitations in share trading, as there had been since the days of the South Sea Bubble.

Gladstone liked big Bills and big Budgets. They were the best way of keeping the Liberal Party united, always preferred by him to party organisation. By 1866 Income Tax was down to 4d and Gladstone 'derived profound and inestimable consolation for the reflection that while the rich have been growing richer, the poor have become less poor'. Exports had risen since 1860 from £130m to £188m. 'There is not a man who labours and sweats for his daily bread, there is not a woman living in a cottage who strives to make her home happy for husband and children, to whom the words of the Chancellor of the Exchequer have not brought hope.' Those were the words of John Bright. A contemporary is quoted by Morley: 'He is in his ministerial capacity probably the best abused and best hated man in the House; nevertheless the House is honestly proud of him, and even the country party feels a glow of pride in exhibiting to the diplomatic gallery such a transcendent mouthpiece of a nation of shopkeepers.' 'They love him much less in the House than they do out of doors,' said Dean Church: 'a strong vein of sentiment is the spring of what is noblest about his impulses; but it is a perilous quality too.'

This was the People's William, already beginning to stump the country, greeted like a king on Tyneside, a lord in Lancashire. Lord Aberdeen thought him too obstinate, Lord Palmerston said he was a dangerous man: 'Keep him in Oxford and he is partially muzzled; but send him elsewhere and he will run wild.'

10
What Did Mr Gladstone Say in 1864?

During the early years of the twentieth century, shortly after Gladstone's death but some forty to fifty years after the relevant words were spoken, this had become a common phrase in the music halls in British cities, the nearest equivalent to popular television comedy of modern times. Mere mention of the name of Gladstone up to about 1930 brought a rejoinder: ' What did Mr Gladstone say in 1864?', although almost everyone had by then forgotten the answer. But the phrase simply meant 'Well, it was bound to happen sooner or later,' or ' I told you so'.

By the late 1840s it was generally accepted by all political parties that the work of the Great Reform Act of 1832 was incomplete. The importance of that Act was that it had broken the medieval mould by which the House of Commons consisted of the representatives of the ancient boroughs, elected by a few privileged voters or office-holders, and of the shires, elected by the forty-shilling freeholders. But the Act had left the country with still only a very small minority of voters and a very incomplete attempt to redistribute constituencies with some reference to population. From 1849 onwards the proposal to introduce a new Reform Bill was mentioned several times in the Queen's Speech. But agreement over details was a different matter altogether. The franchise (the right to vote) and the distribution of votes were distinct questions, but the effect of one on the other linked them in an infinite variety of possibilities. Most people agreed that a 'balance' was desirable, particularly as between town and country, but to agree where the dividing line fell was more complicated.

In 1864 a private member introduced a bill to increase the franchise in boroughs and Gladstone was put up to speak for the Government. Palmerston, the Prime Minister, expressly instructed him not to commit the Government to any particular franchise in the boroughs, and indeed, above all, that the Government must not be bound by any promises in case they should wish to bring in their own bill. Gladstone had already suggested in a speech in Liverpool that an increase in the borough franchise by including some 'articulate artisans' would be just in itself, since the working class paid about one third of the nation's taxes; and he knew, too, that it would strengthen the Liberal Party. But what he said in the House of Commons on 11 May 1864 was this: 'I venture to say that every man who is not presumably incapacitated by some consideration of personal unfitness or of political danger, is morally entitled to come within the pale of the constitution.'

This was radical talk. True, there had been people outside Parliament off and on since the 1790s who had spoken revolutionary words; from the days of Tom Paine and *The Rights of Man* to those of the Chartists in the 1840s. There were radicals in Parliament who might have gone as far as Gladstone did, but certainly they did not include a man of the front rank. The sentence was greeted with 'loud volleys of cheering and counter-cheering'.

Hastily, as the cheers died, Gladstone added his carefully phrased qualifications: 'Of course, in giving utterance to such a proposition, I do not recede from the protest I have previously made against sudden, or violent, or excessive, or intoxicating change.' He then went on to say (in this fairly short speech, thirteen columns in Hansard), perhaps trying to cover his traces by apparently changing the subject, but without much success, that it was important for the country to have 'armies, fleets and fortifications', sustained 'by a sound system of finance, and out of a revenue not wasted by a careless Parliament or by a profligate administration. But that which is better and more weighty still is that hearts should be bound together by a reasonable extension, at fitting times and among *selected* portions of the people, of every benefit and every privilege that can be justly conferred upon them.'

Two MPs at once reported to Phillimore, Gladstone's close friend and legal adviser, that Gladstone had said something that 'would make his hair stand on end'. Disraeli said that Gladstone had revived the doctrine of Tom Paine. In the Press, the speech caused a sensation. The next day Palmerston wrote, in surprisingly moderate terms:

I have read your speech, and I must frankly say, with much regret; as there is little in it that I can agree with, and much from which I differ. You lay down broadly the doctrine of universal suffrage which I can never accept. I entirely deny that every sane and not disqualified man has a right to a vote ... . You did not pronounce an opinion in favour of a specified franchise; but is there any essential difference between naming a six-pound franchise and naming additional numbers which a six-pound franchise was calculated to admit?

In his diary, Gladstone wrote: 'Spoke on the franchise bill. Some sensation. It appears to me that it was due less to me than to the change in the hearers and in the public mind from the professions at least if not the principles of 1859.' Whatever may have been his meaning, it is clear that he is blaming his audience for not understanding what he said, rather than himself for saying it. To Palmerston he replied on Friday: 'I agree in your denial "that every sane and not disqualified man has a moral right to vote", but I am at a loss to know how, as you have read my speech, you can ascribe this opinion to me ... . It requires, I admit, to be construed ...' On Saturday he went to Brighton, where he bathed in the sea, complaining 'water over-warm', and wrote to his brother, Robertson, about his speech: 'I have been astounded to find it the cause or occasion of such a row. It would have been quite as intelligible to me had people said "Under the exceptions of personal unfitness and political danger you exclude or may exclude almost everybody, and you reduce your declaration to a shadow."'

The reader may judge for himself. To the writer (as to Lord Palmerston) this seems to be Gladstone at his worst. He blames the hearer for not reading the small print, and he turns his own argument on its head by confusing the exceptions with the norm. People disliked Gladstone because of his over-refined qualifications, but in this case he was pleading that his qualifications negated his statement altogether. Gladstone had disregarded the clear and reasonable instructions of the Premier. He had spoken as a senior member of the Cabinet, nominated to speak non-committally on one of many issues – the borough franchise – in the field of Parliamentary reform. His statement lacked both tact and circumspection. It was unconnected with what was politically thinkable. Nevertheless, it was probably the most famous sentence he ever uttered.

As it happens, Gladstone had first become a member of Parliament just over thirty years earlier. Just over thirty years were to elapse before his final resignation as Premier. The speech came just halfway through his political career. He was fifty-three years of age. He had served in Cabinet of Sir Robert Peel. He had already presented eight Budgets.

The 'rising hope of the stern unbending Tories' had been left far behind. He was calling himself a Liberal, and his party the Liberal Party – although he could still regale a crowd of Lancashire working men on the significance of what he described as his deep-seated Conservative principles. During the 1830s he had supported the resolution freeing the Commons from their obligation to debate every petition, on the ground that matters must be decided by members within the House, not guided by the petitions of the public. Now he was beginning to stump the country, addressing crowds of working men, inside or outside his own constituency.

The hungry Forties had long receded. The spring tide of Victorian prosperity was flowing: perhaps 1866 is as near as we can get to marking it, yet that was also the year of the collapse of the Overend-Gurney bank, causing the first great panic of its kind since 1720. British commerce and industry dominated the world. They were still growing, but soon the speed of growth would falter. The first major European (in fact, effectively worldwide) slumps lay ahead, the first starting in Austria in 1873, the second in France from over-speculation in 1882. And Britain was about to be left a bystander in Prussia's war against Austria: whence sprung the poison which was to wreak unprecedented sorrow and havoc in 1914.

It would be easy to make too much of this landmark. In some ways, the differences between a Prime Minister's tasks in 1874, when Gladstone's first ministry ended, and 1880, when his second began, seem more significant than those which occurred on either side of 1864. But the famous speech of 1864 was a landmark, nevertheless: and it has the merit of illustrating why Gladstone was both loved and loathed.

Gladstone and Italy:
Garibaldi Visits London

Gladstone's interest in and love of Italy began at school and university with his study of classical authors and of Italian history, not only in ancient times but also during the Renaissance and the Counter-reformation. He read and spoke Italian fluently and Dante was to become one of his 'four doctors'. In 1832 he first entered Italy – from Switzerland where his hopes had been dashed of finding worthy successors to the 'slaughtered saints', the Vaudois protestants massacred for their beliefs and immortalised by Milton. Travelling through the northern states he had then visited Rome and first experienced Roman Catholic services (there were virtually none in Britain). He was both enchanted and dismayed: 'cold and pale spectres of the highest and most powerful domination the world ever beheld'.

In 1838 he travelled extensively in Sicily, typically making elaborate notes on what he discovered – on agriculture, beggars, brigands, cholera, cotton exports, rice production, the sulphur monopoly, wine; as well as fleas and mules. (He later compared his relationship with his mule – 'I could not bring myself to like the brute' – with the Queen's relationship with him in his later years.) These notes became the basis of his *Murray's Guide to Sicily*. Then he visited Rome again (and met Catherine and Mary Glynne there).

With Catherine, Gladstone spent some weeks in Naples during the winter of 1850–1, becoming increasingly critical of the regime and asking himself what he could or should do about it. Rather surprisingly he was permitted on 13 February 1851 to visit the dungeons where political prisoners were incarcerated, and he wrote in a notebook a long account of the appalling conditions he encountered. After his return to Britain he published his findings in an 'open letter' addressed (without permission) to Lord Aberdeen, describing the regime as 'the negation of God erected into a system of government'. Since the Kingdom of Naples was a sovereign power with full diplomatic relations with

Britain, this caused a sensation; although, to be fair, the revolutions throughout Europe in 1848 which had aimed to terminate autocratic rule had received wide sympathy in Britain.

North and South Italy were poles apart. Much of North Italy in the shape of Lombardy and Venetia was still part of the Austrian Habsburg Empire. The rest consisted of small states ruled by petty princes, with the exception of Piedmont (which was part of the Kingdom of Sardinia), ruled by the House of Savoy, a small state with a remarkable history of diplomatic success in contributing to the balance between greater powers. Educated people in its capital Turin were more urbane, more liberal and more cosmopolitan than their neighbours – and they spoke French. Piedmont, notably led by Cavour as Premier, gained the sympathy of Palmerston, Russell and Gladstone, first in the Crimean War, and then in the events momentous for the future of Italy of 1859 and 1860. The Piedmontese ambassador in London knew how important it was 'de luncher avec Lady Palmerston'. There was not much in Palmerston's foreign policy which Gladstone could approve but support for Piedmont was an exception. For Cavour to enlist the support of Palmerston, Russell and Gladstone was to hold a winning hand.

Piedmont had no quarrel with Russia, no interest in Turkey, and no moral and no direct political reason for joining Britain and France in the Crimean War. Yet Britain and France accepted her as an ally and by a stroke of luck (or Allied incompetence), the puny Piedmontese army turned out to be useful. The two great powers could hardly quarrel with Cavour a few years later when in 1860 first Lombardy, and then almost the whole of Italy except Venetia and Rome, became a united Italy. The hornets' nest was stirred up by Napoleon III, who acquired Savoy and Nice. Then Venetia became Italian in 1866, after Bismarck had humiliated Austria in war, and in 1870 the Pope was deprived of the remnant of his temporal power and Rome became Italy's capital.

Cavour got more than he had bargained for. He had no interest in Southern Italy or Sicily, which could be nothing but a drag on the more prosperous North. But in 1860 Garibaldi and the Thousand first conquered Sicily and then the South of Italy as far north as Naples and Caprera. *De facto*, they became part of Italy.

Garibaldi's astonishing exploits thrilled Europe. Born in Nice, he fled to South America in 1834 after being condemned to death for his part in a rebellion against the King of Savoy. There he learnt his trade as a

Surplus Balances in the Exch.r
Can arise only from surplus
revenue.

Sh.d have taken the course pursued by my predecessors —

Surplus revenue must be applied
for the reduction of the National
Debt —

Quite prepared to pay unaccepted
stocks out of the balances.

Reduction of interest on Exchequer
Bills —

Recent Exchequer Bills fell to par.

{ Practice
  since 1817 }

Deficiency Bills —
matter of convenience to the Bank
that the Chancellor of Exchequer
should be under the necessity
of borrowing —

1. That he should expect such
   loans at a lower rate of
   interest

2. Amount

Revenue of the past year.

1. Improvement of the revenue
since my former Estimates.

Estimate 6 mch £54,025 m.
Actual receipt. £54,774 m.
Increase . . . . £749 m.
Whereof Prop. Tax £417 m.
Customs . . . . . £103 m.

2. Surplus taken £2,854 m
   Now shewn £3,524 m.
   Last year's £2,460 m.
   This year unduly
   swelled by say £500000.

   ~~[struck through]~~
   ~~[struck through]~~
   ~~[struck through]~~
                    of 1853

3. The reductions have been in operation for 6, 9, 10 months & up-
   wards
   Amount remitted £2600 m.
   Amount received }
   from new Taxes to Ap. } £700 m.
   5 not over ___ }

4. Or in round numbers
   [   ] remitted 2½ mill
   old [one & a half the new]
   We have a surplus of 3 mill.

State of the Public Balances.

Cr.   Dr.

                                        Balance 5 Ap. 53. £7,859,000
                                                      54   2,778,000

Debt paid off .... £8,042,m   Less by .... £ 5,081 m

Advances, Excess ⎫   N.D. Commrs
over repayments   ⎬ £ 716 m   Stock created   ⎫
                  ⎭   agt. purchase of   ⎬ £ 1,274, m
Reduction of Un- ⎫   Exchequer Bills   ⎭
funded Debt ...   ⎬ £1,718 m
                  ⎭   Exchequer Bonds
                             of 1853 abnt .. £ 420 m.

                    2
                 ─────────   6,775 m
                 10,480 m   3,705 m.
                 ─────────   ──────────
                                                10,480 m.
                                               ──────────

                                                            (By common
                                                             usage)
          Apparent Amount of Deficiency Bills : Brought to
                                                  charge.
In April 1853 .... £ 1,407 m .... £ 300 m.
        1854   £ 5,852 m   £ 5,472 m.
                    ───────────   ────────────
Apparent increase   £ 4,447 m ... £ 5,172 m.
                    ───────────   ────────────
                        445

State of the
Unfunded Debt.

Amount authorised in 1853 £17,742 m.

Minimum point attained ab. £12,897 m.

Less by £1,718 m.

£3,127 m.

£4,845 m.

Amount last quarter ... £16,024 m.

Present amount say .... £16,600 m.

Amount authorised - - - - - - £17,774 m.

We are thus short } £1,174 m.
of the maximum }
say

No present reason to expect that
I shall ~~have~~ occasion to come
' up to it.

The selection of manuscripts described on page 70 in relation to the Budget of 1854 is given in this section. First come the speech notes of 21 March 1854. Then comes the calculation of 'Revenue of the Past Year' dated 11 April 1854, followed by notes of May 1854 on the 'State of the Public Balances'. Above is the 'State of the Unfunded Debt'. The four sheets that follow consist of the speech notes for the debate on Baring's motion on 8 May 1854.

May 54.

{ Debate on
Mr Barings
motion. } NB NB

W. this is matter of praise. NB

"a loss to those who invest
their money in Savings' Banks" NB

Disraeli — Series of errors.

1. Exchequer Bills —
   reduction of the rate.
   "indulgence" to the C. of E.

2. Conversion Scheme
   reading "warnings and
              prophecies." Aug
   ~~giving away the taxes~~
   political cloud. Ap.
                      Aug.

3. Peace Budget.
   no tax to be repealed while
   "there was a chance of this country
   being engaged in war"
   "very great thunder"

   his defence agt my charge —
   "saved you from the succession duty"

4. Error of paying off 3 millions —

5. Tampering with the funds of
   the Savings Banks.

A Baring. Exch⁰ Bills { 1.   Principles.
says
challenge.   { 2.

Debt Conversion - "abortive"

Bank Balances - "public has
the right to the use of its
own deposits -"

One flaw in his speech - its relⁿ
to the proposal he made.

D   Mr Pitt - always successful.
Mr Fox.
Do not worship him in his errors.

You had made in 93 the
after
efforts he made in 98, then
we have been perhaps

Taxes 100 m. +
Debt 500 m. —

We rely on the H. of C. as he did, &
was supported by it

What the H. of C. can do H cannot.

unworthy sneers at Mr. Pitt

Its closing appeal.

The motion.

B   cut Warrants hithow
£6000m.
owing to

not immediate
not a loan

1. Low Balances
2. Margin.
3. Anticipation of taxes.

The amendment.

C
D. idle …

What does it mean?
Is it a vote of want — of confidence?
The want is not denied.
Amount is not objected to.
Exchr Bills are demand impossible
Exr Bonds are refused —
It can only be a loan.
"a loan in a masquerade"

a diminished }
motion. }

"raise it in the usual manner"

"follow as much as possible the
precedents in our possession."

I s appeal. Committee to vote for
the advantage of the
country

meet cost by borrowing.
but borrow at par.—

Cæsus — "equitable adjustment."

Malins — "a myth."

War 29th March   Double Budget   Disraeli — Errors of 1854.

1. Budget of March either inadequate or deceptive.

2. A loan in masquerade.

The Stays —

3. What if Exchr. Bonds had been issued in 1847 —

guerrilla leader in a variety of revolutionary movements. In Montevideo he raised an Italian Legion whose flag was black with a volcano, 'symbol of Italy mourning with the sacred fire in her heart', and clothed his men in red shirts (designed for slaughter houses, where their colour disguised the blood). He spied his future wife, Anita, through a telescope, rowed ashore, snatched her from her husband, and carried her off to his ship, beginning a married life which 'none of the world's famous legends of love surpass in romance and beauty'. He returned to Italy in 1848 and eventually, after a series of adventures in the north, he fetched up in Rome, where a Republic had been established, and led the Tigers of Montevideo in their red shirts in a hopeless resistance against both a Neapolitan and a French army. He escaped and took part in further guerrilla campaigns, Anita eventually dying of fever and privation in Ravenna. Garibaldi fled over the mountains and escaped in a boat, standing in the stern as it left the shore crying 'Viva l'Italia'.

Garibaldi's most remarkable exploit, however, was his conquest of Sicily at the head of the Thousand in 1860. They travelled in two paddle steamers stolen in Genoa (one built in Glasgow). A Royal Navy squadron (sent, of course, to protect British subjects) did not impede their landing at Marsala on the west coast of Sicily, nor later their crossing of the Straits of Messina to the mainland. Success against a large regular army could only be achieved by raising numerous bands of rebels from the local population, by inspiring terror and by bluff. But achieved it was. This was the man who turned up in London in April 1864, in full splendour, with his flowing beard and his red shirt and his grey cloak.

Gladstone had defended the Government's Italian policy in the Commons in 1862, coming down strongly on the nationalists' side, but Italy was still then in a state of flux, if not chaos, although the map looked simpler. There were problems with Modena, the Romagna, the Austrian reluctance to let go, the aggressive French occupation (not for the first time) of Rome; and there were doubts about the motives and the competence of the Piedmontese Government. The 'younger generation' were on Gladstone's side, but he was well aware that British opinion was far from unanimous. Yet he seems not to have reflected at all about what sort of man he would discover in the already almost mythical person of Garibaldi, nor of the ambivalence with which mid-Victorian England would receive him. Nobody seems to have given much thought to a programme of events for the visit of 'General Garibaldi', as Gladstone correctly addressed him. 'I do not know',

Gladstone had written to Palmerston, 'what persons in office are to do with him, but you will lead and we shall follow suit.' But persons in office were not in control. Garibaldi was given a popular welcome as he travelled from Vauxhall station to Stafford House (he stayed with a Duke) of a kind which London had never seen. For five hours the hero 'passed on amid tumultuous waves of passionate curiosity, delight, enthusiasm'. As Gladstone himself later wrote 'We who then saw Garibaldi for the first time can never forget the marvellous effect produced upon all minds by the simple nobility of his demeanour, by his manners and his acts ... his splendid integrity, and his wide and universal sympathies, beside that seductive simplicity of manner ... and that inborn native grace ... the union of the most profound and tender humanity with his fiery valour.' Gladstone, like the welcoming crowd, was bowled over. Disenchantment began to set in when he discovered that Garibaldi was an atheist, with some concession to the Supreme Being of the French Revolution.

'12 April – went to Chiswick and met Garibaldi. We were quite satisfied with him. He did me much more than justice.' It was at some time during this visit that Garibaldi presented Gladstone with a ring inscribed to the 'Precursor'. What Gladstone said of Naples in 1852 had seemed to justify invasion by the Thousand in 1860.

14 April – went, by a desperate push, to see Garibaldi welcomed at the opera. It was good, but not like the people.

16 April. Dined at Lord Palmerston's to meet Garibaldi.

17 April. At Stafford House 5¼–6½ and 9¼ to 12½ on Garibaldi's movements. In a conversation he agreed to give up the provincial tour.

Then, on 20 April, the Gladstones gave their dinner:

Before the door, at night, say a thousand people, all in the best humour: the hall and stair full before dinner. Aunt J in her 89th year stationed in the front. A hostile deputation invaded us at ten: but we ejected them. I settled about tomorrow with Garibaldi, the Duke of S, Ld. Palmerston, and Ld. Shaftesbury. My nerves would not let me – old hack as I am – sleep till after five.

The next day, Thursday 21st, in spite of the sleepless night, he wrote his letters and minutes, rode in the park with Agnes, and had nine to breakfast to celebrate the engagement between Lucy Lyttelton and Lord Frederick Cavendish. The day ended with an anxious night in the Commons, concluded at 7 am, on the 'dangerous subjects of Fire Insurance and Committee on Annuities Bill: which might have shipwrecked both Budget and Bill. The House behaved to me very generously.' But Garibaldi was not quite finished with.

Gladstone set off for Cliveden (the Sutherlands' country palace on the Thames near Maidenhead) at 4.30 on Saturday afternoon, immediately after the Cabinet, took a scull on the river, from which Garibaldi had just landed, and passed 'an evening of great interest'. On the Sunday he had a final tilt at Garibaldi's atheism: 'The utmost I could get from him was that it would be sad if the Italian people should lose its faith.' Then, at last, amidst popular recriminations about the cancellation of Garibaldi's tour, he saw him off at the station.

The radicals had not been pleased that Garibaldi had stayed with the Duke of Sutherland. They said that the Whig aristocrats 'were in a panic lest he should compromise himself with the radicals' and that he was being hustled out of the country. Then it was rumoured (and hotly denied) that Napoleon III had objected to the visit. It came to light that at Stafford House Garibaldi had accepted invitations to visit thirty towns, and that the list was growing longer every day. 'The doctors declared that the General's strength would never stand the exhaustion of a progress on such a scale.' On 17 April Gladstone was 'put up' to express his opinion to Garibaldi, 'to the effect that the hero's life and health were objects of value to the whole world'. Fortunately, Garibaldi announced that if he could not accept all the invitations he could not 'draw a line of preference and would therefore go to none'.

The risks attaching to a grand triumphant tour of Britain by Garibaldi as perceived by the Government were perhaps remote, but they were worrying. Garibaldi had been born in Nice, which had now been filched by Napoleon III. There might have been a public outcry in Britain that it should be returned to Italy. The Italian Government, still in Turin, although constitutional, was much less enlightened than the Government of Britain, with a tiny electorate and the intractable problems of governing the South. Garibaldi was a hero and although wonderfully disinterested in matters political, he was nevertheless a wild card. It was fortunate indeed that Gladstone with the aid of the doctors succeeded in his awkward mission. The episode has its comic side but the consequences of failure might have been serious.

Perhaps mercifully, the Schleswig-Holstein crisis intervened, with the strong possibility of Palmerston leading the country into war in defence of Denmark, and drew public attention away from Garibaldi's abrupt departure.

12

The First Government, 1868–74

Gladstone formed his first ministry in December 1868. He had won the very large majority for those days, of 112. Palmerston had died in harness aged eighty in 1865 and had been succeeded by Earl Russell in the Lords (as Lord John Russell, MP, he had been Prime Minister from 1846 to 1852 and Foreign Secretary under Palmerston). His Government was ousted the next year by the Tories under Lord Derby. Gladstone was now the acknowledged leader of the Liberals, and when Derby resigned from ill health he gave way at last to Disraeli. Thus began a Parliamentary rivalry, the like of which has not been seen before or since.

This rivalry had been focused by the Budgets of 1852 and 1853, although it had been sporadic since the 1840s. Now there was a popular press, an electric telegraph to relay news instantaneously, and a railway system to deliver the papers. There was immense public interest in politics, following the fortunes of the two giants, men of extraordinarily different temperament and character, each of them orators of the very first rank. Their rivalry has been compared with that between Pitt and Fox, but it was more widely known and in many respects far more dramatic – not least in that the pendulum had now begun to swing.

Debate had been going on for years about the next stage of reform after the famous Act of 1832, coming gradually over the course of time to favour an expanded electorate including at least some artisans in the boroughs. The bill which Disraeli introduced in 1866 had been hastily conceived and was much altered in its passage through the Commons in 1867. Its effect was very uneven as between one constituency and another, but it had the effect of producing larger majorities and also of speeding up the swing of the pendulum, especially in 1868, 1874 and 1880 when the contest between Gladstone and Disraeli was at its height; for the new electorate lacked the old traditional loyalties of Whigs and Tories. There was reason to suppose in 1868 that Gladstone's majority might last for the seven years (not five as now) until another general election became mandatory. His Cabinet included several noblemen of old Whig families – Argyll, Hartington, de Grey, Clarendon, Granville – but also some Liberals who had, more or less, made their own way – Lowe, H. A. Bruce, Cardwell, Childers, Goschen, Fortescue; and in time also W. E. Forster and James Stansfeld; and Roundell Palmer, later Lord Selborne.

Gladstone, at fifty-eight years of age, was in his prime, and his first Ministry is still regarded as the most effective of Queen Victoria's entire reign. Astonishing as were his achievements in his seventies and eighties, he no longer then had quite the mastery he showed from 1868 to 1873. His well-honed political skill and dexterity, his extraordinary range of knowledge, his constructive mind, his almost inexhaustible energy and his brilliance as an orator gave him a mastery of the House of Commons which has seldom been equalled. He never lost his nerve (he was 'terrible on the rebound') and he was never afraid to persist with what he believed to be right. He was never dull: the evidence of his ability to marshal detail in a logical argument is a matter of record, as indeed was his ability to 'turn on the steam' as he put it, when he addressed a huge crowd of working men. It is not, perhaps, as easy to recall his extraordinary charm, his delightful manners, his sardonic wit, his quickness of retort. A Prime Minister in the Commons was expected to lead the House. He attended every debate and he steered every bill through all its stages. When we read of his later ministries we are still astonished by his qualities; but it is easy to underestimate the greatness of his prime. He personally initiated all the major bills throughout the Parliament, and in many of them he played a major part in the drafting. He did, however, have several very able lieutenants, notably Forster, Cardwell, H. A. Bruce and (later) Roundell Palmer, who relieved him of much of the burden in their respective fields.

The Government had a mandate to disestablish the (Anglican) Church of Ireland, and this was Gladstone's prime objective. The importance of this issue may seem odd to us now and it is true that it had little relevance to many MPs and to much of the electorate; but it did not seem odd to the vast majority of the Irish population, small farmers and peasants and their large families, almost all (except in Ulster, where anyway the farms were bigger) Roman Catholics. The House of Commons had had about forty years to get used to the idea, which had first been proposed by Peel; but he had had to be content with Catholic Emancipation, which enfranchised the great majority of formerly disqualified voters. The Church was supported by endowments, but the peasants were nevertheless obliged to provide goods or money for the whole ample hierarchy of bishops, deans, archdeacons and parish clergy of a denomination different from their own. The population of Ireland, although declining rapidly, mainly through emigration, was still about 5½ million, not far short of a quarter of the population of England and Wales and substantially larger than that of Scotland. At its peak in the 1840s the population of Ireland had actually been for a few years just over half of that of England and Wales, and more than three times as large as that of Scotland. Gladstone proposed to remove the burden of an alien Church from several millions of people living in dire poverty and, in a bad year, liable to face starvation. He also proposed to alleviate their poverty and bolster their property rights by a Land Act, and to establish a university acceptable to both Anglicans and Roman Catholics.

The Disestablishment Act took up much of the first session of 1869. There was lengthy argument about the precise proportion of the endowments of which the Church should be stripped, in order that they could be transferred to good causes of increased public benefit – an example of Gladstone at his most ruthless.

The Land Act was even more complicated, not least because of the difficulty of establishing exactly what was the law. It depended on time–honoured custom, which might be interpreted differently by landlord and tenant, and in which there were many minor regional variations. There are some salient differences between Ireland and England noted by Gladstone on 17 September 1869. At first sight it appears that he is uncharacteristically mixing the law with the politics:

Land Tenures in Ireland	Land Tenures in England
1 Tradition and marks of conquest, and of forfeiture still subsist.	1 They do not subsist.
2 Landlord does not find capital for improvement.	2 Landlord finds capital for improvement.
3 Landlord frequently absentee.	3 Landlord rarely absentee.

4 Landlords extensively object to leases.	4 Landlords rarely object to leases.
5 In the parts of Ireland not under Tenant-right, the law which gives tenants improvements to landlord is rigidly construed and applied.	6 [sc. 5] The law which gives the tenants improvements to landlord is mitigated, and even in some cases reversed, by local custom.
6 Landlord commonly (in the said parts of Ireland) differs from tenant in religion and politics.	6 Landlord commonly agrees with tenant in religion and politics.
7 Administration of justice, and local discharge of other public duties, not extensively entrusted to landlords, and not conducive to good relation with tenants.	7 Administration of justice and local discharge of other public duties, generally entrusted to landlords, and highly conducive to good relations with tenants.
8 Ireland occupier (yearly) holds by custom.	9 [sc. 8] England. By contract.

Numbers 2, 4, 5 and 8 are the crucial points of law, but the heart of the matter lies in no.1. The English landlord in Ireland was there by conquest – by conquest he had acquired some now unassailable rights. But the Irishman believed that the ultimate or at least the residual ownership of the soil lay with the tenant. This was something which many an English lawyer would never understand: 'upon this state of things comes Palmer with his legal mind.' This was Roundell Palmer, later a notable Lord Chancellor as Lord Selborne, whom Gladstone would not at first have in his Cabinet for this very reason.

The tale is long and intricate. Bright proposed an actual peasant proprietorship, but Gladstone knew that that was not politically feasible. He wanted rents to be fixed by valuation not competition, and he wanted payment for evicted tenants on improvements they had made at their own expense. This compensation the Act achieved, on a sliding scale, and it limited the landlords' power of arbitrary eviction. It was not very effective, but it was a start. It went hand in hand with a Coercion Act, aimed at stopping the violent 'Fenian' outrages, especially in Westmeath; for which Gladstone thought that a committee working in secrecy was required. Disraeli went too far when he complained that the Act 'legalised confiscation, consecrated sacrilege and condoned high treason'.

From July 1869 for many weeks Gladstone had concentrated on learning about Irish land tenure, with much reading, many sessions of listening, much discussion and much correspondence with Chichester Fortescue, the Chief Secretary for Ireland, equivalent of the modern 'Secretary of State', Gladstone's able and trusted lieutenant. He was meanwhile starting to consider the Bankruptcy Bill and the Trades Union Bill, the Parochial Schools (Scotland) Bill and the Endowed Hospitals (Scotland) Bill (master-minded by the Duke of Argyll, who as well as being Secretary for India, was also the Cabinet Scottish member, a sort of informal Secretary for Scotland); as well as (amongst others) the Bishops' Resignation Bill, the Chancery Fund Bill, the Irish Railways Loan Bill, a Cattle Bill (regarding control of disease), the Assessed Rates Bill, the Telegraphs Bill, the Annuity Tax Bill and various financial measures. He was involved in the Committee on the Civil Service, the Marriage Law Commissions, the new site for the Law Courts, the Admiralty and War Office buildings, the Punjab Tenancy Act, charges on the Suez Canal, and the Alabama case arising from the American Civil War. Meanwhile he read *Mansfield Park* and *Pride and Prejudice*, Burke's *Reflections on the French Revolution*, the memoirs of Catherine II and the *Iliad*, as well as many lesser works; went to Box and Cox (at Mary's special desire) and found time to scold Lord O. Fitzgerald, MP for non-attendance at divisions in spite of the Whips. 'I have deserved the reprimand,' was the reply; 'but the very late hours have been rather too much for me.'

Gladstone was at Balmoral from 10 to 25 September; but his work continued every day. On the 25th he took the Deeside train from Ballater to Banchory and walked to Bridge of Feugh (55 minutes), Bridge of Dye (68 minutes) and up the Cairn O'Mount (65 minutes) and down to the Clattering Brig (27 minutes), where he was unexpectedly met by his sister-in-law and niece 'who had kindly come in the carriage' and took him on to Fasque. In 215 minutes he had covered some 14 miles at just over 4 mph, including an ascent of over 300 metres.

In 1866 Bismarck, the Prussian Chancellor, had fought a brief but decisive unprovoked war against his cultural and geographical neighbour Austria, had plundered her territory in the true style of Frederick the Great, and had inaugurated the name of Germany as a State, a 'Nation State' in the terminology of the day, which he labelled 'The German Empire'. He opened the floodgate for others to plunder this most un-nation state, the 'Austrian Empire', now the dual monarchy Austria-Hungary, an amalgam of Habsburg possessions: the Balkans were soon aflame with risings in Montenegro and Bosnia-Hercegovina, names hitherto hardly known in Western Europe. France was on the watch for her share of the pickings, as was the emergent nation state of Italy.

Since the seventeenth century the Prussian State had expanded by marriage and by ruthless politics, acquiring piecemeal large or small territories in Western Germany. Western Germany consisted of a large number of small states, a kind of power vacuum which Napoleon had filled with his 'Confederation of the Rhine'. After his defeat in 1815, the Congress of Vienna made the fatal error (but what else could they have done, it may be asked) – of making Prussia the dominant state in the West – subject to the independence of the Netherlands and (though the name came a little later) Belgium. Bismarck, having disposed of Austria, proceeded to provoke France into declaring war on him with the objective of confirming the German Empire's mastery in the West. The result was the humiliation of France, the removal of Napoleon III, the Paris Commune and the German annexation of Alsace and Lorraine.

Ever since the demise of Charlemagne in the ninth century the control of the banana-shaped area with the Rhine as its backbone in the north and the Po in the south has been a key to strategic and economic power. The 'Netherlands' (including Belgium) are well known as the 'cockpit of Europe'. What was Britain to do in the face of Bismarck and the huge Continental armies? She was a helpless bystander. She was, however, a party to the guarantee of the independence of Belgium. But what could she do about that? Could she send 20,000 soldiers (a puny force in comparison with the German and French armies) – or even 10,000 – to Antwerp? The answer from the War Department was no. It was not possible.

The British Army, in spite of the Crimean War, was more or less unreformed since Wellington's day. Understanding the British dislike of a 'standing' (i.e. regular) army in peacetime, Wellington had anyway tended to hide it away in colonial garrisons. But the right of officers to purchase their commissions for money created a vested interest which could not be reshaped. A gentleman who had paid good money to command a regiment was not going to see it restructured and renamed.

In practice, therefore, the argument in favour of promotion by merit came second to the need for restructuring; but until purchase was abolished restructuring could not begin. The tactics of the colonels who led the opposition to abolition in the Commons provided the first example of obstruction, later to be made so painful by the Irish. When it went to the Lords, the bill was not actually rejected, but more cunningly its effect was indefinitely postponed. The very next morning Gladstone announced that the purchase of commissions had been abolished (as it had first been permitted) by Royal Warrant: that was Gladstone at his best. He brought the Lords to heel because abolition by Warrant could provide no compensation: by Act it could, and did.

Cardwell then reformed the whole regimental structure, above all giving the line regiments their county names and giving each two battalions 750 strong (against the old 500). He introduced short service (six years with the colours, instead of twelve) and he thus created a large reserve of trained men. The infantry was rearmed with modern Martini-Henry rifles. The Regiment of Artillery was much increased and, like the infantry, to some degree localised, but attempts to rearm it with breech-loaders were effectively obstructed by its officers.

Cardwell worked tirelessly for three years to provide Britain with a modern army. He exhausted himself in the effort, retired to the House of Lords, and was no more heard of. But the first evidence of his inestimable service to the nation became clear before the end of the Government's tenure.

In three respects he had still not succeeded. The cavalry regiments were officered by men of such powerful aristocratic connections that he decided to leave them alone. Retaining their arcane numbering as Dragoon Guards, Dragoons, Lancers and Hussars, each regiment with a tiny strength of 250, they played little further part in war until 1939. Secondly, Cardwell could not shift HRH The Duke of Cambridge as Commander-in-Chief; and thirdly, largely because of this he could not create a central, or 'general', staff.

The Army reforms stimulated a powerful vested interest against the Government; but the money which had to be found in the crisis which had led to them – the Franco-Prussian War – led to a tactical error by Lowe, the Chancellor of the Exchequer, who tried to introduce a tax on matches, a new product employing many poor workers in London, mostly women, in sulphurous conditions. Lowe was delighted with his Latin pun on the tax stamp which was to appear on every box: '*ex luce lucellum*'. But the protest march by thousands of these pathetic workers was so moving that Lowe had to abandon his proposal and raise income tax instead. His reputation never quite recovered, and Gladstone later removed him, becoming Chancellor of the Exchequer himself.

Meantime, under the aegis of W. E. Forster, came the Elementary Education Act. Gladstone had reached the conclusion that charitable bodies alone could not provide the nation, especially in the large towns, with what was required. The intractable problem was to decide what religious teaching, if any, there should be in these state schools. In the early stages of the debate, there was a good deal said in favour of a secular state curriculum, with voluntary bodies providing religious education in the schools. Gladstone, though a convinced Anglican, had always been sympathetic and liberal in his attitude to nonconformists. Eventually a not altogether satisfactory compromise was decided on – namely that there should be Christian religious instruction but without 'dogma'; that is to say, it would be mainly scriptural, and not denominational. Thus Britain, in most respects rather behind France and Germany, acquired free compulsory education for all until the age of fourteen. Gladstone also wanted to redistribute the endowments of moribund ancient schools to modern good causes, but although he set great store by the Endowed Schools Act it was a failure. The small commission of three he appointed had neither the ability nor the clout, nor the administrative support to identify, let alone tackle, the target schools.

In 1871 the Home Secretary, H. A. Bruce (later Lord Aberdare), brought in a Licensing Bill. Drunkenness was a serious social problem, wreaking havoc in many lives and families and especially evident in the lower social classes. The bill was draconian, and produced a storm of protest from breweries and publicans. For technical reasons it did not enlist the full support of the temperance organisations and it had to be abandoned. The second bill in 1872 was less drastic but still contentious. A bishop declared in the House of Lords that he would rather see England free than England sober, but the Act was passed and severely enforced.

Gladstone, who enjoyed wine throughout his long life and had it copiously provided by his wife, with raw egg beaten up, to sustain him in his longer Parliamentary speeches, was undoubtedly convinced of the need for regulation, and once convinced about the rightness of a bill he seldom gave in; but a strong reason for persisting was the strength of nonconformist support for the Liberal Party. In doing so he brought down on his Government the opposition of a very widespread and wealthy vested interest. Of all the vested interests which were challenged by his reforms, this was by far the most powerful. It had a vast if informal organisational framework – the pub, which henceforward became a Tory forum. Thereafter the brewers were a main source of Tory funds. To his brother Robertson, Gladstone wrote 'We are borne down in a torrent of gin and beer.'

Morley makes the point that Gladstone always did what he considered right without regard to what people might think of him. The Licensing Bill was a case in point. It brought serious unpopularity to the Government when it had already passed a number of measures which were whittling away its majority. In 1871 Gladstone thought of retirement. He had no inclination to take notice of the lessons which Aberdeen, Palmerston and others had tried to inculcate: be careful not to make the Government unpopular, and do not open up to the Opposition too many potential points of attack. Gladstone was a shrewd Parliamentary tactician in achieving what he wanted to, but he was seldom willing to trim his sails. Yet Morley points out that this characteristic sometimes evoked unnecessary opposition on quite trivial or even eccentric issues. A classic example of his persuading himself that he was not so much right as in the right was the patronage of the rectory of Ewelme in 1871.

This desirable church living had been within the gift of an Oxford Divinity professorship, by which the professor could take it for himself, substantially increasing his income but not his work: he could put in a poor curate to take care of that. This advowson (a right of appointment) had been removed as part of the programme of university reforms emanating from the 1854 Act, and had been transferred by Act of Parliament in 1871 to the Crown, that is to say to the recommendation of the Prime Minister; but, to sweeten the pill, the living had to go an Oxford man. Gladstone first offered it to a distinguished Christ Church don, Jelf, who refused. He then offered it to another distinguished scholar, Harvey, who was a Cambridge man. Harvey expressed some doubt, was reassured, and accepted. He then duly had to be made a fellow of an Oxford college in order that he could become a member of the University Convocation, which was the technical qualification. There was, however, some doubt (not more than doubt) whether his membership achieved by this route satisfied the requirements of the Act. All this was above board – nothing was concealed – but unease began to surface, and Gladstone wrote to Harvey to reassure him that the presentation was valid. As may be imagined, this splendid opportunity for satirical comments was not neglected by members of Parliament, university dons or journalists. H. A. Bruce, the trenchant originator of the Licensing Act, gave his verdict with perhaps uncharacteristic moderation: 'Gladstone spoke with great vigour and eloquence on the Ewelme Case; but I think that, with the best possible intentions, he placed himself in a wrong position.'

It was an important part of Gladstone's Parliamentary tactics not to 'overlap' legislation. Nevertheless a number of bills were often running at one time, occupying a long period between first reading and royal assent. The precise chronology need not concern us. The University Tests Bill was introduced in 1870; when passed, it opened Oxford and Cambridge to men of any denomination or none. From this measure sprung many of the ablest entrants to the professions, especially the burgeoning Civil Service, now recruited by competitive examination; but none for commerce and industry, which would have nothing to do with universities, nor universities with them.

In 1872 the Ballot Act was passed, introducing secret voting. It was contentious, but did not engender as much popular enthusiasm as one might expect. The declining influence of aristocratic property owners and the advent of the new electorate had decreased the proportion of voters who might be intimidated: except in one case – that of Ireland, which the Government had not taken into account. Strangely enough, it was a young protestant landowner, Charles Stewart Parnell, who saw at once that an Irish National Party could now be created. Their growing influence was already apparent in the results of the General Election of 1874.

The last major reform of Gladstone's first Ministry was the Judicature Act of 1872. It did away with the chaotic residue of the Middle Ages, by which there were two systems of law, common law and equity, the former administered by three courts, all with unlimited jurisdiction, and the latter by the Court of Chancery. Common law depended exclusively on precedent; equity on the other hand had been developed to apply the concept of fairness, or justice with a small 'j'. There were also four specialised courts, of Admiralty, Probate, Divorce and Matrimonial Causes, and Bankruptcy. Gladstone brought in Roundell Palmer (Lord Selborne) as Lord Chancellor, and he more or less single-handedly drafted the most elaborate bill which the complexities of the old structure made necessary. He had the advantage of general agreement by the leading figures in the legal profession, although there was much debate over detail and some of Selborne's arrangements were later modified. However, he set up the 'Supreme Court of Judicature' which is still easily recognisable as the High Court of today, together with the Court of Appeal. He wanted to abolish the final appeal to the House of Lords (in effect a group of senior judges holding life peerages) but was overruled.

In international law, still in its infancy, Gladstone accepted the verdict of the court then in Geneva (later transferred to The Hague) giving judgment against Britain in the case of the *Alabama*. The *Alabama* had been a heavy modern battleship, an ironclad 'ram', built at Birkenhead during the American Civil War for the Confederacy (the Southern States) and not prevented by the Government from joining its navy. Legally, of course, the United States was a sovereign power and the confederates were rebels. The *Alabama* sank a good deal of United States' shipping and Gladstone agreed to pay the damages decided by the Court in the room in Geneva still known in commemoration of this landmark case as the Alabama Room.

In 1873-4 a small but interesting war in Africa provided the first evidence of the success of Cardwell's reforms. The Government decided to use the Army to suppress the regime of 'King Coffee' (the Ashanti warrior Koffi Kari-Kari) which was promoting the slave trade on the Gold Coast. Sir Garnet Wolseley was given command of a small army and was put in charge of the whole administration of the area and of the forts along the coast. He took with him a full and efficient staff and a picked body of officers, many of whose names later became famous. Quite young men raised their own native regiments, some of which had to be driven forward from behind (through boundless and trackless tropical forest) rather than led from the front; as later testified by Sir Evelyn Wood's autobiography, *From Midshipman to Field Marshal*. Wolseley had to get to Kumasi, deal with Kofi, and return to the coast within two months, before the rainy season. He succeeded triumphantly, giving rise to a new phrase to describe a neat and successful operation, 'All Sir Garnet'.

Gladstone was exhausted by five years of Herculean labour and the Government's majority was becoming uncertain. Several by-elections were lost and Disraeli's invective about 'extinct volcanoes' and 'blundering and plundering' was beginning to ring true. The Government by its reforms had made many enemies, and it had not yet at its disposal a Civil Service capable of efficiently administering all its legislation, which consequently brought in its wake a fair amount of muddle. Several by-elections went against the Liberals.

In spite of these problems, Gladstone introduced his Irish University Bill early in 1873. It was to be primarily for the benefit of Roman Catholics, but it was hoped that it would be acceptable also to Anglicans and Presbyterians. Cardinal Manning, Gladstone's old friend now head of the English Roman Catholic Church, supported it, but the Irish hierarchy opposed it, and there was a good deal of opposition from Protestants on both religious and educational grounds. It was defeated on its second reading by precisely three votes, forty-three Liberals voting in the majority. Gladstone resigned.

It was Disraeli's leadership which had led to the defeat. Gladstone of course recommended the Queen to send for him. But Disraeli was too cunning to take the bait. He would not attempt to form a Government without an assured majority. Gladstone had to resume: he made some adjustments, removing Lowe and Bruce. But in January 1874 the Government lost another by-election and Gladstone stated that Parliament would be dissolved. At the general election Disraeli was returned with an assured majority. Gladstone resigned the leadership of the Liberal Party and announced his retirement.

13
Gladstone the Scotsman

Gladstone was of pure Scottish descent on both his father's and his mother's side. His grandfather Thomas became a successful corn merchant in Leith, the port of Edinburgh. Thomas's son John migrated to Liverpool, becoming one of its many prosperous traders, and, as we have seen, Gladstone himself was born in Liverpool. When John retired he bought the estate of Fasque, in Kincardineshire, in 1830, with a massive barely completed 'trophy' house which had ruined its builder, Sir Alexander Ramsay. John strove to improve the methods of his tenants, emphasising the importance of drainage and persuading them to use the carefully selected seed-corn which he provided.

Fasque was thus Gladstone's family home for some eight or nine years before his marriage. He became attached to the house and especially to the countryside, where he enjoyed shooting and walking. In the early years he would travel quite frequently by ship from Liverpool to Glasgow, and he spent a good deal of time at Fasque after 1846, occasionally with his family, when he was for a short time out of Parliament and for some years out of office. He was able to reserve a turret room for his work and his studies.

From Sir Walter Scott Gladstone learned about the old life of the Highland clans and of Edinburgh (where his own romantic tribute was the restoration of the Mercat Cross in 1885). He first came across Scott's work in his last Eton summer holiday in 1826, reading *Woodstock* as soon as it came out, *The Bride of Lammermoor* the next week and *Waverley* the third. The following year he read *The Antiquary*, *Rob Roy*, *The Heart of Midlothian* and *The Two Drovers*, becoming a lifelong devotee. In his Temple of Peace in Hawarden there were only two pictures on the walls, nearly all the space being taken up by bookshelves: one of them was a fine engraving after Raeburn's last portrait of Scott.

John Gladstone was an MP for some years, representing diverse constituencies potentially winnable by a rich man, and he received a baronetcy from Peel, largely in recognition of his philanthropic work, although he did not at all approve of Peel's decision, supported of course by William, to repeal the Corn Laws, nor of the subsequent repeal of the Navigation Acts. He was becoming deaf and argued his point 'always at the top of his voice', still expecting his dutiful son, even when Chancellor of the Exchequer, to make copies of his letters. After John's death in 1851 Gladstone fell out with his eldest brother, Thomas, as a result of their political differences and for some years there were no visits until the brothers were reconciled in 1874.

It was at Fasque that Gladstone first encountered the problems of his sister Helen, a clever lady of strong character who revolted against her narrow upbringing in a remote Scottish mansion. Rows and tantrums went from bad to worse, and laudanum, to which she soon became addicted, was prescribed to calm her. Her masterstroke of anti-paternal tactics was to convert to Roman Catholicism. Most of her later life was lived in Germany, where Gladstone visited her from time to time.

In his early years as laird of Fasque, John Gladstone attended the kirk in Fettercairn, and he established a family vault in the kirkyard. But in 1847 William persuaded him to build an Episcopal church only a hundred yards from the big house: it was one of the first of many built on Scottish estates and in towns and villages in subsequent years. The consecration of St Andrew's, Fasque, came at the height of Gladstone's High Church particularity, inspired by his friends in the Oxford Movement. There was much rehearsing of the chanting of psalms in place of the hymn-tunes of the Scottish metrical versions. There was terrible embarrassment when the unfortunate clergyman, Mr Teed, turned up without his 'gown'. The household servants were, of course, expected to attend, the females neatly attired in their caps. The parson was accommodated in a substantial house next door to the factor, where against strong competition he led one of the easiest lives of all the clergy in Britain.

About the same time, together with his friend J. R. Hope (later Hope-Scott of Abbotsford), Gladstone conceived the foundation of Glenalmond College, and he persuaded his father to contribute to the cost of the magnificent buildings in the Perthshire countryside. The original intention was to provide a college for Episcopal ordinands as well as a boys' school, but this came to nothing. Every Scottish bishop was a member of the Council, with the Primus as chairman. Gladstone's objective was to persuade the Scottish gentry to educate their sons in Scotland instead of sending them to Rugby or Shrewsbury, or even as far afield as Eton or Harrow. A few years later he thought he would fail unless, as he put it, he could 'obviate the Scotch accent'. After a slow and anxious period, the school grew in the 1880s under Warden Skrine, and flourished. On Gladstone's first visit he inspected the buildings and on his second, in April 1851, he paid for his choice of an isolated rural site by having to walk there for the consecration of the chapel, eight or nine miles 'carrying my bag for lack of any other porter'. He attended the services on 1 May from '11 to 3.40 and again 5 to 6½ ... the chanting was of a noble vigour'. There were two long, irrelevant sermons. The evening was not wasted: 'Conv. with Wordsworth [the Warden who had been persuaded to migrate from Winchester] on Church and State – Bp of Aberdeen (on Papal Aggression) – Bp of Argyll (on Laymen in Synods) – and others.' He then set out at 11.30 pm and walked down to Perth, got to Laurencekirk by train at 4 am and walked to Fasque: '18m between supper and breakfast'.

He was back at Glenalmond in October for a Council meeting. Towards the end of the summer term of 1857 he attended the examination and prize day: 'Banquet at 2. I made a speech according to order on classical education. Left the College much pleased with all I had seen.' In the train from Perth, he 'got from a Newcastle man a good lecture on the Iron Trade'. Thereafter he visited the College when he could, or held the meetings in Edinburgh on his annual visit to the capital during his term from 1859 to 1865 as Rector of the University.

Gladstone liked to visit Scotland every year, especially – if he could – in August and September. He enjoyed some extensive tours of the Highlands, mostly staying at great houses, and he visited Dingwall to keep in touch with his mother's family and friends. In September 1858 he went to Scourie – almost as far north-west as you can go. He sprained his ankle on his morning walk on 22 September, then walked thirty-one miles – stopping at Glen Dhu for luncheon. 'This loch and Quinag from it are very grand.' He got to Dunrobin the next day and had the sprain properly tended: 'On the way I could only douch it in the burn.' His long tour in 1872 included the descent of Glencoe, 'rather a nervous business'. He was minister in attendance at Balmoral during several years – 1864, 1869, 1871 and 1873; he must have particularly enjoyed the time he stole for a walk up Lochnagar. Then in 1874 he visited Fasque for the first time for some years for the sad occasion of a niece's funeral – the little coffin placed in the family vault near that of his beloved Jessy. The brothers were reconciled, and there were many visits thereafter, up to 1891.

Gladstone's retirement after 1874 was the result of his exhaustion after five years as Prime Minister, and it was not very long before he felt the urge to return to the political stage. He had had no intention of retiring as a writer. On the contrary, he had intended to use his pen more than he had previously had time for. Provoked, however, by Disraeli's offhand attitude to Turkish atrocities against Christians, he could no longer stand on the sidelines, and he wrote his most famous pamphlet, on the Bulgarian horrors, in September 1876. In 1877 he was elected Rector of Glasgow University. The next year he announced that he would not again contest his Greenwich constituency, and in January 1879 he accepted nomination for Midlothian, the ancient county (as opposed to borough) constituency of what was still occasionally called 'Edinburghshire'. The idea was proposed, and the campaign orchestrated, by Lord Rosebery, whose immense wealth sprang from the expansion of Edinburgh and whose seat Dalmeny was on the coast not many miles north of the city. Rosebery was to enter Gladstone's Cabinet in 1885 and to become Foreign Secretary in 1886.

Gladstone took his time before accepting the nomination, consulting the Liberal Whips and others, but he promised his full energy should he accept, and he was as good as his word. His journey from Liverpool to Edinburgh on 24 November was, he recorded, 'really more like a triumphant procession'. All the stations where the train stopped were crowded – people had come from towns and villages simply in the hope of getting a glimpse of him. Regarding the whole of southern Scotland as his oyster, he began with a speech at Carlisle on 24 November 1879 and finished there at the railway station on 8 December, but on that return journey he also spoke at Preston, Wigan and Warrington stations and finally at a procession in Chester. He noted down on 11 December his schedule of thirty speeches in fifteen days (including Sundays, when of course he did not speak) addressing 86,930 people. The largest audience, reckoned at 20,000, was in the Waverley Market at Edinburgh, and the most testing day was 5 December at Glasgow, where he spoke four times. John Morley was there, and his description of the day and of the campaign as a whole is probably still the best that has been written. People came, he says, from as far as the Hebrides, and where there were six thousand seats, the applications were for forty or fifty thousand. But the real audience was, of course, much larger. The electric telegraph enabled the typesetters to get to work even before a speech had ended, the advent of paper free of duty meant that there were daily editions, and the railways enabled them to be distributed. When Gladstone got home he had not only to deal with overwhelming sacks of mail, but with the proof-correction of 255 pages of his speeches, duly published in Edinburgh in two volumes.

The objective was to attack Disraeli's policies, 'Beaconsfieldism'. But the subjects Gladstone covered, like the audiences to whom he spoke, were diverse. Audiences of working men were treated just as if they had been the House of Commons. One opponent said that Gladstone's verbosity had become 'a positive danger to the Commonwealth' and another that his performances 'were an innovation on the constitution, and aggravated the evil tendencies of democracy'.

Meeting Disraeli, so to speak, on his own ground, the main subject of the campaign was the attack on the Government's foreign and impe-rial policy, and Gladstone enumerated six principles which Britain should follow: to foster the strength of the Empire by just laws and economy, to preserve the world's peace, to support the Concert of Europe, to avoid needless and entangling engagements, to allow the promotion of freedom to govern our foreign policy, and to acknowl-edge the equal rights of all nations. He spoke of Disraeli's policies towards Turkey, Russia, Cyprus, India; of 'the sanctity of life in the hill villages of Afghanistan', of the 'invasion of a free people' in the Trans-vaal; of the destruction by artillery of 10,000 Zulus defending their hearths and homes with their naked bodies. There were fiscal and financial matters too, replete with statistics, especially in the speech at the Edinburgh Corn Exchange. 'Not for a moment did he lose his hold', not even 'in the middle of his most formidable statistics, nor at any point in the labyrinthine evolution of his longest sentences.' It was in the previous year that Disraeli, in one of his most effective speeches, had referred perhaps with some justice to the 'sophisticated rhetorician inebriated by the exuberance of his own verbosity'.

The earlier part of 5 December, the day at Glasgow, signalled a rest from politics. In his inaugural address at the University Gladstone described the salient feature of the age as, on its material side, the discovery of the secrets of nature, and the progressive subjugation of her forces to the purposes and will of man. On the moral side, if these conquests had done much for industry, they had done more for capital:

if much for labour, more for luxury; they had variously and vastly multiplied the stimulants to gain, the avenues of excitement, the solicitations to pleasure. The universities were to check this: 'the habits of mind formed by universities are founded in sobriety and tranquillity ... they tend to self-command, self-government, and that genuine self-respect which has nothing of mere self-worship, for it is the reverence which each man ought to feel for the nature that God has given him, and for the laws of that nature. The Christian tradition must be sustained by intellectual dignity and argument... . Thought is the citadel.' There was 'a steeplechase philosophy in vogue – sometimes making short cuts to the honours of universal knowledge.'

Gladstone then spoke at the luncheon, and thirdly to an audience of 6,500 in St Andrew's Hall on the wickedness of the Government's foreign and imperial policy. Finally, he spoke to the large audience assembled by the Glasgow corporation in the City Hall with praise for the city and its citizens. It was fourteen years since he had been honoured with the freedom of the city.

The next year, 1880, he was back on what has been termed the Second Midlothian Campaign, from 16 March to 5 April, with a further round of speeches prior to the general election, in which he was elected with 1,549 votes. He had also been nominated for Leeds, where he was elected with 24,622 votes. The figures are a commentary on Disraeli's Reform Act of 1867, ill thought out and hurried through Parliament, creating a gross imbalance between the number of voters in boroughs and those in the shires. Elected now in two constituencies, Gladstone opted for Midlothian and Herbert Gladstone was then adopted as candidate for Leeds, which he represented for many years. Beaconsfield was toppled and in May, forty-eight years after first becoming an MP, Gladstone entered the House of Commons as Prime Minister for the second time, also taking the office of Chancellor of the Exchequer.

In 1885, 1886 and 1892 Gladstone was re-elected for Midlothian. It was during the 1885 campaign that he unveiled the restored Mercat Cross. A painting by W. A. Donnelly, now at Hawarden, vividly depicts the scene.

In the early stages of planning his first Home Rule Bill for Ireland, Gladstone declared that an important principle was that nothing would be done for Ireland that could not be done for Scotland, and in principle he was willing to support the idea of Scottish self-rule. But he declared that the issue was not 'ripe' and that more consultation was needed with the people of Scotland. He certainly would not have attempted to run two Home Rule Bills in double harness. It seems, however, that he would not have expected a full century to pass before Scotland received a measure of devolution.

14

Gladstone the Christian

Throughout his life Gladstone was intensely aware of the presence of God. This belief was implanted in what in early adulthood he described as the very narrow Evangelical discipline in which he was brought up. In this his mother was a strong influence, as also was his older sister Anne. Both were invalids, and he often took Anne for an airing in Liverpool, pulling her bath chair ('Drew Anne in chair' refers to traction, not artistry). She died in her teens. But because he derived from them no methodical teaching or theology, and no concept of what the words 'The Church' might mean, he rather played down their influence. It was nevertheless fundamental to his life. He never suffered from any kind of doubt about the existence and the all-seeing and all-forgiving nature of God. Knowledge and thought about the Church – the 'Holy Catholic Church' of the Creed – came later.

In spite of receiving no formal religious instruction at Eton, although there was a daily service in Chapel, Gladstone felt called to become a clergyman during his time at Oxford, but was dissuaded by his father, who pointed out that the influence of a parish priest would be very limited. Gladstone often noted in his diary the disappointingly small number of undergraduates who attended the communion services in the Cathedral (which was also the college chapel), showing that he had by now recognised the centrality of that service, and had already moved far from his early Evangelical upbringing. He had a group of friends at Christ Church who were of the same persuasion, some of them members of the 'Weg,' his essay society, with whom he kept in touch, notably in the eventual formation of the lay brotherhood, the Engagement. Not long after he had gone down from Oxford this school of thought developed into the Oxford Movement led by the Tractarians, dedicated to the recognition of the Church of England as the Catholic Church: the reformed Church deriving from Christ himself the power to forgive and the authority of the Apostolic Succession. Gladstone himself, however, declared that he was not a Tractarian, that he had not read the Tracts, and that he would not be labelled as a member of any party. Thus, although he believed the Church of England to be the Holy Catholic Church in England, he never took a dogmatic stance and was notably sympathetic towards dissenters. (In Scotland, where the Presbyterian kirk was the established Church, he himself as an Episcopalian was a dissenter.) He refused to condemn anyone 'truly united to Christ by faith and love, whatever may be the faults of his opinions'. This tolerance he attributed to the mother of his Eton friend James Milnes-Gaskell, and he wrote in later life that his conversation with her 'supplied me with the key to the whole question ... . It is now my rule to remember her in prayer.'

Gladstone was (and is) often described as a High Churchman and insofar as he considered the Church of England to be 'the Holy Catholic Church', with the communion service at the centre of its liturgy, that is a valid description. Certainly it applied to quite a long period during his middle years when he could indeed have been validly described as a 'High Churchman', worshipped in London at All Saints, Margaret Street and involved himself in the tight discipline of the Engagement; but in the end his tolerant breadth of view prevailed. This process was hastened by despair when two of his closest and most admired friends, Manning and Hope-Scott, became Roman Catholics.

In spite of his tolerance and breadth of view, Gladstone was hostile to the Roman Catholic Church, even at the stage when he himself was close to deserving the label of 'Anglo-Catholic'. It is difficult, if not impossible, to identify the origin of this condemnation of Rome, but it would have been part and parcel of his early Evangelical upbringing. Before he first attended a Roman Catholic Service (in Italy in 1838) he already deplored the historical claim of the Papacy to universal domination. His study of the counter-reformation at Eton, followed up at Oxford, contributed to this view, as did his admiration for Archbishop Laud as the great systematic reviver of the Church of England as the Holy Catholic Church. Of the reputedly intolerant Laud he said 'I find him the most tolerant of them all.' He realised that Puritanism was far less tolerant than Laud's Anglicanism and far less reasonable. His study of Laud informed him of the Greek Orthodox Church as a willing ally against the primacy of Rome. Gladstone had read a good deal about Protestantism and the counter-reformation in Italy; and he was aware of the scandalous history of the Papacy prior to the

Reformation. His knowledge and sympathy for the Orthodox Church heightened his sense of outrage at the Bulgarian and the Armenian atrocities.

What Gladstone especially deplored about the Papacy was its claim of domination. When this claim was extended by the doctrine of Papal Infallibility in 1870 he was genuinely shocked. In broad terms this move was a Papal reaction against the growth of anti-clericalism in general throughout Roman Catholic Europe, and in particular against the virtual termination of the temporal power of the Papacy in 1870, when Rome became the secular capital of the new state of Italy and the Pope's dominion was confined to the Vatican City. Pope Pius IX (Pio Nono), hailed on his election in 1846 as a liberal, had reacted ardently against the claims first of the 'Roman Republic' and then of the Italian kingdom. It became Papal policy – a counter-productive if not a fatal policy – to endeavour to replace the temporal power by inevitably political, or semi-political, Concordats with nation states, designed as the new national bulwarks of Papal authority. The doctrinal running-mate of the temporal Concordats was thus the claim to *ex-cathedra* infallibility.

The increasing importance of authority in Roman Catholic thinking was labelled as 'ultramontanism', and when the claim of infallibility was linked to the right of the Church not to submit to the State, the new label 'Vaticanism' appeared. It seemed to Gladstone as to his liberal Catholic friends, especially Lord Acton and the German Dr Döllinger, that the Papacy was abandoning its time-honoured and reverenced dependence on history and on reason in favour of an unqualified assertion of authority. As usual, his pen came to his service and he published his condemnation in *Vaticanism*; as usual, too, it included some unconventional arguments, but it was on the whole an attack on authority – as opposed to reason, reason as a key in the search for truth.

Anti-Puritan by nature, as well as in his discovery that the Puritans of the seventeenth century were less tolerant than the Laudians, Gladstone condemned the anchorites, hermits of the early Christian centuries, believing that they had almost succeeded in leading Christianity away from the joyfulness of life which to him was its essence. The concept of monasticism was anathema to him. It was the joy of life in the Homeric world which led him to see it as part of God's creation. The Greek appreciation of beauty, especially the beauty of the human form, was part and parcel of his Homeric joyfulness: Gladstone found it to be in sharp and telling contrast to the images used by the Roman Church throughout Europe – not a single one of which, as he commented, deserved to be described as a work of art. Some of the passages in his diary, especially his self-examinations at his birthdays, if taken alone, could give the impression that he was obsessed not by the joyfulness of life but by sin. The theme in fact is forgiveness and renewal.

Gladstone was convinced by the doctrine of the Fall of Man, the fall from grace of Adam and Eve in the Garden of Eden. But the question whether the book of Genesis was literally true was not one which much concerned him: the truth lay in the concept of the imperfection of Man and the mercy, redemption, atonement, forgiveness of God. He believed in God as Creator, but if he was a 'creationist' (to use a modern label) then he was a creationist in a sophisticated sense. He had no serious difficulty in accepting the validity of geology. He was open-minded about Darwin's *Origin of Species*, if not perhaps wholly convinced. He believed that if indeed life had evolved by an almost infinite series of small steps, then this was a far more wonderful manifestation of God's creation than the Genesis story. No doubt he would have been equally willing to regard with an open mind, ready to be convinced by evidence, later refinements of the general theory of evolution.

Several commentators, including Morley, said that Gladstone was not interested in science. This was not the case; but Gladstone was not much interested in science as a challenge to religious belief. Geology and the theory of evolution interested him, and he was a keen reader of what might be called 'popular' science, but was really science for the layman. He read numerous books about scientific discovery, especially astronomy with its expanding vision of the universe. He had a first class degree in mathematics, which included optics, and spherical trigonometry was bread and butter to him. He had studied statics and dynamics, too. It has to be stated, however, that there is one piece of remarkable negative evidence: namely that when he went to visit and converse with Darwin at home he did not mention the fact in his diary; and this in spite of the fact that his diary was a diary of record, almost always including everywhere he went and everybody he met. In the face of a good deal of evidence of his interest in, and inclination to accept, the theory of evolution, it is not easy to explain this omission.

The battle of belief which Gladstone fought was not a battle against science, but a battle against the claim that scientific evidence was the only route to truth. In the context of the battle, the notion of scientific evidence was narrower than it would be today. Scientific evidence, in the language of the time, was evidence which could be 'seen', what we would call observable evidence in a rather narrow interpretation of that phrase. Gladstone's main opponents were Fitzjames Stephen, who might well be called a common-or-garden atheist, and T. H. Huxley, a scientist whose simple opinion was that what could not be seen could not be true. Against them Gladstone did his best to assert that the 'unseen world' was also a source of truth. Thus, since the protagonists were arguing from different premises, their disputes were somewhat unproductive. But since each side held its opinion with passionate sincerity, the battle continued unabated, notably in the meetings of the Metaphysical Society and its journal the *Contemporary Review.*

Gladstone faced two problems in conducting the battle. The first was that his opponents included not only scientists who took the view that what science did not or could not demonstrate could not be true, but also non-scientists of all shades of opinion from those who were vaguely agnostic to atheists who refused to accept the scriptures, or religious experience, as valid routes to truth. The second was that if he argued on the basis of 'received wisdom' he was treading on or near the ground which the Papacy was using as the argument in favour of its monopoly of religious truth, namely 'Authority'. As always, when he felt passionately about truth or justice he was not slow to leap into the fray, yet he was in a cleft stick. He found no difficulty in following St Augustine, one of his four 'Doctors', in the view that what the world judges to be true is true, but he received with – to put it mildly – a degree of scepticism Manning's defence of Vaticanism in a paper to the Metaphysical Society showing that 'Legitimate Authority is an Evidence of Truth'. He wrote a good deal about probability but on the whole his writings during the battle of belief do not seem satisfactory.

It was Lyon Playfair who turned out to be Gladstone's greatest support in communicating, interpreting and advising the Liberal Governments on science. He was a brilliant Scottish chemist who had studied under Liebig and in the Giessen laboratories in Germany and worked with Bunsen. A Gladstonian Liberal, he became Postmaster-General in 1873 and introduced Gladstone's idea of the halfpenny postcard. A polymath, he was put to work by the Government to report on the cattle plague and on the condition of the large towns of Lancashire; to advise on the drains of Buckingham Palace; and to chat with the Prince Consort in his fluent German about the use of sewage as fertiliser at Osborne. He became the Government's adviser on scientific education, was Professor of Chemistry at the new Government-inspired School of Mines, and it was he who proposed the Victorian Museum, duly to become the V & A. Gladstone admired him, roped him in as Deputy Speaker to deal with obstruction in the Home Rule debates, and raised him to the peerage in 1892.

Gladstone attended church at least twice every Sunday and three times when there was an appropriate opportunity. He listened attentively to every sermon however humble the preacher. In Hawarden church he sat in the front row and in very old age he would rise in his seat, ear trumpet to his ear, to catch every word spoken by the unfortunate curate. On every weekday when he was at Hawarden he walked up to church by the private path he had created through the park for the service at 8 am. He took immense trouble during his middle years over the composition of sermons for the benefit of the servants at household prayers. Yet he was regularly accused by his opponents of self-righteousness, hypocrisy and unctuousness. The verdict lies in the ear of the hearer. It was more of a strength than a weakness for a politician to be convinced that he was right, and Gladstone's most admirable characteristic was to fight for what he thought was just and fair without much regard for the political consequences. He was undaunted in defeat. There were times when worry and overwork made him ill and he had one or two periods of severe insomnia; but these problems were not brought on by fear of defeat, and his ability to rebound was astonishing. The fact that he always thought he was right infuriated his opponents and was sometimes perceived with strong reservations by his supporters. The borderline between personal conviction and self-righteousness can be a narrow one. He was criticised by supporters and opponents alike for the long and elaborate qualifications which larded his apparently endless but perfectly constructed sentences, and what was worse was his expectation that his audience would construe every nuance of his meaning. He was certainly guilty of sophistry on occasions. As an old and cunning Parliamentary hand, he was sometimes guilty, too, of deliberate obfuscation: many skilled and experienced politicians are guilty of that, but few have performed with the labyrinthine virtuosity with which he could provide a meaningless answer if the occasion demanded one. It was hardly thinkable that a person so intensely religious could never thank God for his success or see an opportunity for action in some just cause as one provided by the Almighty.

When Gladstone was addressing a big non-Parliamentary audience he would deliberately 'turn on the steam', but what comes across in his speeches in the House of Commons is not ranting but sweet reasonableness, perfect clarity, lucid argument and a great deal of wit. He could evoke loud and continuous laughter from any audience. He was earnest, and he did not tell jokes, but as his confidence grew so did his lightness of touch.

Two of the keys to Gladstone's thought are his diary and his library. Each is unique: no other diary of a politician covering anything approaching the timescale of 1825 to 1896 exists; but the diary is not literary or descriptive. It was not written for an audience. It was a private record of the way he spent his time: a sort of account book for his Creator. His library was equally his own personal tool for the knowledge he wished to acquire. He was always keen that others should be able to benefit from his books: and that indeed was the entire motivation for founding St Deiniol's Library. But he collected books not in order to create a library on this subject or that but simply because he wanted to read them. His reading and his writing were at nobody's behest. His scholarship – notably his theology and his Homeric studies – was entirely individualistic, if not idiosyncratic, and indeed in the eyes of the academic world eccentric and occasionally even 'dotty'. His theological and Homeric works were apt to receive savage reviews; yet, on the whole, when you read them you find much that is logical, cogent and in particular sweetly reasonable. There is certainly a similarity between his politics and his literary leisure pursuits. The driving force was deep personal conviction.

We have seen that, except for his father's influence, he might well have become a clergyman. People have often said that if he had not become Prime Minister he would have become Archbishop of Canterbury. But this is to misunderstand his qualities and his restless personality. The House of Commons suited him because it was a forum for discussion and an engine of change. The Church of England is not quite the same. He would have been a wonderful archdeacon in the style of Gerald of Wales. He might even have become a bishop in Victorian times, when (within strict limits) originality was still recognised as a virtue. But it is hard to think of him as an archbishop. It has often been said (and no doubt often will be) that he was the greatest Anglican layman of his time. So, in a way, he was. But if one reflects, one has to swallow hard before saying even that.

15
Gladstone on Homer

I THREE PHASES OF HOMERIC STUDIES

Gladstone's main publications on Homer, omitting numerous articles in learned periodicals, can be considered in three periods: his magnum opus, *Studies on Homer and the Homeric Age*, published in 1858; secondly, what was essentially a revision of that work's more controversial conclusions in *Juventus Mundi* in 1869; and thirdly, as representative of his later ideas, *Homeric Synchronism* in 1876. His theories attracted plenty of hostile criticism, notoriously from Macaulay, a brilliant if not a profound writer with an utterly different mindset from that of Gladstone: Macaulay, the archpriest of the 'Whig interpretation of history' which tends to look upon history as a story of human progress.

The best way to form a judgement of Gladstone's works is to read them; but anybody who is sufficiently interested to do that would do well to use as a guide the two long relevant chapters in David Bebbington's *The Mind of Gladstone* (Oxford, 2004) and perhaps also F. M. Turner's *The Greek Heritage in Victorian Britain* (New Haven, Connecticut, 1981). There is, however, a short cut; and that short cut is to read Gladstone's valedictory address as Rector of the University of Edinburgh, delivered over the course of a little more than two hours in 1865 under the title of 'The Place of Ancient Greece in the Providential Order'. Gladstone included the text, with some notes, in volume vii of his *Gleanings of Past Years*, published by John Murray in 1879.

The address was given some four years before the advent of *Juventus Mundi*, but Gladstone was nevertheless willing to publish it some fourteen years later. Thus it gives the essence of his revised message about the Homeric age, and above all it conveys his enthusiasm and his sheer joy in his subject. Whilst in full flow he considerably shortened his text (he must have detected that the attention span of his audience would not stretch much beyond two hours), and anyway his willingness to

Cabinet.

June 1 (11 am) 1872.

v Treaty of Washington. Mr Fish's
telegram. recd this morning.
Answer considered & agreed on.
Alteration made in wording of
laws Officers at the end — with ref.
to *before* expression of the power
of Adjournment at Geneva.

v Chancellorship of the Duchy of
Lancaster.

o Salary of Ld advocate.

v Tichborne Case — question. Not
the fact

Ref. chapter 12, The First Government. Cabinet agenda for 1 June 1872. The meeting lasted from 11 am to 4 pm: each item is ticked when concluded. The first item deals with the *Alabama* case (see further coverage on pp. 3–5 of this section) – a discussion on the contentious Treaty of Washington under which Britain agreed to accept the judgment of the international court. Perhaps the third item, marked with an 'O', was not resolved. The fourth item is on the celebrated Tichborne inheritance case, then being argued in court, when an Australian, Arthur Orton, claimed to be the presumed dead Roger Tichborne.

v Education Bill Scotland.
  As to Board – Endeavour to
  put Given article, accepting
  Mr Leyce: fight Garden at ba
  entrance –

v Russell's Salary – If the question
  be raised, vote for it as originally
  engaged by Mr. of Ed.

v Ld Lifford's motion for a committee
  on Irish Land Act –
  Oppose on the ground of time –

v French Communists,
  acq. the Govt of strong feeling of Parlt
  & that we must keep peace.

v Answer Ld Buckhurst that
  he wd not go back on any question
  of the premises or engagements
  between the Cmmt.

See caption facing page (above)

Mem. for sending Guards Band to America to go forward.

Do of Richmond Officers address.

ABOVE AND FACING PAGE A proposal by Lord Lifford for a committee to debate the Irish Land Act is rejected 'on the ground of time'. The ticklish problem arises of French communist refugees in Britain after the suppression of the Paris commune: 'Acquaint Fr. Govt. of strong feeling of Parliament.' The agenda include discussion of some items which would be considered insufficiently important nowadays; but Gladstone's Cabinet had to decide how to respond in Parliament. (The 2nd Lord Buckhurst, incidentally, was to introduce the Acrobats Bill to the Lords the following month.) The penultimate item confirms that the Guards Band shall go to the USA – the days of a more assertive redcoat presence there had been over now since the War of 1812.

BELOW Gladstone's memoranda for the Cabinet's discussion of the *Alabama* on 1 June 1872 are a masterly summary of the conditions he proposes. The final section demonstrates the Government's courage in submitting judgement to an international court, and the necessity of avoiding any sense of British humiliation as a result. 'Cabinet is summoned at 11. These are my first impressions. The two Governments appear to be agreed…'

1. That cases of bad faith & wilful misconduct should not be brought within the scope of the proposed agreement which deals with pecuniary compensation.

2. That in cases of failure to observe neutral obligation through want of due diligence, claims are ~~not~~ to be made in respect of the remote or indirect consequences of the injurious acts growing out of such failure.

3. That if an agreement can be concluded upon this subject between the two countries the President will covenant to make no claim at Geneva in respect of the indirect losses set forth at Washington to show no further proceeding would be taken upon or in respect of them

4. That (in the words of the Fish's Telegram) there is not "any such "difference of object between the two Governments in the definition & limitation which each desires to place upon the liability of a neutral as to prevent an agreement

on the language in which to express
it, if time be allowed for the exchange of views by some other means
than the Telegraph—"

The British Government could
not without exciting the grave
displeasure of Parlᵗ & people of this
country sign a form of words
which does not conform to the
views of either Govᵗ in respect of
wilful misconduct, & which immediately after being signed would
become the subject of negotiation
with a view to its abrogation.

But in order that the objects
of the two Govᵗˢ may be attained,
& that the Arbitration at Geneva
may proceed, they will with readiness
agree
to extend the time allowed for the
Arbitrators to meet at
Geneva, & they have provided
Sir E. Thornton with full powers
for this purpose

Wᵐ G June 1. 72

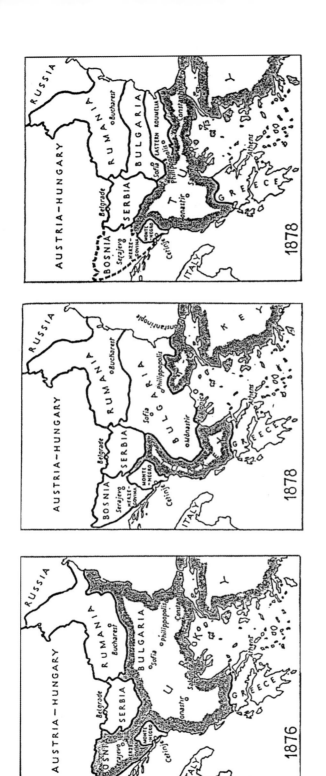

SCALE IN MILES

| 0 | 100 | 200 | 300 | 400 | 500 |

The Balkans 1876–78 (chapter 16)

CENSUS FIGURES FOR THE UNITED KINGDOM
1801–1891

ENGLAND AND WALES.	Total	Increase	
		Decennial	Per Cent (a)
1801	8.892,536	-	-
1811	10,164,256	1,271,720	14.00
1821	12,000,236	1,835,980	18.06
1831	13.896.797	1.896.561	15.80
1841	15,914,148	2,017,351	14.48
1851	17,927,609	2,013,461	12.89
1861	20,066,224	2,138,615	11.90
1871	22,712,266	2,646,042	13.21
1881	25,974,439	3,262,173	14.36
1891	29,002,525	3,028,086	11.65
SCOTLAND			
1801	1,608,420	-	-
1811	1,805,864	197,444	12.27
1821	2,091,521	285,657	15.82
1831	2,364,386	272,865	13.04
1841	2,620,184	255,798	10.82
1851	2,888,742	268,558	10.25
1861	3.062.294	173.552	6.00
1871	3,360,018	297,724	9.72
1881	3,735,573	375,555	11.18
1891	4,025,647	290,074	7.77
IRELAND			
1821	6,801,827	-	-
1831	7,767,401	965,574	14.19
1841	8.175,124	407.723	5.25
1851	6,552,385	+1,622,739	+19.85
1861	5,798,967	+753,418	+11.50
1871	5,412.377	+386.590	+6.67
1881	5,174,836	+237,541	+4.39
1891	4,704,750	+470.086	+9.08
ISLANDS			
1851	143,126	-	-
1861	143,447	321	0.22
1871	144.638	1.191	0.83
1881	141,260	+3,378	+2.34
1891	147,842	6.582	4.66

Census figures dramatically illustrate the rise and fall
of the population of Ireland, and its proportion to that
of England and Wales and of Scotland (chapter 17)

April 4th · 1878

[Tennyson]
Robert Browning
[J. A. Lorre]
James Stuart.
Edward Burne-Jones
G. W. Balfour
Hallam Tennyson
Margaret Cowell Stepney

8 May 1884
Octavie Hill
M. de Laveleye
Mr Mivart

15
Arthur Blunt
Ld Rowley   }   3 buffoons
George Russell
Anna Swanwick

22
John Morley
Andrew Carnegie
Lord Morley

Gladstone gave breakfast parties on most Thursdays at 10 am when he was in London, inviting a mixed group of guests from various walks of life. As he grew older his daughter Mary masterminded them and wrote sometimes robust comments in indelible pencil in the Breakfast Book, where the guests (or occasionally she herself) entered their names.

confine the essence to 'what may be termed an address' compelled him to omit a substantial amount of detailed evidence and some of the still controversial conclusions which he drew from it. But it is a satisfactory starting point.

Having read the address (which is summarised in the second section of this chapter), the reader might be tempted to dip into the magnum opus, for Gladstone's methodical arrangement detailed in the Contents makes it a wonderfully dippable book. He begins the work by stating his objective: that Homer should be studied at the universities in a far more extensive way than in his own days, for the mere schoolboy could hardly be expected to understand the nature and characteristics of the Homeric Age.

> Nevertheless, Homer's free and genial temperament gives him a hold on the sympathies of the young. The simple and direct construction of his sentences allows them easy access to his meaning; the examination of the sense of single words ... is within their reach; while the large and varied inflexions of the Greek tongue, in Homer's hands at once so accurate and so elastic, make him peculiarly fit for the indispensable and invaluable work of parsing... .

This seems nowadays an optimistic assessment of the achievements of the average sixth former.

Gladstone begins the work with the date and authenticity of Homer, and then launches into a very long section on the ethnology of the ancient races, much of which was soon to be brought into question as archaeological and other scientific knowledge expanded. His conclusions, largely drawn (as he himself stated) from the Homeric epics themselves, did not stand up to the kind of scientific inquiry which was soon to develop but which he can hardly have dreamed of. Yet one can only admire the thoroughness of his research and the perceptiveness of his conclusions about kingship and lordship in the section of more than 100 pages, still under 'ethnology'.

The second volume is on the subject of 'Olympus, or the religion of the Homeric age', and this was the one most challenged by critics and most altered in *Juventus Mundi*. It was in itself a challenge to the new, dangerous and controversial view expressed by Jowett, then a don at Balliol College, that the supernatural elements of Biblical revelation needed to be explained in terms of ordinary life. This challenged

Gladstone's conviction that the Christian religion was a revealed religion. British, and most particularly German scholars, were abandoning the idea of revelation, particularly a great 'initial' revelation near the beginning of time, and were looking at all religious development as a 'natural' process. Unlike Gladstone's Olympus, they argued that the earliest Greek deities were derived from the forces of Nature. It was on this subject that Gladstone, wading increasingly through German (and British) scholarship as the 1850s rolled on into the '60s, most obviously modified his views. But I shall leave him to draw his own conclusions in his address at Edinburgh.

Gladstone has been accused of detecting 'providential' revelation to the Greeks prior to the revelation of the Christian gospel to the Jews. The accusation is false. What he saw was not a precursor of Christian revelation but a revelation parallel to that vouchsafed to the Jews in the pre-Christian era. And indeed he makes the point that later Greek civilisation provided essential ground for the spread of the Gospel: the conquests of Alexander the Great, he said, were short-lived but left behind them an altered culture, capable of receiving Christianity.

In conceding that the Gods – at least those of the second rank – owed their origin to Nature, Gladstone seems to have invented a word 'anthropomorphuic' just before it is found in use without the 'u' – which he then dropped. Personification, he points out, is a common device of civilisations. Homeric society differed from Judaic in the central place it gave to the beauty of the human form.

The character of Gladstone's argument in his magnum opus was to draw conclusions by inference from the Homeric text. We may here and there doubt his premises, and we may not accept his conclusions, but we must marvel at his knowledge, his logic, and his profound understanding of Homeric life. His conclusions depended on probability. Probability in his hands was that of a rigid logician and an accomplished mathematician. (There is a long essay in the subject of probability in *Gleanings*.) When he turns to social and moral questions in his sections in the Olympian Pantheon, his work on the place of women in Homeric society and his analysis of the rules of marriage and sexual behaviour make wonderful reading. As to the Table of Kindred and Affinity and the difficulty of explaining why marriage to an aunt may have been acceptable in rare cases on Olympus, he provides the Homeric vocabulary for father and for mother-in-law, brother- and sister-in-law, son- and daughter-in-law, and stepmother ('or the lawful wife in relation to a spurious son') – used only once in Homer; and finally, for a husband's sister-in-law, 'a relationship not expressed by any word in the English and many other languages'. He also explains why concubinage is acceptable, under strict limitations, for soldiers long and far from home.

In the third volume, which in some respects is the most readable and interesting, after dealing with politics (which I shall mention briefly in another essay), he deals with the Trojans, with geography, and with the plot of the *Iliad* (an important subject in view of Grote's contention – which had been aired by Coleridge as early as the 1820s – that the epic derives from several distinct sources) and then goes on to the sense of beauty in Homer (referred to in the Edinburgh address), the use of number and the sense of colour, before stepping on to the more speculative ground of comparison with Virgil and Tasso (and, *en passant*, Dante and Milton). Finally, he deals with the characters of Hector, Helen and Paris and (mercilessly) with the decline ('declension') of the great Homeric characters in later Greek literature and drama. He makes no bones about his scorn for the dramatists' willingness to dumb down their presentation in pursuit of ratings, their 'absolute dependence on popular taste', the 'general obliteration of the finer distinctions', and the 'mutilation' of the characters of Helen and Ulysses in Greek theatre. The work ends with Homeric characters in Shakespeare and Racine. Whatever its limitations, Gladstone's *Studies on Homer and the Homeric Age*, three volumes, 1,722 pages, would stand the test of a lifetime's work by many a more than ordinary man.

The final period of Gladstone's work and writings on Homer was in some respects the least satisfactory. He was much excited by Schliemann's belief that he had excavated the site of Troy, and there was disagreement between Schliemann and Gladstone about the dating of the siege of Troy and of Homer's account of it. Both men were on very uncertain ground. Reluctantly, Gladstone later agreed to write a preface to Schliemann's work on Mycenae. He was equally excited by the interpretation of cuneiform tablets and at the Chaldean story of a flood similar to Noah's. But Gladstone's *Homeric Synchronism* of 1876 and his other late works were too ready to draw conclusions from recent and incomplete research. His last work was *Landmarks of Homeric Study* in 1890, something of a mixture of his older and his newer conclusions. Perhaps the most Gladstonian characteristic of all these books was the irresistible urge to put pen to paper and to share his enthusiasm with his readers.

2 THE ADDRESS AT EDINBURGH UNIVERSITY, 1865

There is nothing more calculated than a précis, even if larded with quotations from the original text, to dumb down the spirit of an author, or even more so the spirit of an orator. A reading of this address is a short cut to an appreciation of Gladstone's Homeric studies, especially in their relation to Christian revelation; but it cannot convey the full flavour of Gladstone's absorption in the Homeric world, even if it suggests what most particularly concerned him. A shortening of the short cut must be even less satisfactory. But one has to begin somewhere.

Gladstone opens by emphasising the manifold ways in which Greek civilisation has influenced later periods. Yet there has been a 'practical indisposition to regard ancient Greece as having had a distinct, assignable and most important place in the Providential government of the world'. It is his object to correct this view, and he devotes the first part of his address to the improbability of an all-seeing and all-powerful God having neglected to endow any other than the Jewish people with some form of providential wisdom. He deals at length with Eusebius' condemnation of all pagan systems of religion, and shows that most Christian apologists followed suit. The Christian writers' objective was to 'sweep from the world a crying and incurable moral evil, not to construct a universal philosophy of the religious history of man'. But if we believe in the essential soundness of the text of scripture ... 'we must then believe that the Hametic and Japhetic races ... brought with them (in their migrations, and development) the common religious traditions'.

Jewish idolatry was never anthropomorphic – 'thus was kept vacant the sublime and solitary place which the Redeemer of the world was to fill.' Gladstone then illustrates at length the 'anthropomorphic genius' of the Greeks. 'To Apollo is assigned the healing art, the general office of deliverance. He remains to the last the perfect model of the human male form and is assigned by tradition the conquest alike over death and over the might of the rebellious spirits.'

Every ancient religion except the Greek involved the worship of nature and of animals, which the early Hellenic system steadily rejected and eschewed. The eagle of Zeus, the falcon of Apollo, the peacock of Here, the owl of Pallas, stood no higher than accessories to the figures they attended. The 'rude and formless art' of Egypt is condemned. Gladstone deals (in 'rude and rapid outline') with the Greek annexation of manhood to deity and the reciprocal incorporation of deity into manhood; the profound reverence for human life and human nature. Human sacrifice, common in other religious and notably in Rome, is not found in Homer. Incest, polygamy, abortion, the exposure of infants, have no place in the Homeric poems. The intense admiration of human beauty in Homer exceeds that of any author in any country. The law of force is dethroned. The place of women in Homeric society was infinitely more enlightened than in the Jewish tradition.

With his eye on the Roman Church he points out that 'over the whole continent of Europe there is scarcely at this moment an object of popular veneration which is worthy to be called a work of art'.

Then 'I must shortly touch on their philosophy. The true meaning of the famous saying that Socrates called down philosophy from Heaven would seem to be that he gave expression to the genius of his country by propounding, as the prime subject for the study of man, the nature, constitution, and destiny of man himself.' The Greek mind was to some degree the secular counterpart of the Gospel, and became the predominant intellectual factor of Christian civilisation, although 'all the wonders of the Greek civilisation heaped together are less wonderful than is the single Book of Psalms... .

'Melchisedic, the type of Christ; Job, one of the chosen patrons of faith and patience; they, after all, were of blood foreign to the patriarchal race.'

There is then a sustained attack on the 'thousands of anchorites' in the early Christian church who

foreswore every human relation, extinguished every appetite, and absorbed every motive, every idea, every movement of our complex nature in the great but single function of the relation to the unseen world... . The internecine war with sin, the very essence of Christianity, seems to have been understood by them as a war against the whole visible and sensible world, against the intellectual life, against a great portion of their own normal nature ... severing the Gospel from all that is beautiful and glorious in creation.

Then comes the peroration: 'We live in times when the whole nature of our relation to the unseen world is widely, eagerly and assiduously questioned'; and Gladstone refers to St Augustine's observation about periods 'when the power of putting questions runs greatly in advance of the pains to answer them'. Who, he asks, can with just and firm hand sever the transitory from the durable, and the accidental from the essential, in old opinions? Who can combine reverence and gratitude for the past with a sense of the new claims, new means, new duties of the present? Who can do battle for the truth and yet hold sacred the freedom of enquiry and cherish a chivalry of controversy like the ancient chivalry of arms?

> Let us embrace this persuasion, that Christianity will by her inherent resources find for herself a philosophy equal to all the shifting and all the growing wants of the time. ... The Christianity which is now and hereafter to flourish, and through its power in the inner circles of human thought to influence more adequately than now the masses of mankind, must be such as of old the Wisdom of God was described.

16

From 'Bag and Baggage'
to 'Peace with Honour'

Controversy over the Eastern Question, which had involved Britain in the Crimean War twenty years earlier, gripped the country between 1876 and 1878 in a way in which no other issue has done before or since in time of peace. The nearest parallel is perhaps the Suez crisis of 1956, in which the whole country took sides, entirely without regard to people's normal political alignments; but that was short-lived and uncomplicated by comparison. It also lacked a unique dramatic feature of this Victorian crisis, namely that the two leaders, Disraeli and Gladstone, occupied positions more extreme than that of their colleagues, and therefore polarised a situation in which there would otherwise have been room for a good deal of compromise. And not only that: the fringe supporters on each extreme, either in or with the aid of the press, did their best in intemperate terms to draw public perception of the positions of the two leaders ever further apart.

The Eastern Question in simple terms was this: how was the vacuum to be filled caused by the decline of Turkey, the Ottoman Empire now in a state of decay, which had dominated south-eastern Europe for more than four centuries? Rumania, Bulgaria and the Balkans were largely Christian areas which had been under Moslem rule, in intensely mixed racial groups. For example, the 'Big Bulgaria' (see map in illustration section 4) which was proposed as a means of ensuring political stability or perhaps Russian domination, according to one's point of view, would have included only a minority of Bulgarians, and a great variety of other races. As to the Balkans, the verb 'Balkanise', in common currency from the nineteenth to the twenty-first century, emerged precisely in order to describe this characteristic.

The independence of the southern part of Greece from Turkish rule in the 1820s marked the first chapter, complete with its romantic associations; the Crimean War the second; and the third began with risings in Herzegovina, Serbia, Bosnia and Montenegro in the 1870s. They were hotly resisted by the Turks, just in time to enlist the services of Russian Pan-Slav volunteers on the Austrian side, including Vronsky in the final chapters of *Anna Karenina*. At an early stage, after the murder of the German and French consuls by a Turkish mob, Russia, Austria and Germany proposed an armistice to enable a reform programme by Turkey to take place. Known as the 'Berlin Memorandum', it was surprisingly rejected by Disraeli, who feared Russian motives and distrusted both Bismarck and the Austrian Foreign Minister Andrássy. Disraeli proposed to follow the British tradition of supporting Turkey, and called the British Fleet to Besika Bay.

The tale of Disraeli's subsequent actions is complicated both by the changing situation, his complaints of incompetence about Foreign Office information and advice, his disregard of the views of his Cabinet colleagues, and by a series of misjudgements due to some extent to the poor state of his health, aggravated by counter-productive medical treatment. Disraeli was always something of a loner. He had few close friends and socially he always most enjoyed the company of women, notably his wife Mary Ann and Queen Victoria. Gladstone had had a warm regard for Mary Ann, and on occasions he would call on her at Grosvenor Gate after a debate in order to show that there was no ill-will. She was older than her husband and when she collapsed at the age of eighty Gladstone made a kindly reference to her health in the Commons. Disraeli thanked him with tears in his eyes, following this with a letter. It was only in Disraeli's last years, after Mary Ann's death, that his rivalry with Gladstone became bitter and indeed eventually developed into something like mutual hatred. When he was not at Downing Street Disraeli lived and worked alone at Hughenden. Apart from Monty Corry he could not even tolerate the company of a secretary and, certainly in relation to his Eastern policy, his Cabinet was not much consulted and was notoriously at sixes and sevens.

A hopeless rising in Bulgaria was suppressed in a barbaric manner, fully reported in the British press, by irregular Turkish troops. Partly because his policy was to support Turkey, Disraeli persistently denied the severity of these atrocities, even after they had been confirmed by impeccable sources.

Some time after the first reports of the burning of villages and the rape and massacre of women and children, long after Disraeli could (without necessarily having to make any material changes in his policy) have acknowledged his horror of the atrocities, Gladstone emerged on the scene from his retirement at Hawarden and, abandoning his chosen literary pursuits, wrote in a few days in the Temple of Peace his most famous pamphlet, *The Bulgarian Horrors and the Question of the East*. He then hastened to London – in spite of his lumbago – to check some facts, took the text to his publisher John Murray, and read the proofs, all in a matter of days. The pamphlet sold 40,000 copies in three or four days, and 200,000 over the course of the coming weeks. It was followed by an open-air speech in pouring rain (for which Disraeli gave thanks) at Blackheath (in Gladstone's Greenwich constituency) to a audience of some 20,000.

The pamphlet included a powerful dramatic passage which has often been quoted:

An old servant of the Crown and State, I entreat my countrymen, upon whom far more than perhaps any other people of Europe it depends, to require and insist that our Government, which has been working in one direction, shall work in the other, and shall apply all its vigour to concur with other states of Europe in obtaining the extinction of the Turkish executive power in Bulgaria. Let the Turks now carry away their abuses in the only possible manner, namely by carrying off themselves. Their Zaptiehs and their Mudirs, their Bimbashis and their Yuzbachis, their Kaimakams and their Pashas, one and all, bag and baggage, shall, I hope, clear out from the province they have desolated and profaned. This thorough riddance, this most blessed deliverance, is the only reparation we can make to the memory of those heaps on heaps of dead; to the violated purity alike of matron, of maiden and of child; to the civilisation which has been affronted and shamed; to the laws of God, or if you like, of Allah; to the moral sense of mankind at large. There is not a criminal in an European gaol, there is not a cannibal in the South Sea Islands, whose indignation would not arise and overboil at the recital of that which has been done, which has too late been examined, but which remains unavenged; which has left behind all the foul and all the fierce passions that produced it, and which may again spring up in another murderous harvest, from the soil soaked and reeking with blood and in the air tainted with every imaginable deed of crime and shame. That such things should be done once, is a damning disgrace to the portion of our race which did them; that a door should be left open for their repetition would spread that shame over the whole. Better, we may justly tell the Sultan, almost any inconvenience, difficulty or loss associated with Bulgaria,

> Than thou reseated in thy place of light,
> The mockery of thy people and their bane.

We may ransack the annals of the world, but I know not what research can furnish us with so portentous an example of the fiendish misuse of the powers established by God 'for the punishment of evil-doers and for the encouragement of them that do well'. No Government ever has so sinned; none has so proved itself incorrigible in sin, or which is the same, so impotent for reformation. If it be allowable that the executive power of Turkey should renew at this great crisis, by permission or authority of Europe, the charter of its existence in Bulgaria, then there is not on record since the beginnings of political society a protest that man has lodged against intolerable misgovernment, or a stroke he has dealt at loathsome tyranny, that ought not henceforward to be branded as a crime.

The best remembered of all these ringing phrases is the strange one 'bag and baggage'. The supposed inventor was Stratford de Redcliffe, the British Ambassador at Constantinople during the Crimean War, but Scott had used it in *Waverley* of the highland army during the 1745 rebellion. From one of these sources it had caught Gladstone's ear, as it has subsequently caught the ear of millions. These three words were the most famous he ever wrote, just as his unguarded sentence in 1864 constituted the most famous words he ever uttered.

The fact is that the pamphlet, and the horrors it described, caught the mood of people of every class in Britain. Nothing like the atrocities had ever before trespassed on their lives. Tennyson, Ruskin, Burne-Jones, Darwin and Delane (the influential editor of *The Times*) joined leading historical writers of the day – Carlyle, Froude, Acton, J. R. Green and Bishop Stubbs – in sympathising publicly with Gladstone's view. There was also a good deal of intemperate support, including attacks on Disraeli's Judaism, from 'popular' writers – invoking equally crude responses.

For Disraeli the question was how to restrain Russia without a fight, but his attempt to demonstrate Britain's determination was not helped by Gladstone. This gave the Russian 'Pan-Slavists' a freer hand to fight their cause as a mission to free the long-enslaved Christian states. This in itself reinvigorated the contest between the two great protagonists in both Parliamentary and public speeches.

Somewhat contrary to expectations, Turkey defeated Serbia, and Disraeli had to bring pressure to bear on Turkey to end the war and embark on yet another – this time in theory more fundamental – programme of reform. Lord Salisbury, who was in the Cabinet as Indian Secretary, was the British delegate at the Constantinople Conference. His ability to master all the elements of the situation, to inspire trust and confidence and to show himself a skilled, shrewd negotiator made his name as a statesman of the first rank and brought him forward as Disraeli's probable successor. The Turks do not seem to have believed that Britain would leave them to face defeat by a British washing of hands. Salisbury knew that Britain could not join Turkey in a war against Russia. He was convinced, too, that however frightening the Russian threat might seem, the Czar would stop short of Constantinople. But the Constantinople Conference broke up in disagreement. Disraeli does not appear to have realised that the policy of both Salisbury and the Foreign Secretary, Derby, was different from his own. British policy had simply come to a halt. Negotiations continued between the various parties, but it was becoming clear that war between Russia and Turkey was now more than probable. When it eventually broke out, Britain declared her neutrality, provided that what she saw as her essential interests were preserved: namely that Constantinople should remain Turkish, and that the Straits should be free for navigation – by the British Fleet, of course; and that the Suez Canal should also remain free and beyond the sphere of the war. The Russians agreed.

The war lasted from April 1877 to the end of January 1878. Russian armies became committed to difficult Balkan campaigns and their main advance was halted by Turkish victories, and then by the defence of Plevna. Meanwhile to the British public, well informed by press reports, the old fear of Russian ambitions pushed the Turkish atrocities into second place in public concern. In the end, Russia did prevail, and in spite of Turkish pleas for an armistice, Russian troops occupied Adrianople. Disraeli was determined to hold firm. Derby hesitated, but the Cabinet ordered the Fleet to steam through the Dardanelles to Constantinople, and in spite of Gladstone's vehement opposition, Parliament granted £6 million for military purposes. Derby and Carnarvon, the Colonial Secretary, resigned. The situation became most alarming. Russian soldiers, who had continued to advance after the armistice, could see the British warships. To Gladstone's disgust, the music-hall song caught on everywhere:

> We don't want to fight
> But by Jingo, if we do,
> We've got the men, we've got the ships,
> We've got the money, too.

But a truce was arranged: Russia would not occupy Gallipoli, and British troops would not land; and this turned into the Treaty of San Stefano, with a big Bulgaria and an independent Bosnia (as well as Serbia, Rumania and Montenegro) giving Russia the control of the Black Sea coast and overriding influence in the Balkans. Russia also annexed parts of Armenia in 'Asiatic Turkey' but did nothing to help the oppressed Christians in the Turkish areas: it remained for Gladstone to take up their cause to their intense and lasting gratitude, although the terrible events in both Turkey and Russia in 1914–18 were grossly to exceed the horrors of the 1870s. Salisbury succeeded Derby as Foreign Secretary and it was his work which brought about the Congress of Berlin. The Great Powers agreed to modifications to the Treaty of San Stefano, and Disraeli returned to London in triumph proclaiming 'Peace with honour'.

This was the last scene in the drama, a drama summed up by three words written by Gladstone and three words spoken by Disraeli: 'bag and baggage'; 'peace with honour'. The curtain fell. The nation remained divided in the '*envoi*', a dual *envoi* to each of the two heroes.

Disraeli had put Britain – or had put Britain back – on the world map. The Berlin Congress was followed by a period of peace in Europe lasting thirty-six years. Peace after Vienna had lasted thirty-nine years. Disraeli had dreamed of British hegemony from the Levant to the frontiers of India: jingoism remained unabated and eventually Britain emerged on the victorious side in the war to end wars.

But Gladstone had asserted Liberal values, and it was Gladstone who, after Midlothian, won the election of 1880, and set about dismantling Beaconsfieldism. Disraeli (now the Earl of Beaconsfield) was as dismayed and as surprised as Gladstone had been to be ousted in 1874.

Finally, there is a postscript. The Congress of Berlin was both preceded and succeeded by several secret or semi-secret agreements between pairs of Great Powers, including one between Britain and Turkey by which Britain agreed to support Turkey's position in Asia in return for the British occupation of Cyprus. (The island was duly surveyed, to the standard of the British Ordnance, by a young army officer, Herbert Kitchener.) Cyprus would provide the Mediterranean Fleet with a base east of Malta – and would thus enable Britain to fulfil her part of the obligation to support Turkey-in-Asia. But the harbours of Cyprus became redundant in a vast cloud of black smoke from the guns of the Royal Navy when in July 1882 Gladstone consented to the bombardment of Alexandria, thereafter the main British naval base in the Eastern Mediterranean. Without Alexandria Britain would certainly not have been able to retain her fleet in the Mediterranean and to keep open the Suez route to India during the Second World War.

There is no better summary of events or fairer judgement on Disraeli's policy than in Robert Blake's *Disraeli* (1966). He pays tribute to the first study which, by access to the secret Russian correspondence, was able to make an authentic judgement on Russia's intentions: this was Professor Seton-Watson's *Disraeli, Gladstone and the Eastern Question*, published in 1935, a detailed and still valid account. It is a fine vindication of Liberal policy, music to the ears of the Gladstonian. Yet it is too hard on Disraeli, who may have overestimated the Russian threat, but who never wanted or courted war. As Blake points out, Disraeli – like Churchill in the 1930s – knew that a stance against aggression would have been futile unless it could be backed by force.

17
Gladstone and Ireland

Gladstone's political involvement with Ireland was so long and so complicated that in order to make it comprehensible to the general reader it needs to be separated from all the other political events – worldwide – with which the Government was dealing at the time and treated on its own. There is something Gladstonian in this treatment. 'Spoke on Transvaal', he noted on 25 July 1881, 'and voted in 314:205. But I am too full of Ireland to be *free* in anything else.' The course of Irish affairs can be divided into phases, although of course these phases were not necessarily evident at the time.

Part of the complication lies in the recurring theme of whip and carrot. There was a Coercion Act, suspending civil liberties (including sometimes *habeas corpus*, the right to trial before imprisonment) or creating special penalties for acts of violence or terrorism; and there was also a carrot, a concession to economic or political demands. Either the whip or the carrot might come first; or they might be deployed simultaneously. Equally unproductive was the change of policy with each new government. This was a powerful factor in eventually convincing Gladstone of the desirability of Home Rule: he became aware that a consistent policy from Liberal and Conservative Governments was impossible.

THE STATE OF IRELAND

On taking office as Prime Minister for the first time, Gladstone had disestablished the Irish Church (1869) and had passed the (first) Irish Land Act 1870. These two important measures have been dealt with under the heading of the First Government, and after sketching the historical background, we shall take up the tale on his return to power in 1880.

The social and economic condition of Ireland was appalling. The great majority of the population lived at starvation level in primitive cottages on very small farms. The fertility of much of the land was inadequate for cereals, even with the very low yields expected from better land at that period, so the inhabitants were obliged to rely on potatoes; but there was not enough land to allow for the fertility of the soil, such as it was, to be maintained, nor for the risk of disease to be reduced, by rotation. The population increased, but the amount of land available did not. In the event of a poor crop, the alternatives were starvation or emigration.

Most of the agricultural land consisted of large estates owned by English landlords, some of whom were absentees living in London or on their English estates. The Irish estates were run by agents who had few duties other than extracting rent or evicting those who could not (or would not) pay. It was not the custom for landlords to make improvements to land or buildings, and evicted tenants were paid no compensation for the improvements which they themselves had made. (There were exceptions, especially in the north and in counties around Dublin, with fertile land, large farms, specified rights for tenants and enlightened landlords; but these did not affect the vast majority.)

THE HISTORICAL BACKGROUND

Most of the Irish – perhaps four out of five – were Roman Catholics, but, as we have seen, until 1869 the established Church was Protestant. It was the Church of England, with a very full complement of bishops in their dioceses, deans and canons, archdeacons and clergy all expecting a decent living. Some of the costs of this Church were met from endowments but much had to be paid for compulsorily by the whole population, mostly Roman Catholic.

The Protestant Church, like the English ownership of land, was the product of conquest. The Irish, refusing to accept the Reformation, had remained staunchly Catholic, threatening Tudor hegemony in Britain and, worse still, being potential allies to Britain's Catholic enemies, especially the Spanish. Queen Elizabeth involved herself in a costly series of Irish wars, with limited success. Two generations later, Oliver Cromwell took up the cudgels with unprecedented ferocity and finally, when the Catholic James II was replaced in 1689–90 by the Protestant William of Orange (William and Mary were joint sovereigns not by divine right but by Act of Parliament), William put the cap on it, notably with the 'plantation' of Ulster, the only part of Ireland to have subsequently a Protestant majority.

Throughout the eighteenth century, then, Ireland was ruled by aristocratic English families, the eldest sons owning the land and the younger sons or other men of good English family and Oxford education becoming bishops. But Ireland had her own Parliament, with its House of Lords and its House of Commons, and as the century wore on the Irish House of Commons began to acquire a distinctly national flavour.

THE ACT OF UNION, 1801

The French Revolution (1789) – the storming of the Bastille, the Tennis Court Oath, the flight and later the execution of the King and Queen, the massacres in La Vendée and the Reign of Terror – horrified the English, and with good reason. In London Tom Paine identified the Rights of Man, and the French identified Ireland as a potential ally, even staging what turned out to be a futile (to the point of ridicule) invasion. Consequently William Pitt (Prime Minister since 1784) decided to abolish the Irish Parliament by what Gladstone, ninety years later, called a 'gigantic, but excusable, mistake', namely the Act of Union of the Kingdom of Ireland with the Kingdom of Great Britain.

Acceptance of the Act of Union required plenty of persuasion, but with the armies of revolutionary France, now led by Napoleon, sweeping the Continent and the British facing national disaster, Pitt was in no mood for half-measures. Money and peerages, or promotions in the peerage, were offered galore, and the Union became a fact. Ireland sent a hundred MPs to Westminster and elected twenty Irish representative peers (elected for life) to the House of Lords. The electoral system was that of England. Most of the voters were obliged to vote as their landlords wished. Not until the secret ballot act of 1872 was it feasible for an Irish national party to be formed in the House of Commons.

OBSTRUCTION

Charles Stewart Parnell, although himself a Protestant landowner, realised that the secret ballot provided the opportunity to create an Irish Nationalist Party. For political reasons his policy was, on the whole, to act within the law, but within a few years he trod very close to the brink of lawlessness and his success in forming the Irish party led by the early 1880s to increasing violence in Ireland, generally described as 'Fenianism'. With up to 85 MPs willing to vote on the single issue of Ireland, Parnell potentially held the balance between Liberals and Tories. He was willing to accept whatever he could get from either party.

Parnell set about systematically obstructing the business of the House of Commons by endless speeches ('filibustering'), points of order (questioning whether the rules of the House were being adhered to) and motions that a particular speaker (often Mr Gladstone) 'be not heard'. A huge amount of time, too, was wasted debating minute details of proposed Irish legislation. The most famous occasion was the sitting of 41½ hours from 31 January to 2 February 1881. This was brought to an end by the Speaker simply deciding to adjourn the House.

The Cabinet was by then already devising rules to prevent obstruction, first by devolving some business to 'grand committees' ('devolution') and secondly by the famous 'guillotine', by which a debate could be brought to a close. The elaborate new rules were eventually passed during a special session in October 1882. Gladstone, aged seventy-three, exhausted, began to suffer from insomnia, gave up the Chancellorship of the Exchequer, and made plans to retire.

Parnell, a ruthless tactician, underestimated the hostile reaction of English MPs and the English public. The one thing that many MPs wanted was to get rid of the Irish from the House of Commons. In one way of course this helped Home Rule on its way: but it also led to a fatal flaw in the First Home Rule Bill in 1886 which gave the Irish limited powers in Ireland but removed Irish MPs from the House of Commons. This was what is now called 'The Midlothian Question' (regarding Scottish MPs) turned inside out.

THE LAND LEAGUE AND THE SECOND LAND ACT

The Irish Land League in its origins was a political movement devoted to the transformation of the system of land ownership and the rights of farmers, but in its effectiveness it became a popular movement with the simple objective of alleviating the current problems of the Irish tenant farmer, and in order to achieve their objective, many Irish farmers were prepared to resort to violence. This difference between the Central Committee and the 'grass roots' of the League was what Gladstone sought to exploit in his Second Irish Land Bill.

The Bill was planned in 1881 and introduced in April 1882 after two Coercion Acts in January and March. The Land League was proscribed and Parnell was jailed for what may well be called, to use a Gladstonian phrase, inciting violence.

The carrot followed the whip, and it was a big one, mainly because its purpose was to split and destroy the Land League, but also because Gladstone's avowed legislative tactic was to present the Liberal Party with 'big' Bills, which, in Colin Matthew's words 'would enable its public, political effect to be established and dramatised'. Long debates in the House of Commons were therefore to be welcomed. Gladstone's speech introducing the Bill took 2¾ hours.

In practice, the Bill introduced 'the three Fs', fair rent, fixity of tenure, and free sale, which had been recommended, to Gladstone's surprise, by a Royal Commission. His initial delight had soon been tempered by fear that so far reaching a measure would be politically unachievable, at least for the time being. He refused to embark on the theoretical question whether or not the three Fs were included in the Bill. He certainly would not countenance the removal of the landowners, as the Land League's Committee wished: this alone might have – one can almost say 'would have' – solved the Irish Question, but he saw that it was politically impossible, and future events proved him to be correct. The only other development which would have been essential to Ireland's economic prosperity was the creation of larger farms; but as far as Gladstone was concerned, the economics could follow the politics if the Irish wished: 'I decline', he said, 'to enter into the economical part of the question.'

Thus, although the Bill in practice introduced just those reforms which the 'grass roots' were clamouring for and thus 'castrated' the Land League, the salient point to Gladstone was not the change in law but the means of enforcing it. This was his trump card: the tenant farmers of Ireland would have recourse to a Land Court to settle their grievances. In May 1892 Parnell was released in Kilmainham jail after talks between representatives known as the Kilmainham Treaty, with the promise of an Arrears Bill. (The difficulty of letting off farmers from arrears of rent was, to say the least, intractable, but it seemed to be the price of pacification.) Gladstone wrote in his notes of the Cabinet of 1 May 1892, 'The moment is golden.'

PHOENIX PARK: 6 MAY 1882

Within a few days of Gladstone's recording the golden moment, disaster intervened. Lord Frederick Cavendish, the newly appointed Irish Secretary (that is the Minister, second only to the Viceroy, and a person of Cabinet rank whether or not actually with a seat in the Cabinet) and Thomas Burke, the senior civil servant, were stabbed to death in

Phoenix Park, Dublin, taking a stroll and within sight of Government House. The wild gang responsible for this unprecedented murder of a politician had mistaken their target. Lord Frederick was a close friend of the Gladstones, formerly Gladstone's Financial Secretary at the Treasury, younger brother of his Cabinet colleague, the Marquess of Hartington. They were sons of the Duke of Devonshire, members of one of the most distinguished Whig families, with huge estates in Ireland as well as their seat at Chatsworth. And Lord Frederick was married to Lucy Lyttelton, Catherine Gladstone's niece. The murder was thus a severe personal blow, and Gladstone could not help feeling a degree of responsibility. Moreover, Cavendish was an advocate of, and the Government's acknowledged expert in, the policy of Land Purchase, that most difficult of all Irish legislative proposals. Had he lived, the scheme sketched out in 1881 might well have emerged in more thorough and considered legislative form than it did two or three years later.

The murders caused horror throughout England, and indeed even brought a secret offer from Parnell to resign; but the incident had little effect on the main stream of politics, and within a week Gladstone was introducing the Arrears Bill, running mate of the Coercion ('Crimes') Bill. In due course much attention was given (without much fruit) to the future of local government in Ireland, and broader questions about the need to satisfy the leaders of Irish constitutional opinion started to receive the Cabinet's attention.

THE 'HAWARDEN KITE': DECEMBER 1885

Plans for Ireland thus received a good deal of thought in the Cabinet between 1882 and 1885, but the Government's main preoccupations were elsewhere: with what became known as the Third Reform Act, 1884, and with problems in Afghanistan, Egypt and, above all, the Sudan, with the news in February 1885 of Gordon's murder at Khartoum.

Gladstone had been Prime Minister since 1880 and had faced many contentious issues. The murder of Gordon focused the Opposition, and in June 1885 the P.M. warned the Cabinet that they might be defeated on the Budget. They were, and resigned, Lord Salisbury forming a minority Government pending a general election at some future date. (The maximum period between elections was then seven years.) Gladstone took on his role as Leader of the Opposition with extraordinary zest: there had been talk of retirement at various stages since 1881, but not now. In July he opened a secret channel of communication with Parnell's mistress, Katherine O'Shea. She had married, socially and financially, somewhat beneath her family background, Captain O'Shea, who had been Gladstone's channel to Parnell when, and after, he had been in jail. She was clever and discreet, and an ideal intermediary.

Gladstone was beginning to come round to some kind of Home Rule Bill. On 19 September 1885 he wrote in his diary: 'I have long suspected the Union of 1800. There was a case for doing something but this was like Pitt's Revolutionary war, a gigantic though excusable mistake.' In November he received a 'Proposed Constitution' from Parnell and the same month he wrote a 'sketch':

secret no.1. 14 November 1885.

1   Irish Chamber for Irish affairs.
2   Irish representation to remain as now for Imperial affairs.
3   Equitable division of Imperial charges by fixed proportions.
4   Protection of minority.
5   Suspension of Imperial authority for all civil purposes what-
     soever.

Simultaneously, Salisbury's Conservative Government was itself beginning to come round to the idea of Home Rule: and, having opposed coercion largely as a means of getting rid of the Liberals, they had never actually been obliged to espouse it. Gladstone was very uncertain of bringing round the Liberal Party, but he was confident that on this issue they could probably be persuaded not to oppose the Tories. Moreover, as he and Parnell both perceived, the great advantage of a Tory bill was that they would get the support of the Lords.

At this stage Herbert Gladstone flew the 'Hawarden Kite': in fact he flew it in London, in confidential interviews with three responsible journalists. He had discovered in London 'a regular plot on foot among a section of the [Liberal] party to shelve the Irish Question, to keep the Tories in office, and to prevent under any circumstances my father forming a Government'. His response was to make it clear to journalists that his father was coming round to Home Rule, and he must have known that the essence of what he said would not remain private; but he probably went too far, showing them almost a copy of Gladstone's secret notes. On 17 December Mr Gladstone's 'Scheme for Home Rule' and 'The Authentic Plan of Mr Gladstone' appeared in the press.

Some historians, including Sir Richard Ensor, judged that the Hawarden Kite tipped the balance against the prospect of the Conservatives introducing a Home Rule Bill, and that ultimately it therefore led to the defeat of Gladstone's second Bill in the Lords in 1894. But the matter is more complicated. Gladstone himself was dilatory about trying to bring round the Tories, and the Tories themselves did nothing.

Gladstone knew Arthur Balfour, Salisbury's nephew and successor as Conservative Prime Minister, well. He was a friend of the family and often stayed at Hawarden. The two met 'accidentally' (i.e. by chance) at Eaton Hall on 15 December and Gladstone said to Balfour 'what he will probably repeat in London'. The next day he drafted a letter to Balfour saying that it would be a 'public calamity if this great subject should fall into the lines of party conflict' and offering his support if the Conservatives put forward a 'complete settlement'. But he did not send the letter until 20 December: 'We felled a good ash, read Burke, Dicey. Suspended the Balfour letter,' he wrote on the 16th. Moreover, when Balfour got the letter he did not take it as Gladstone had intended, but reported it to Salisbury more as a point of political tactics than a clear proposal from the Liberal leader that the Conservatives should introduce a Home Rule Bill; which would receive Liberal support.

Herbert Gladstone was acting as Gladstone's secretary at the time, for Gladstone had no official secretary when out of office; and he had a good deal of experience of Ireland, having been involved in negotiations around the time of the 'Kilmainham Treaty'. It would have been better if he had not flown the kite, but it cannot be asserted that it changed the course of history. Gladstone was already considering forming a Government to introduce a Home Rule Bill. He continued to give the Conservatives the opportunity to act; but they did nothing. The problem was how to get rid of the Government without damaging the future prospects of a Liberal Bill, and Gladstone shrewdly, but on the spur of the moment, chose to challenge them on 26 January 1886 on a point of agricultural policy: 'We beat the Government, I think wisely, by 329: 250' he wrote in his diary. Lord Salisbury resigned.

THE FIRST HOME RULE BILL

On Monday 1 February 1886 Gladstone returned from Osborne on the Isle of Wight where he had had to travel by rail to kiss hands with the Queen who described him as 'this half-crazy and really in many ways

ridiculous old man'. In his diary he wrote: 'I kissed hands and am therefore Prime Minister for the third time. But as I trust for a brief tenure
only. Slept well, D.G.'

His Cabinet lacked many of the old hands, especially Hartington,
and Granville was demoted to make way, at the Queen's insistence, for
Rosebery as Foreign Secretary. Spencer was brought back from Ireland,
becoming Lord President of the Council, because Gladstone wanted his
support in the Cabinet. John Morley, inexperienced in government, yet
an ideal choice, became Irish Secretary, with Lord Aberdeen as Viceroy.
G. O. Trevelyan became Secretary of State for Scotland and Joseph
Chamberlain was somewhat sidelined as President of the Local
Government Board, but sadly these two powerful voices were to resign
over Home Rule.

Home Rule was proposed in the form of a Government of Ireland
Act and a Land Act (the third), linked together in a 'Siamese twinship'.
The Land Bill was discussed in Cabinet first, to give Gladstone time for
reflection and preparation on Home Rule, but would come second
before the House of Commons. It was a very bold measure, and it was
necessary not so much in order to please the farmers and peasants, as to
give the landowners the option of an escape route. The Government
would guarantee a massive loan at 3% to enable the Irish to buy their
land. Gladstone reduced his proposed sum to cover the first four years
from £120m to £50m for tactical reasons, because he saw that Parliament would increase the amount if the project were successful. For this
radical proposal he was willing to add what might amount to over 4%
to the National Debt. Instead of paying rent to a landlord, the farmer
would borrow at 3% to pay for his land.

The Home Rule Bill had to settle the following questions: What sort
of 'Assembly' should Ireland have? What powers should this Assembly
have? Should its members also sit at Westminster? Who should pay?

Gladstone followed the precedent of Canada as far as he found it
practicable, but he did not find it practicable on Defence. Uncharacteristically, for he always preferred to follow historical precedent, he came
up with a highly imaginative and complicated scheme which would
both protect minority interests and accommodate conservative opinion.
(He personally hoped that many of the landowning families would stay
in Ireland, even without land, as the natural leaders of society.)

There was to be one chamber, but made up of two 'Orders' (he
borrowed the name from the *ancien régime* in France). The 'Second

Order' would consist of 202 county and borough (and university) members, to include at first the 101 Irish MPs, to be elected at least every five years. The 'First Order' would consist of 28 Irish Peers and 75 members elected for ten years on a '£25 occupier' franchise, for which candidates had to be property owners. Each Order (i.e. a majority of each Order) could call for the Orders to vote separately; thus the First Order had a veto similar to that of the House of Lords.

It is easy to see why it would not have been acceptable to Parliament at this stage simply to remove the Irish party from Westminster to Dublin, even if also retaining them at Westminster with limited powers. This Assembly, essentially called 'a legislative body' in the Bill, was to have legislative power except in defence and foreign and colonial matters, and it was permitted to raise indirect taxes except on trade (free trade being sacrosanct). The Irish would pay income tax ('like everybody else' as it might be expressed in the twenty-first century) but in return they would receive a lump sum for expenditure in Ireland. Although this lump sum was conceived as a proportion (at first 1/14th, then 1/15th) of the total revenue, in the Bill it was proposed in figures, as two annual fixed sums (£4,236,000 plus £360,000 to service their share of the National Debt). The main figure was to remain unaltered for thirty years, which as things turned out would have given Ireland a very good bargain.

All this was acceptable to Parnell, as was the eventual decision to remove the Irish members from Westminster, a move strongly (and perhaps surprisingly for a man of such a subtle and penetrative mind) advocated by Morley. The arguments are too finely balanced, and too intractable, and too well known to modern readers, to be worth repeating. But one difference from modern Scotland was the long-standing, united and ruthless Irish National Party at Westminster, whom many English would be thankful to be rid of; whereas on the other hand the Westminster Parliament governed not only the United Kingdom (including Ireland) but also the Empire on which the sun never set. Of course, the removal of the Irish from Westminster encouraged separatism.

Gladstone realised that the Bill might not pass, but he decided that it must be so far reaching and important that neither the Liberal Party nor the House of Lords would dare to negate its main purpose by amendment before passing it. Always positive, always optimistic, he told the Commons in what turned out to be prophetic words that this was 'one of those golden moments of our history; one of those opportunities which may come and may go but which rarely return, or if they return, return at long intervals, and under circumstances which no man can forecast'. As usual, he did little of what would now seem natural, to canvass individual backbenchers or the press in order to win votes. Until the vote on the second reading was taken, he thought that he might win, and he worked undaunted to that end. He actually told the Party that if the second reading was passed he would withdraw the Bill, revise the clauses on Irish representation at Westminster, and reintroduce it in the autumn.

The Bill was defeated on the second reading on 7 June 1886 by 341 votes to 311. 'Upon the whole we have more ground to be satisfied with the progress made, than to disappointed at the failure. But it is a serious mischief.' The next day Gladstone persuaded the Cabinet not to resign (which would be 'abandonment of the cause') but to hold a general election. The result was a disappointment, partly because the immediate dissolution of Parliament did not leave time for a well-organised election campaign. The Liberals were reduced from 333 to 196 and the Tories increased from 251 to 316. The Unionists now had a majority of over 100, including 74 Liberals. The second 'golden moment' had passed. The Government resigned, but Gladstone told the Cabinet that he would lead the Opposition and, as Rosebery noted, 'all applauded'.

THE SECOND HOME RULE BILL

Gladstone did a great deal of private reading about Ireland and there was much discussion about Irish legislation when the Liberals were in opposition, both in Cabinet and with the Irish. There were long negotiations with Parnell, who actually visited Gladstone at home at Hawarden in December 1889. These discussions were confidential, but they were direct, no longer depending on the secret route through Mrs O'Shea. Parnell's demands were within what the Liberals considered politically acceptable and feasible. Through the whole period of opposition Gladstone strove to maintain the 'primacy of Ireland' in the Liberal programme.

In December 1890, however, Parnell was obliged to resign after Captain O'Shea had sued for divorce; not simply because of the divorce case but largely because he handled the situation with uncharacteristic ineptitude. Eventually Justin McCarthy, journalist and Irish MP, after meeting Gladstone, successfully challenged Parnell's leadership, partly at least on the basis of Gladstone's view that its continuation would be disastrous for Ireland. Parnell was heavily defeated. (He died the next year.)

The loss of Parnell, though to Gladstone inevitable in the circumstances, was a severe blow to him, undoing much that had been achieved and prejudicing future success. Home Rule now might be postponed for years. 'The struggle in that case must survive me, cannot be survived by me.' But, characteristically, he soon bounced back.

The result of the general election in 1892 was not surprisingly an improvement on 1886, but Gladstone had hoped for better. The Liberals had 272 seats against the Tories' 268; but the Irish Home Rulers had 80 votes to add to the Liberals, whilst the Liberals' Unionists added 46 to the Tory Opposition. The Cabinet included six men who were to be members of the 1905 Liberal Government and four – including the P.M. – who had been in Palmerston's Cabinet in 1866. John Morley was Gladstone's most valued support.

The Second Home Rule Bill was very different from the first. It proposed two Houses and an executive similar to the Cabinet. It was to devolve some powers to Ireland gradually over a set period of years: legislation on land, the judiciary, the police and finance. This would make the initial measure less radical in character and would allow flexibility over details in the light of experience. In finance, the fixed sum of the First Bill was to be replaced by a complicated but carefully considered system which, however, was hastily and radically altered at the Committee stage after a major error in the calculations of the civil servants had prejudiced its credibility. The Committee decided that all Irish taxation would be collected in Ireland, and one third of the proceeds would then be paid to the 'Imperial' Exchequer to pay for defence and all the Irish items not devolved. This perplexed Gladstone, who knew that though simple in outline it would be devilish in detail, although from the outset he had left much detail open for the Committee to refine. He personally piloted all the clauses through sixty-three days of debate, until the guillotine fell.

The principal alteration from the First Bill was that eighty Irish MPs would still be at Westminster. It was proposed that they would vote on Irish and Imperial, but not British, questions. The boundary could only be settled, with an unwritten constitution dependent on precedent and convention, by experience. But there was one essential question, which could and should have been answered, and was not:

would they be entitled to take part in a vote of confidence, which could break a government? Again, the Committee provided a simple answer – but one which could have left contention wide open for the future – and the eighty Irish were to be members of the Commons without restriction.

The Bill passed its third reading by 34 votes after 82 sittings on 1 September, the session having been extended. Exactly a week later it was defeated in the Lords after a short debate by 419 votes to 41.

18

Gladstone the Conservative, the Liberal, the Radical

I THE CONSERVATIVE

Gladstone entered Parliament in 1833 as a Conservative. He had been brought up at the feet of George Canning, whom John Gladstone had persuaded to stand as MP for Liverpool in 1812, guaranteeing the formidable sum of £10,000. This, he realised, might be the cost of an election in which four candidates, three of them famous and the other having the support of the Tory Corporation of the town, were contesting two seats: Brougham and Creevey as Whigs, Canning and Gascoyne as Tories. In fact the election, fought and won under John Gladstone's brilliant tactical leadership, cost £9,000. What made it worth it? The answer lies in the coincidence between the political stance of John Gladstone and that of George Canning in 1812.

Business in Liverpool was in a bad way. Merchants were facing ruin as a result of the blockade of Continental Europe regarded by the Government as vital in the war against Napoleonic France. John Gladstone was one of the few who had come to believe that the war would not be won without the blockade, and he supported the policy by which it was enforced by Orders in Council. The hostility of the United States made matters worse. John Gladstone's route to survival was not by making objections but by finding alternatives. This was the stage at which he began to invest in West Indian sugar plantations. But above all he wanted to trade with India, and he even believed that Indian cotton might replace American cotton and save Lancashire. This required the removal of the East India Company's monopoly; and Canning had expressed his support for terminating it, contrary to the official Government view that unregulated trade with Asia would not work because of religious and cultural differences: 'Let us try,' said Gladstone. 'We will take our chance and abide by the consequences.' Canning's brilliance quickly caught Gladstone's imagination.

Canning's political career had been nurtured by the reforming ideas of Pitt which had had to be abandoned on the outbreak of war in 1793. He was more responsive to changing times than most Tories, though the battles for Catholic emancipation and Parliamentary reform lay in the postwar future. Canning was a Tory who regarded Church and State, and an aristocracy of landowners, as the pillars of the Constitution, but he was willing to think about the future and he dedicated himself to his discipleship of Pitt. His ideas precisely enunciated those of Gladstone in 1812. Canning, then, can best be described at that time as a progressive Tory: the label 'liberal toryism' came later, but it was a label familiar to William Gladstone as he grew up. Canning ceased to represent Liverpool in 1822. Disillusioned, he was about to embark for India as Governor-General. He visited John Gladstone in Liverpool for the last time. With him was his son, Charles, the future Earl Canning (who actually did become Governor-General of India), then aged nine, just three years younger than W. E. Gladstone, who described him as 'very intelligent'. But at that juncture Castlereagh committed suicide; and Canning stayed in Britain.

From Gladstone's education grew his own respect for British institutions. The customs of the House of Commons – the sole effective Parliamentary institution in Europe – were aped in the Eton Society and the Oxford Union.

Gladstone used to say that Aristotle, St Augustine, Dante and Bishop Butler were his 'four doctors': that is to say his four teachers. He felt that it was to these four that he owed his understanding of the political and religious institutions which he revered. If we look at his reading on a wider basis, we shall find confirmation of this cast of mind. Let us consider his absorption at one stage in the novels of Sir Walter Scott, the Prayer Book of Cranmer and the epic poems of Homer. Each one of these diverse works revealed the nature and history of ancient institutions which captivated him. Scott, the antiquary, carried Gladstone in to the bygone world of the old Scottish kingdom. Cranmer in the Book of Common Prayer had adapted, translated and reformed in matchless English prose the Latin liturgies of medieval Christendom. Interpreting the rubric in the spirit of Archbishop Laud, and approving the moderate reforms of 1661, Gladstone discovered as much about the nature of the Church as he ever learnt from Bishop Butler. Homer revealed an almost magical unsullied civilisation near the beginning of recorded time: a world which, indeed, had much declined with the passing centuries by the time of classical Greece; but a world which had provided the fertile ground on which Christendom could take root, and a world whose unrivalled culture, linguistic, literary, intellectual and artistic, though lost from view during the Dark Ages, was the foundation of European thought.

To Gladstone the State was an organic institution, with a being of its own and a totality greater than the sum of its parts. The objective of his first book, *The State in Its Relation to the Church*, was to show that the State ought to have a conscience. It seemed to him at that time that the conscience of the State should be the Established Church. Before long he had modified his view in two respects. He saw that the Established Church, even if it could recover and contain some of the lost elements of its early latitude, could not of itself fulfil this role; and he saw that the notion of a conscience in the State could not be clearly defined. It is a strange psychological slip which drives so many critics to refer to his title as 'The Church in Its Relation to the State'. (The Italian translation actually carried that title.) But Gladstone was writing about the State, not the Church, as he himself often had to protest. The book was much savaged by the critics, but it ran to several editions and it was widely read for many years. And, after all, the question it sought to answer was one that has concerned political philosophers throughout the ages. Colin Matthew says that Christianity with its emphasis on the individual superseded Aristotle in Gladstone's mind, a point which is attested by Gladstone's individual conviction of what was right, and certainly the individual plays a role in nineteenth-century liberal thinking. But this did not negate Gladstone's respect for the old institutions of Church and State as being something more than the sum of individual persons.

Gladstone's mode of thought was that of the historian: if he asked himself why an institution was as it was, his answer was historical: that was the way in which, by hand of God and man, it had evolved. Steeped in history and nurtured on Aristotle's *Politics*, he believed in monarchical and aristocratic government. His deep respect for the Crown and his conviction that it was the solemn responsibility of the old landowning families to play their part in government prevented him from ever becoming – in spite of long and repeated provocation – an out-and-out radical in his attitude to the Monarchy or the House of Lords. The Commons should be composed of select men elected by

select voters, voters who must be what modern jargon calls stake-
holders. Soon after the Reform Act of 1832 the Commons resolved no
longer to adhere to the time-honoured custom of debating every petition made to them by members of the public. Gladstone strongly
approved, for it was the responsibility of the members of the elected
House itself to decide what questions should be debated, or should be
the subjects of legislation. In those days it was easy for an individual
member to put down a motion or to introduce a bill. The dangers of
democracy became especially apparent to Gladstone as Chancellor of
the Exchequer. It was difficult enough to resist demands for profligate
expenditure from parties in the House itself. To enable demands to be
open to popular opinion would be fatal. This was the main motive of
his objection to a more democratic system in the 1850s and 1860s. His
ideas for widening the franchise were eventually linked to the fact that
working people paid something like one third of the total revenue in
taxation.

The Tory or Conservative Party was open, as we have seen, to liberal
ideas. Pitt, Liverpool, Canning, Peel had confirmed its role as a reforming party. But when it came to the repeal of the Corn Laws by Peel in
1846, a major rift appeared in the Tory ranks, which was never healed
but eventually lost its significance with the lapse of time. The label 'Peel-
ite' long survived to describe the Tories who had taken the 'liberal' side.
It was the great achievement of Disraeli to reinvigorate the Tory Party
as a party, and as a party of reform. Before either Disraeli or Gladstone
had finally achieved the undoubted leadership of the Conservatives and
the Liberals, or at least the undoubted succession to leadership when
Derby and Palmerston disappeared from the scene, there were many
who believed that it would be Gladstone who became the Tory leader.
Gladstone did indeed hesitate for years before eventually, and irrevoca-
bly, throwing in his hand with Palmerston. When he did so, one of his
considerations was 'the question of Disraeli': in other words, by the
time he did make his decision, Disraeli was too firmly harnessed as successor to the Tory leadership to dislodge: and if Gladstone could not dislodge Disraeli, he could not see himself as a Conservative.

The many reforms which were undertaken in those years between
1846 and 1859 were not the monopoly of Whigs or of Tories, of
Conservatives or of Liberals. Gladstone was a leading light in many of
them – colonial self-government in Canada, Australia and New
Zealand, the reform of the Civil Service and the universities for instance

– but it was not beyond Disraeli to catch the Whigs bathing and to make away with their clothes; and the second Reform Act, of 1867, was a Conservative act.

2 THE LIBERAL

The length of time it took Gladstone to come out as a Liberal in 1859 was typical of the man. He liked to turn a question over in his mind for a long period before the best course of action became clear to him; but once he had made up his mind he was difficult to shake. He had none of the characteristics of the modern political party manager. In this he had much in common with his Whig contemporaries: Granville assumed that he would not attend the inaugural meeting of the National Liberal Federation in 1877. This might have trapped him in policies he did not wish to pursue, for which he could not obtain Parliamentary support. He did indeed commit to paper, or declaim in a speech, the principles governing Liberal policy; but they were principles which he himself, not the party, had resolved. He did not like to dilate on Liberal political theory: his approach was often pragmatic – he saw the Liberals as a party of action, and in so far as he had a policy for retaining party loyalty it was the policy of action: of big debates and big bills. In this respect he was slow to change with the times and as the years rolled on – and his eyesight declined – he became less and less concerned with maintaining the sympathies of his backbenchers. He was not interested in them, he did not recognise them, and he did not stoop to court them. This was politically inept, except in so far as it respected their independence of view.

Chamberlain founded the National Liberal Federation in 1877, at a moment when Gladstone was investing huge effort to bring the country round to his opposition to Disraeli's Eastern policy. In view of Gladstone's star quality, Chamberlain was keen to enlist him in his inaugural ceremony in Birmingham, and to this end he was willing to give Gladstone a free hand. The occasion was a stupendous one, though not very satisfactory to Gladstone in that the audience numbered 27,000 and the acoustics were appalling. Thereafter he did attend and speak (as the star turn) at several annual meetings of the Federation all over England but it did not have much continuity of action; and it was Chamberlain, not Gladstone, who had founded it. The National Liberal Club Gladstone approved of, gave it his stamp, and attended its official functions;

but he never used it as a club. It was the meeting place for the newer Liberals, not the Whigs. There was a Central Liberal Association, a useful postbox but perhaps not much more. During his later Governments Gladstone did, in spite of his age, make occasional very demanding provincial tours – in the West Country and South Wales, for instance – to marshal and encourage Liberal voters. But he never liked the idea of a Parliamentary Liberal organisation.

As late as 1885 Gladstone appealed to individual thought and action although it should be combined with corporate efficiency.

> This aim is noble but difficult ... nothing would induce me to change it for the regimental discipline which brings the two minorities, each in a well-fused mass, into the voting lobby. For this valued freedom, and this abundance of variety, cherished in the Liberal party, have not disabled it during the last half-century from efficient action. For more than two-thirds of that period the Liberal party has held power, and fully nine-tenths of our useful legislation has been due to its inspiration and its labours. What modern Britain at this moment is, she has become substantially through the agency of the Liberal party.

Harcourt, at the very end of Gladstone's political career, put a different point of view: 'Mr Gladstone has already twice brought the Liberal party to grief – first in 1874 and afterwards in 1886. He does not care a rush for the party. So long as the party suits his purposes, he uses it. The moment the question of his own personal convenience turns up, or he finds himself out of touch with the party, he is ready to discard it regardless of consequences.' As usual, Harcourt was too blunt to enlist much support for his views.

The ideas and policies of Disraeli and Gladstone in the third quarter of the nineteenth century represent the emergence of the modern Conservative Party, and of the Liberal Party until its collapse in the shadow of the Labour Party's socialism in the 1930s. Both Conservatism and Liberalism, in British political terminology, coincided with the high tide of Britain's greatness, not only in her political institutions but also in her commercial, industrial and imperial supremacy. Both Conservatism and Liberalism in this context derive from respect for the institutions which eventually emerged from the political struggles of the seventeenth century. The definition of the two modes of thought depends

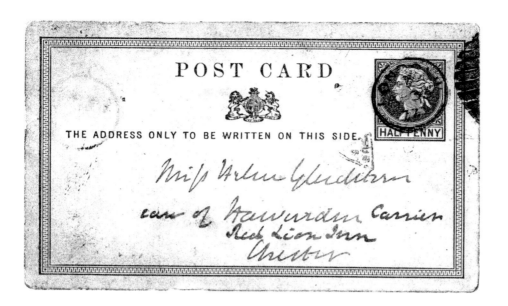

A postcard, Gladstone's invention. The penny post, started in 1840, had transformed communication. Gladstone suggested that short 'uncovered' messages should cost only a halfpenny; and he often made use of them himself.

"EIGHTY" CLUB.

DINNER

TO THE

LABOUR REPRESENTATIVES.

SPEECHES BY

MR. B. PICKARD, M.P.

(PRESIDENT OF MINERS' FEDERATION)

MR. E. HARFORD

(SECRETARY OF AMALGAMATED SOCIETY OF RAILWAY SERVANTS.)

MR. SYDNEY BUXTON, M.P.,

COL. READE, and SIR W. LAWSON, BART., M.P

AT THE

WESTMINSTER PALACE HOTEL.

On Wednesday, May 23rd, 1894.

MR. HERBERT GLADSTONE, M.P.

IN THE CHAIR.

Secretary: J. A. B. BRUCE, 2, Middle Temple Lane, E.C.

Gladstone wanted to see working men in Parliament but he never seems to have mastered quite how that could be achieved in practice. All the same, a large group of working men were MPs less than ten years after his death. During the 1890s some meetings and dinners orchestrated by Herbert Gladstone and others were held for working men, most of them – if not all – involved in local government. The objective clearly was to familiarise them with the idea of becoming MPs. Only very few trades union representatives seem to have been invited. (See chapter 18.)

Sursum Corda

Wm Gladstone
Jul 30, 95.

[In compliance with our request that he would favour our readers with a motto which they might constantly use, Mr. Gladstone was good enough to send us the autograph, "Lift up your hearts," which we again reproduce. No other phrase could have better summed up his own aim and character as a Christian statesman.—Ed. *S. M.*]

Lyddell Sawyer, photo, 230 Regent Street, London.

Gladstone was said to address audiences of working men as if they were the House of Commons, and when requested to choose a motto for popular consumption he wrote it in Latin. The editor provided a translation.

my relations with Liber-
alism (as incorporated in party)
Began in 1846.... (479)
Took form in 1852.
Checked in 1855
Sealed.. in 1859 (349)

Gladstone wrote this note in about 1896, before his operation for
cataract, in large handwriting characteristic only of that period

Charles Parnell visited Hawarden in December 1889: see chapter 17.
(Five years later Margot Tennant married the widower H. H. Asquith
who made his name defending Parnell in court.)

ABOVE The Prince and Princess of Wales, with their daughter Princess Victoria, visited Hawarden on 10 May 1897. (See chapter 19.)

BELOW There was a Colonial visitation in July, coming to Britain for the first gathering of its kind: George Reid (NSW, Australia), Richard Seddon (New Zealand), Wilfrid Laurier (Canada) and Sir Lewis Davies (Canadian Minister of Fisheries) were photographed with Gladstone.

1. I, William Ewart Gladstone, of Hawarden Castle, make this my last Will and Testament, and hereby revoke every former Will and Testamentary document.

2. Commending myself to the infinite mercies of God in the Incarnate Son as my only and sufficient hope, I leave the particulars of my burial to my Executors, specifying only

(a) that it is to be very simple; and also private unless they shall consider that there are conclusive reasons to the contrary

(b) that I desire to be buried where my wife may also lie

(c) that on no account shall any laudatory inscription be placed over me

The opening of Gladstone's will, written in his own hand (enlarged) in a penny notebook

Thomas Smith   April 24. 1898

mag Benson   April 29. 1898

Lucy S. M. Tait   ". ".

Arthur Godley   9 May 1898

Margaret Cowell Stepney   10 May -

G W E Russell   May 10. '98

Rendel   13 May. 1898

John Morley   May 13. '98

Rosebery   May 13. 1898.

Edith H Desmarez   May 19th /90

W. B. Richmond   May 21. 1898

J. Armitstead   May 31. 1898.

Lucy Phillimore.   July 8. 1898

Arthur Godley   1-3 Oct 1898

A dotted line in the Visitor's Book marks the end of an era: John Morley and Lord Rosebery were amongst the last to see Gladstone before his death

Baron de Goltstein de Oldenaller
(Representing Their Majesties The Queen, and The Queen Regent of the Netherlands).

Monsieur F. E. de Bille
(Representing Their Majesties The King and Queen of Denmark).

His Excellency Lieutenant-General Annibale Ferrero
(Representing His Majesty The King of Italy).

His Excellency Monsieur de Staal
(Representing His Imperial Majesty The Emperor of Russia).

His Royal Highness Prince Christian of Schleswig-Holstein, K.G.

His Royal Highness The Duke of Cambridge, K.G.

His Royal Highness The Duke of Connaught and Strathearn, K.G.

Preceded by the following Officers of their Royal Highnesses Households :—

Colonel the Honourable C. G. C. Eliot.	Colonel A. C. F. FitzGeorge, C.B.
Lieutenant Sir Charles Cust, Bart., R.N.	Colonel Alfred Egerton, C.B.
Captain G. L. Holford, C.I.E., M.V.O.	Sir Francis Knollys, K.C.B., K.C.M.G.

The Earl of Pembroke, G.C.V.O.
(REPRESENTING HER MAJESTY THE QUEEN).

The Duke of Norfolk, K.G., Earl Marshal.

Supporters of the Pall.		*Supporters of the Pall.*
George Armitstead, Esq.		The Lord Rendel.
The Earl of Rosebery, K.G.	THE	The Duke of Rutland, K.G.
The Right Honourable Sir William Vernon Harcourt.	COFFIN.	The Right Honourable Arthur J. Balfour.
The Earl of Kimberley, K.G.		The Marquess of Salisbury, K.G.
His Royal Highness The Duke of York, K.G.		His Royal Highness The Prince of Wales, K.G.

William Henry Weldon, Esq.,
Norroy King of Arms
(Representing Garter King of Arms,
Sir Albert W. Woods).

The Reverend Stephen E. Gladstone
(Chief Mourner).

The Right Honourable Herbert J. Gladstone.	Henry N. Gladstone, Esq.
Albert C. Gladstone, Esq.	William G. C. Gladstone, Esq.
S. Deiniol Gladstone, Esq.	Charles A. Gladstone, Esq.
The Reverend Harry Drew.	The Very Reverend the Dean of Lincoln.
Edward G. Wickham, Esq.	William G. Wickham, Esq.
Walter L. Gladstone, Esq.	Sir John R. Gladstone, Bart.
John E. Gladstone, Esq.	Richard F. Gladstone, Esq.
The Honourable and Reverend A. T. Lyttelton.	Viscount Cobham.
The Honourable Robert H. Lyttelton.	Colonel the Honourable N. G. Lyttelton.
Lord Penrhyn.	The Honourable and Reverend Edward Lyttelton.
The Bishop of Rochester.	The Right Honourable John G. Talbot.
E. J. Thornewell, Esq.	Robert Gladstone, Esq.
Lord Wenlock, G.C.S.I., G.C.I.E.	Sir Reginald Hardy, Bart.

Former Private Secretaries of the Deceased.

Right Honourable Sir Algernon West, K.C.B.	Lord Welby, G.C.B.
Sir William Gurdon, K.C.M.G., C.B.	Sir James Carmichael, Bart.
Sir Arthur Godley, K.C.B.	Honourable Spencer Lyttelton, C.B.
Horace A. D. Seymour, Esq., C.B.	Sir Edward W. Hamilton, K.C.B.
George Leveson-Gower, Esq.	Henry Primrose, Esq., C.B., C.S.I.
Hans G. L. Shand, Esq.	George H. Murray, Esq., C.B.

The Physicians to the Deceased.

Sir Thomas Smith, Bart., M.R.C.S.	William Dobie, Esq., M.D.
Samuel Herbert Habershon, Esq., M.D.	H. E. J. Biss, Esq., M.D.

A page from the official programme for Gladstone's State Funeral (see chapter 19) more on the practical realities of political life than on philosophical musing. In this sense 'Gladstonism' and 'Liberalism' are much the same. Britain was different from Continental Europe in this respect. Here, Liberalism depended on the nurture of existing institutions: in Europe it was a dream to be achieved by the destruction of autocratic regimes – in Russia, Germany, Austria, Italy, Portugal and Spain. France was different, but in place of the rocklike permanence of British Parliamentary government, it suffered regime changes in 1804, 1815, 1830, 1848–52 and 1870.

Gladstone believed in minimal government. When he came on the scene in 1833 Britain was out of date – the ideas of reform of the late eighteenth century had been put on hold for twenty years throughout the struggle first against revolutionary France and then against Napoleon's bid to dominate Europe. Pitt's progressive ideas had indeed been revived by the 'Liberal Tories', and old restrictive legislation had been removed or modified more than is generally recognised. A start was being made on the reform of the ancient poor law, of local government, and of Parliament with Catholic emancipation and, of course, the Great Reform Act of 1832. But many institutions were ossified in ancient form, and there was reluctance to interfere with them by political means. Minimalist government was the key to Gladstone's ideas. Apart from having to fund the vast National Debt, acquired by financing in the French war – not only the Royal Navy and the Army but also the armies of our Continental allies – the sole major expense of Government was to pay for the armed forces; and in the days of simple and slow technical advances this could largely be done *ad hoc* in time of war. Budgets were small, and revenue depended on a labyrinth of customs and excise duties, designed either to raise money for the crown or to protect Britain from foreign competition. Education and welfare of every kind were left to charity. The relief of the poor was designed to discourage applicants for assistance. There was no professional Civil Service in the modern sense.

Addressing an audience of savings bank depositors on the theme of 'Thrift' as late as 1890, Gladstone justified State intervention by the establishment in 1861 of the Post Office Savings Bank as doing no more than providing a facility which people could use if they wished, disclaiming his belief in what would nowadays be called the 'nanny state'. Thrift, he said, has been encouraged by 'judicious legislation – not by what is called "grandmotherly legislation" of which I for one have a great deal of suspicion – but by legislation … which, like your savings bank, helps the people by enabling the people to help themselves.'

Commerce and industry were interfered with only fitfully in order to regulate abuses. As has been shown, joint stock companies were simple associations between small groups of investors, mainly for shipping. Industrial capital was still mostly provided by entrepreneurs from their own profits. Agricultural capital was provided by landlords (including many independent farmers, large and small – the yeomanry, the glory of old England). Only with the advent of railways was an amount of capital required to create something remotely resembling a substantial modern company; but there were still restrictions on trading in shares and there was no way of limiting individual liability. With railways, Acts of Parliament were needed to facilitate 'compulsory' purchase of land – but they were private acts, and it was not until 1844 that Gladstone introduced a Railways Bill for general regulation. What the Government did was not to regulate commerce and industry but exactly the opposite: to remove the ancient obstructions and burdens of taxation and restrictive laws. In 1852 the House of Commons came to the conclusion that Britain was a nation of free trade.

Gradually the Government stretched out its tentacles: to elementary education, for instance, in 1870, when it had become clear that private charity could not provide what was required. Nevertheless minimalist government remained a reality throughout the reign of Queen Victoria. It lay at the heart of Liberal policy. Freedom was the secret of prosperity.

Behind the practicalities lay the philosophy. Individual freedom – of thought and word and belief – was the heart of liberal thinking. 'Laissez-faire' became the watchword, but to most people it meant not a general concept of freedom but free trade. 'Free trade' became in the course of time more than a liberal practice, it became a principle. The market was the creator of wealth – just as Adam Smith had said a hundred years before. Gladstone remained a spectator (with but a couple of Acts as small reliefs) as British agriculture, still the finest in the world, suffered in the face of imported prairie wheat in the 1870s and 1880s.

Reform was a Liberal principle. To be a Liberal was to be a reformer. Once the Liberals and the Conservatives had decided in favour of free trade and Parliamentary reform, the ways parted. The Tories were willing to reform institutions which were manifestly corrupt or evil, but they were reluctant to trespass on vested interests. The Liberals were willing to invoke the wrath of brewers and publicans in their efforts to curb the manifest evils of drunkenness; the Tories were not. The Liberals wanted the Army efficiently officered; the Conservatives preferred the old system of purchase. Gladstone's first Government was the first for many years to achieve a strong majority in the Commons. This opened the floodgates of Liberal reform, in every case opposed by the Conservatives; and if the Conservatives were beaten in the Commons, there was always a second line of defence in the House of Lords.

At the heart of Liberal thinking were justice and fairness. Perhaps Gladstone's foremost quality was to set aside tradition and prejudice in order to create a fair society. It was this quality which led him to conclude that Home Rule provided the only means of fostering justice for Ireland. He was far from being an egalitarian, but he believed essentially in an inclusive rather than an exclusive society, and this included his conviction that women should obtain equality of status with men.

The Liberals were avowedly supporters of nationality, or self-determination; the Conservative approach was much more cautious, wary of upsetting the status quo. This is a large part of the reason for the Liberal admiration for Bismarck: he had attacked the 'ramshackle' Habsburg empire, which inhibited self-determination in Hungary, northern Italy and the Balkans; and he removed the vestiges of the old princely rule in the small regimes of western Germany. It was the Liberals who hastened to the support of Montenegro, Bosnia and Hercegovinia, and Bulgaria. Nationality was of special importance to Gladstone because it involved religious freedom, especially in the tottering Turkish Empire. To him the words 'Holy Catholic Church' in the creed meant the Christian Church wherever it might be, most especially the Greek church which had been strongly invoked in the seventeenth century as Britain's ally in the contest against Papal domination. Bismarck's ruthless 'Kultur-Kampf' against the Papacy was another reason why Gladstone admired him.

The growth of self-rule in the British colonies was largely the fruit of Liberal thinking, especially the development of the system in Canada, Australia and New Zealand which evolved into 'Dominion Status'. The Liberals – successors of the Whigs – supported the emporia of British trade around the globe, and the strategic bases (especially coaling stations, as the century wore on) of the Navy which ensured Pax Britannica. But they opposed the annexation of territory for its own sake and the rivalries and entanglements which it involved. The Ashanti War was needful for the suppression of slavery. The Zulu War was not. The paradox by which Gladstone found himself entangled in Egypt when the French sailed away was like an exception which proved a rule. The objective of the 1880 Government was to dismantle the imperial policy of 'Beaconsfieldism'.

Gladstone was a man of peace but he dissociated himself strongly from what was labelled the 'Manchester School', led by Cobden and Bright, which considered wars to be things of the past, superseded by other means of settling differences. 'However much you may detest war,' he said in 1880 in Edinburgh, '... however deplorable wars may be, they are among the necessities of our condition; and there are times when justice, when faith, when the welfare of mankind, require a man not to shrink from the responsibility of undertaking them.' It was partly Gladstone's long-past responsibility for the Crimean War, as a member of Aberdeen's Cabinet, which led him to feel a responsibility for curtailing Russian expansion in the 1880s; indeed, as the survivor of that Cabinet he considered himself the representative of its collective responsibility. (There were actually two other survivors still active in politics.) Afghanistan, whose geography made it almost ungovernable, was a case in point. Uganda was another area from which the Liberals withdrew. As to Egypt, Gladstone was drawn into the bombardment of Alexandria by the Mediterranean Fleet in 1882 partly by Bismarck's skilful diplomatic duplicity, Britain having been left holding the baby by the entirely unexpected withdrawal of the French: their fleet had to sail away because they were prohibited from any act of war without prior approval of the National Assembly.

As far as rescuing Gordon from Khartoum was concerned, Gladstone and his Cabinet realised that any notion of 'holding the forts' in the Sudan was pure make-believe. The whole idea of the British Army imposing order in that vast country was fanciful. Gordon had not acted with the prudence which his orders, even when strongly tempered by the situation as he found it, required; but Gladstone made the gross error of dilatoriness in the face of an urgent need to rescue a beleaguered British force, and his reputation suffered sorely as a result: this was a case where he ought to have acted, despite his distaste for war, as he did in the cases of Egypt and the Ashantis.

Throughout the periods when he was Chancellor of the Exchequer, Gladstone fought a running battle with the War Department and the

Admiralty to contain expenditure. A battle over the Naval Estimates was the last battle of his political career. He had not fully grasped what was afoot, and in 1893 he found himself in a minority in his own Cabinet. After a meeting with Spencer, First Lord of the Admiralty, and much agonising, he moved an amendment to a motion by the former Tory First Lord on the need for a powerful Navy. He won by thirty-six votes, but in his diary he wrote 'The situation almost hopeless when a large minority allows itself in panic and joining hands with the professional elements works on the susceptibilities of a portion of the people to alarm.'

In a memorandum of January 1894 Gladstone wrote the noble words which might well stand as his epitaph:

> I shall not break to pieces the continuous action of my political life, nor trample on the tradition received from every colleague who has ever been my teacher. Above all I cannot and will not add to the perils of the coming calamities of Europe by an act of militarism which will be found to involve a policy, and which excuses thus the militarism of Germany, France or Russia. England's providential part is to help peace, and liberty of which peace is the nurse; this policy is the foe of both. I am ready to see England dare in the world of arms; but not to see England help to set the world in arms.

Then, during 1895, Gladstone was the guest of Sir Donald Currie on a Baltic cruise in his ship the *Tantallon Castle*, and he witnessed the ostentatious opening ceremonies of the Kiel Canal, with the Kaiser's yacht steaming between the lines of German warships. 'This means war,' he said.

The Kiel Canal enabled the German fleet to switch from the Baltic to the North Sea and to provoke Russia or Britain (or, as it happened, both of them) almost on a whim. Two years later Admiral Tirpitz became German Minister of Marine and thus began the great arms race which was to end with the Battle of Jutland in 1916 and the surrender of the German Grand Fleet in Scapa Flow in 1919. Could Gladstone, the man of peace, have prevented this? It is not easy to think that, even if he had been in his prime, he could have done. His argument in 1893 was that British naval supremacy would not be at risk by the saving of some money and by not being party to a 'race'. But the ships were not the ships of Nelson's day, which could be laid up for decades and recommissioned by purchasing a few miles of rope and acres of canvas, recruiting a few hundred tars and bringing a captain out of half-pay.

A year after Tirpitz's first naval programme Gladstone died at the age of eighty-seven: as Lord Salisbury said of him 'He kept the soul of England alive.' There is a nobility in his pleas for peace, but Europe was perhaps already too far down the road to Armageddon.

3 HOW RADICAL WAS THE G.O.M.?

Gladstone's long experience taught him that the average political life span of a Liberal peer was ten years. After that, he would on average have become a Conservative. He was, of course, referring to political peerages, granted to MPs who had earned promotion or whom it would be convenient to kick upstairs: what he called 'the common ruck of official barons'. It did not apply to men like Tennyson, Leighton, Acton or Playfair. He was merely observing a common phenomenon, that people become less enthusiastic about reform as they grow older. Gladstone was an exception to that rule; so, oddly enough, was Campbell-Bannerman, a member of Gladstone's last Cabinet and Liberal Prime Minister from 1905 until his death in 1908.

Starting as a Conservative, albeit a liberal Conservative, Gladstone had become a Liberal Chancellor, 'The People's William', and the leader in 1868 of the greatest of all Victorian reforming Governments. As he evolved into the 'Grand Old Man' he espoused policies which were generally regarded (certainly by his contemporaries) as more than merely liberal: they were radical. His ideas about votes for working men, and his attempts to find a way by which working men could become MPs fall into this category. They included meetings in London for working men involved in local politics, to which a few trades union leaders were also invited. On at least one occasion a meeting was followed by a dinner with speeches, orchestrated by Herbert Gladstone. From the 1850s he was much concerned with the recognition of the rightful place of women in society, especially in education and in the right of entry to the professions. It is true, however, that if his vision was radical, and even if he took bold practical steps towards making it a reality, his methods remained, on the whole, those of a reformer.

Colin Matthew describes the Home Rule Bill as being a classically Whig measure, but I am doubtful whether that phrase can be made to apply to the 1880s and 1890s. Gladstone had anyway come to realise that a Home Rule Act on its own would be barren: the old English Protestant ascendancy had to go. This could be achieved by giving tenants recourse to a land court and rights of purchase. The policy spelt the end of a ruling class and it failed because of opposition by the House of Lords. Thus Gladstone's successor Rosebery saw it as his duty to show that it was Liberal policy either to abolish the Lords or to curtail its veto. That was Gladstone's political legacy. If he had not been too old, he would surely have asked for a dissolution and he would have fought an election on this issue. As it was, he accepted the verdict with a degree of resignation, and made off on a tour of Scotland. But that degree of resignation was comforted by his acceptance that, although the House of Lords had wrecked most of the other Liberal measures as well as Home Rule since 1880, the time to remove its power was not yet ripe. Just as he had wanted to deprive the Irish landowners of their power over their tenants, yet had hoped that they would remain in Ireland and play a responsible part in society, still owning their land; so he may have felt that a second house ought to survive in the interest of stable government, and that it should be reformed by a gradual process.

It has sometimes been suggested that Gladstone's obsession with Ireland – his insistence that his Cabinet should be in agreement about the 'primacy' of Irish legislation – prevented Liberal Governments from getting ahead with more general Liberal programmes. It has also been suggested that the Grand Old Man had run out of steam as a Liberal thinker. There is some truth in the former suggestion, but none in the latter. Gladstone's achievement had been astonishing. Having won an election on Home Rule he became Premier for the fourth time at over eighty years of age, and he devised and then piloted his very complicated bill through all its lengthy stages in the Commons. When the Liberals returned to power in 1905 the party did indeed have a new programme, as one would expect. It also had a new kind of Cabinet. The Commons majority included more than ninety working men as Labour or Lib-Lab MPs. Gladstone's programme was still at the heart of Liberal thinking: with the rights of agricultural tenants, working men in the Commons, and the emancipation of women as leading issues. But the House of Lords was more obstructive than ever, and heading for disaster. Within two years the Government did bring in an Evicted Tenants' Bill for Ireland, but perhaps for the time being the country had had too big a dose of Home Rule. In substance Campbell-Bannerman's policy (1901–8) was the successor of Gladstone's and in 1907 he picked up a proposal made by John Bright in 1884 and moved a resolution that 'in order to give effect to the will of the people as expressed by their elected representatives, the power of the other House to alter or reject bills passed by this House must be so restricted by law as to secure that within the limits of a single Parliament the final decision of the Commons should prevail'. He explained in detail how this might be achieved, and his resolution was passed by a huge majority. Still the House of Lords took no notice. Two years later began the battle which led, in 1911, to what Campbell-Bannerman had proposed. For the first time since the 1880s a progressive Liberal programme, indeed a Gladstonian programme, became a possibility.

The Liberal Party had, as Gladstone claimed, made middle and late Victorian Britain what it was. Starting as a Conservative in the first reformed Parliament he had eventually in the 1860s become decidedly a Liberal and then, as he advanced into old age, people began to speak of him as a radical. In spite of all his conservative instincts he masterminded the transition from aristocratic to democratic government: indeed it was his respect for British institutions which enabled the transformation of government to be managed without any major destabilisation. The so-called two-party system did actually match its name in the era of Gladstone and Disraeli. It took an outsider, the distinguished French historian Elie Halévy, to point out that both 'two party' and 'system' had been misleading labels for the greater part of the eighteenth and nineteenth centuries. But, in the time of Gladstone and Disraeli, W. S. Gilbert's sentry could convince his audience that every boy and every girl that's born into this world alive is either a little Liberal or else a little Conservative.

19

The Queen and Mr Gladstone 1871–98

The Gladstone manuscripts include some 4,500 letters, memoranda and telegrams from Gladstone to the Queen and about 1,700 from her and from her private secretaries, about half and half, to him. Only a few documents in this large collection are of interest. In 1934 the well-known Liberal historian Philip Guedalla published a book under the title of *The Queen and Mr Gladstone* covering 800 pages, consisting of 150 of 'Commentary' in seven chapters, chronologically arranged, the last entitled 'Antipathy', dealing with the gradual deterioration in the relationship. The remaining pages reproduce a selection of about 1,500 of the 6,000 documents, illustrating the 'Commentary', most of them rather dull, couched in the polite and formal style of communication between the Sovereign and her minister. The book would have been almost as valuable with the Commentary alone, supported by a small selection of the manuscripts, mainly of those written by the Queen.

A few of the documents show the Queen in a very bad light. Her uncoded critical telegram on the receipt of the news of the death of Gordon in Khartoum, her acceptance of Lord Salisbury's resignation as Prime Minister 'with regret', her instruction to Gladstone to read to his Cabinet her letter on the condition of the Navy in December 1893, all demonstrate only too vividly her inability to master her prejudices and come to terms with her role as a constitutional monarch. George III in the 1760s, lacking her experience and having greater constitutional influence over the choice of his ministers, had done better.

There were of course other occasions when this unwelcome characteristic obtruded: in her refusal, for instance, to agree to a peerage for Sir Garnet Wolseley (the very model of a modern major-general) and her refusal to permit the Second Home Rule bill to be entitled 'For the Better Government of Ireland'; but these and similar episodes, often trivial, are no more than illustrations of an attitude. Perhaps only once did she catch Gladstone seriously at fault. This was on the occasion of his cruise in Sir Donald Currie's *Sunbeam* when he landed on foreign soil without having obtained her consent. What niggled her, however, was not his technical error but the fact that he was being indulged in just the kind of royal progress which she would have preferred to reserve for herself. The King of Denmark invited the Gladstones to dinner to meet the Czar, the King and Queen of Greece and the Princess of Wales, all with a full supporting cast of royal persons.

Part of the problem, as Giles St Aubyn points out in his life of Queen Victoria, was that she was jealous of Gladstone's fame. From Midlothian onwards, his political tours were triumphal progresses. Often he did no more than step out of a railway carriage to address a crowd, many of whom had travelled miles simply in order to catch a glimpse of him. This is why the Queen continued to complain about the impropriety of politicians making speeches beyond their home ground. Gladstone would perhaps have agreed with her in the 1840s but by the 1870s things had changed. Railways, the electric telegraph and cheap newspapers had seen to that.

The Queen's supposed remark that Gladstone addressed her as if she were a public meeting is as well known as Disraeli's success in charming her. Gladstone was known for his invariable politeness and patience, whomever he might be addressing, whether on paper or by word of mouth. It was not his manner that the Queen disliked, though she found him rather hard going, earnest and humourless (and his memoranda were too long for her), but his measures. When she was displeased Gladstone was not a lone target. Her complaints were open to all around her. Gladstone and the Queen got on well, even very well, until about 1871 when he mildly attempted to persuade her to postpone her Balmoral holiday for a week until Parliament rose. That summer she had given full support to the Army Bill which was hotly opposed in the Commons, especially by members close to those who surrounded the Queen, and she made no difficulty over the proposal to abolish the purchase of commissions by royal warrant. Gladstone paid a public tribute to her, speaking of the 'undiminished and ever warm affection of the country towards Your Majesty' when it was proposed by some left-wing members that she would do well to retire. She duly thanked him 'for his kind expression and defence of her'. She had also been most helpful in 1869 in discouraging the House of Lords from rejecting the Bill, passed by the Commons, to disestablish the Irish Church: firmly but tactfully she had made her contribution to prevent a constitutional impasse. Admittedly, even then Gladstone had complained 'But how much better if not 600 miles off.' The idea that she might stay a little longer in London in August 1871 upset her. 'The Queen will not stay where she is, worked and worried and worn'; and 'What killed her beloved husband? Overwork and worry. What killed Lord Clarendon? The same. What has broken down Mr Bright and Mr Childers and made them retire, but the same: and the Queen, a woman, no longer young, is supposed to be proof against it all... .' Then, 'No earthly political object', she wrote, 'can be gained by her remaining a week longer, except gratifying a foolish and unreasonable fancy.'

Gladstone and his colleagues did not perhaps act with exemplary circumspection in the way they attempted to influence her, but on the other hand Gladstone was seriously worried by mischievous critical suggestions from 'radicals' about the monarchy. The Prince of Wales, for whom Gladstone tried to find a role, invariably with opposition from the Queen, was as always helpful; and Princess Alice was 'very sensible of the mischief'. But this was the defining moment. To Lord Granville he wrote: 'The repellent power which she so well knows how to use has been put in action towards me on this occasion for the first time since the formation of the government. I have felt myself on a new and different footing with her... . On account of her natural and constant kindness as well as her position, I am grieved.' From then on there were bright moments – even at Balmoral that year – and as late as 1873 when 'Granville told me last night that she had never known you so remarkably agreeable', but their relationship gradually deteriorated, with serious consequences.

The reasons for this decline are not difficult to diagnose. After the death of Prince Albert the Queen always felt lonely. When she felt exhausted she became more determined, not less. In 1870 she lost her closest friend and adviser, her Private Secretary General Grey, who died after a series of strokes. Henry Ponsonby, who succeeded him, was already an experienced and diplomatic courtier, and he became the Queen's close and trusted adviser, more sensitive even than Grey in trimming his sails to every squall and compensating by his tact for Grey's firmness. Grey was an old hand before the Queen had acquired the stubborn self-assurance of her later years; Ponsonby (six years her junior) was the right man for his time. Nonetheless there was a gap before Ponsonby had found his feet. Gladstone complained to his wife in 1871 that 'that Speech of Dizzy's savours of his usual flunkeyism' and during Disraeli's Government from 1874 to 1880 he became her closest and most trusted friend; but it would not be just to suggest that

Disraeli dispensed poison against the Liberals or their leader. He was more positive than that, and less dishonourable. Gladstone's difficulty after 1880 was not so much the Queen's dislike for him as her dislike of his dismantling of 'Beaconsfieldism' and more importantly that she missed Disraeli the man, always sympathetic, always a listener, always a flatterer. Gladstone had mauled him: that she did not like. Gladstone had belittled Disraeli's insistence that the Queen should be Empress of India. But already Disraeli was ill, and he died in 1881.

Far more serious constitutionally was the Queen's attitude to Home Rule. She dreaded the general election of 1892, writing in her diary 'should these wretched Home Rulers come in, it is to be hoped they will not last long'. She was persuaded that it would be as hopeless to send for Rosebery or any other candidate as it had been to hope for Hartington or Granville last time round. 'Mr Gladstone', she wrote, 'has brought so much violence into the contest and used such insolent language that the Queen is quite shocked and ashamed.' 'By an incomprehensible, reckless vote, the result of most unfair and abominable misrepresentations at the elections, one of the best and most useful governments [Lord Salisbury's] have [*sic*] been defeated.' ... 'The danger to her vast Empire ... entrusted to the shaking hand of an old, wild, and incomprehensible man of 82½, is very great.' When she sent for him, Gladstone noted that she was 'cautiously polite, in nothing helpful ... after dinner a little unfrozen'.

As Gladstone complained, she lived her whole life in the company of people to whom home rule was anathema, all of them directly or indirectly connected with the ascendancy in Ireland which he intended to destroy. Far from using her influence to moderate the action of the House of Lords in opposition to an act passed in the Commons, at least perhaps so to speak to bring the parties to the table, she did all she could to destroy her Government. This is not to say that she could or should have persuaded the Upper House to pass the measure, but it was her clear constitutional duty to see whether it might be possible to prevent the contemptuous treatment which the bill received. The Upper House destroyed also the other important legislation of the government – notably Asquith's Employer's Liability Bill and Fowler's Local Government Bill. Rosebery, Gladstone's successor, warned the Queen that his duty would in due course be to propose either the abolition of the Lords or the removal of its veto, although he realised that without another victorious general election this would not be feasible. The Queen consulted the Prince of Wales, who agreed with her that an attack on the Lords would be a threat, too, to the monarchy. The Conservatives achieved a majority in 1895 and the matter was eventually postponed until the last years of the Prince's reign as King Edward VII.

The Queen's treatment of Gladstone on his final retirement did not do her much credit. There were three brief interviews: before the third, Gladstone wrote out his resignation. He handed it to the Queen, who did not read it. Gladstone wrote: 'Not one word was said of the resignation; and it seems that if it was accepted it was in some way accepted before it was tendered.... Not one syllable proceeded from Her Majesty either as to the future or the past.' Gladstone much resented the way he had been treated. She did not ask him to sit. 'The same brevity', he wrote, 'perhaps prevails in settling a tradesman's bill when it reaches over many years.' Ten days later he wrote a delightful description of the mule which had carried him across Sicily in 1838 concluding: 'I had been on the back of the beast for many scores of hours; it had done me no wrong: it had rendered me much valuable service. Yet it was in vain to argue. There was the fact staring me in the face, I could not get up the smallest shred of feeling for the brute, I could neither love nor like it … what the Sicilian mule was to me, I have been to the Queen; and the fortnight or three weeks are represented by 52 or 53 years.'

The Prince of Wales did his best over a long period to make some compensation for the Queen's attitude towards Gladstone and the Liberal Party, and the Princess showed great kindness towards Catherine. Three times he invited the Gladstones to Sandringham. He visited them at Hawarden. He presented them with a fine and generously inscribed inkstand for their golden wedding. He tried to get them invited, against the Queen's veto, to Prince Arthur's wedding. The Prince of Wales and Prince George, the future King George V, whom Gladstone liked and esteemed, acted as pall bearers – that is to say they walked alongside the bier, together with three Prime Ministers, at the state funeral. The Queen inquired what advice had been sought and what precedents followed. The Prince of Wales replied that he had sought no advice and knew of no precedents.

The story is a sad one. It marks the last occasion on which a Sovereign deliberately and significantly acted contrary to constitutional practice. It also records a deterioration in a relationship which, if seldom cordial since the death of the Prince Consort, had nevertheless been courteous and correct to the point of generosity by both parties for some thirty years – from the early 1840s at least to 1871. The point at issue was Gladstone's eventual perception that not only Home Rule but also the end of the English aristocratic ascendancy in Ireland would be necessary to bring justice – and peace – for Great Britain. Whether his Irish Land legislation would have ended that ascendancy, even perhaps, as he hoped, retaining the old English landowners in residence as leading families in the community, cannot be known. Whether a more correct line of policy by the Queen could have moderated the opposition of the House of Lords and provided a compromise is also unknowable, and improbable. Two matters were settled, one by the Parliament Act of 1911 which removed the permanent veto of the Lords, and the other by the Irish rebellion of 1916. As George V said to his Prime Minister Ramsay MacDonald at the opening of the Stormont in 1930 'What fools we were not to have accepted Gladstone's Home Rule Bill. The Empire now would not have had the Irish Free State giving us so much trouble and pulling us to pieces.'

20

Gladstone in Wales

Gladstone's first visit to Wales was at the age of fifteen. With his brother Tom he left Liverpool by the steam-packet *Prince Llewellyn* ('dined on board, pretty well, ½ crown a head, delightful sail'), arriving off Beaumaris ('beautiful place of Lord and Lady Bulkeley above it'), sailed on to Bangor Ferry ('just above the bridge') and got on a rickety and poor coach to Caernarfon where they stayed at the Uxbridge Arms, 'a <u>very good</u> inn and moderate enough'. There is a full account in the diary of their return journey along the coast to Bagillt, and then by boat right up to Chester, 'a very curious and respectable city'. The navigation was 'very difficult; at low water those who know the fords may easily walk across'.

Nearly thirty years later Gladstone took his family on their first Welsh holiday, staying at Penmaenmawr but also making a long expedition to mid-Wales and Snowdonia, starting with a sixteen-mile walk over the hill to Llanwrst, then Dolgelly ('Golden Lion good' – surprisingly for 'whenever you go to Dolgelly, remember the Lion Hotel, for you'll sure get a pain in your belly, and nobody answers the bell'); Machynlleth – 'tried Cader Idris, clouds prevented one reaching the top'; Barmouth (an early bathe), then to Harlech and 'I walked over to Bedgellert, Willy riding with me... . Goat at Bedgellert very good.' The whole tour, ending as it began at Penmaenmawr, is splendidly described in the diary. Then Willy was kept at home from school 'on account of a bad boil, probably the result of over-exertion', but he had to do Tasso with his father in the evenings. On the return journey to Hawarden, they stayed with the Williamses (by then named Hay-Williams Hay) at Bodelwyddan: 'Sat up late reading the detailed accounts from Sevastopol: wh. were for England grievous.'

The next Penmaenmawr holiday, in 1859, was much curtailed for Gladstone, who went for just three days to see Catherine and the children there: detained by Cobden's visit to Hawarden, where the commercial treaty with France was hatched, and afterwards to London for a Cabinet on the nature of treaties with France and China – and intense evening meetings with the beguiling M. Summerhayes, including 'a scene of rebuke not easily to be forgotten, 10–1¾'.

On every Penmaenmawr holiday Gladstone valued the sea-bathing for its therapeutic qualities. Some years he recorded in his diary every bathe he took: 'it is a most powerful agent.' In a letter to the Duchess of Sutherland in 1860 he wrote: 'we are exceedingly happy at Penmaenmawr, between Italy, heath, hill and sea all taken together. I do not know if you are acquainted with the Welsh coast and interior; but I am sure you would think it well worth knowing, both for the solitary grandeur of the Snowdon group, and for the widely diffused and almost endless beauty of detail. It is a kind of landscape jewellery.' In 1863 he wrote of the South Stack Lighthouse 'with its grand and savage rocks. They are very remarkable, one part for masses of sheer precipices descending in columns to the sea, the other for the extraordinary contortion which the rocks have undergone from igneous action and huge compressing forces... . The gliding days recall to mind the busy outer world from which we are so well defended.' This is the pre-Cambrian rock so wonderfully exposed on the extreme north-westerly cliffs of Anglesey. As the holiday drew to a close 'bathed 25th and last, finished book III of the Politics of Aristotle with Willy. I must not turn my back upon this place without recording my thanks to God for the health and happiness of our large party during the month of our stay. Read Tacitus. Gems of English Poetry. Off at 2½ for Llanrwst.' This was a walk over the hills of about twenty-five miles. The next day they returned to Hawarden via Denbigh. Once again, in 1867, he reports 'We are nine, all together, and alone.' Sea bathing, hill walking and round games were the order of the day – and 'cricket round the hat with the very young folks'. In 1868, now celebrities, they were 'drawn up by the working men from the station to our house with much enthusiasm'. As usual, on the first evening 'Arranged all my things forthwith and so equipped my little room with its glad sea view.' But the next day 'terrible parcel of letters and papers from Hawarden'. This was his last visit for some years: in December he became Prime Minister.

In 1874 he was back. From the house 'the outline of the hills I think seems even more beautiful than it used.' But by now it was backgammon, not Latin, with Willy; and with young Harry, not cricket round the hat but conversation on his forthcoming career in India. By 1882

Lucy Cavendish was taking the house; but 'the people recognise us and are beyond anything kind'. In October 1896 'we came once more to our old haunt of Penmaenmawr to fortify ourselves against the coming winter; the house, now much more comfortable than ever, has been lent to us by the Darbyshires [his old friends and landlords] and here we may stay until perhaps the second week in November.' He was eighty-four and almost blind. This was the last entry but two in his diary.

2 CHURCH AND POLITICS

Gladstone's first foray into Welsh politics was canvassing for his brother-in-law Stephen Glynne in the Flintshire county election of 1841. The nomination at Flint was 'a tempest from beginning to end'. There was a riot at Mold: 'bribery, faggotry, abduction, personation, riot, factious delays, landlords' intimidation, partiality of authorities; all together, but *faggotry* in particular (the temporary splitting of estates to produce extra votes), have defeated Stephen for the moment.' But Stephen petitioned, and the House found in his favour in May 1842.

In 1843 Gladstone found two reasons to doubt whether he should accept Peel's invitation to join the Cabinet (at the age of thirty-four) as President of the Board of Trade. One reason was his disapproval of the opium wars against China. Peel persuaded him that the Cabinet inherited a situation which they could not entirely undo. The second was the proposal to amalgamate the two ancient dioceses of North Wales, Bangor and St Asaph, in order that a new diocese of Manchester could be established. This proposal had been approved by Parliament in 1836, to take place on the death (bishops died in harness in those days) of the Bishop of St Asaph and had received general support in the Anglican Church. But objections arose locally and then became widespread. There were four very ancient dioceses in Wales, St David's, Llandaff, St Asaph and Bangor, still akin to the old pre-Norman dioceses in England in small essentially rural centres, and all within the Province of Canterbury. This ancient heritage was much valued in Wales. The dioceses had been founded by celebrated Celtic saints long before most of the English dioceses were thought of. Moreover, it had been at St Asaph that the Bible had been translated into Welsh; and although the population of North Wales was not great, the area was. Gladstone, now married into a family living in Flintshire, supported the opposition. Peel was astonished that he should consider it a resignation

[177]

issue. Gladstone's friends Manning and Hope persuaded him that he would not be acting dishonourably if he were a member of a Government whose policy in remote particular instances he disavowed.

When he was Prime Minister, Gladstone had to recommend candidates for consecration as bishops and here we find ambivalent entries in his diary and letters: on the one hand he recorded the end of a 'long and interesting search' to find a suitable Welsh-speaking Bishop of St Asaph; on the other, he complained that Welsh appointments caused him twice as much trouble as English ones, apparently because there was more lobbying from the rank-and-file, and more tiresomeness about particular candidates' suitability. The Anglican Church in Wales had suffered neglect in the past, and in the nineteenth century it paid the penalty in the shape of a huge growth in non-conformity. Some bishops had been absentees, coming perhaps only once to their diocese for a visitation. In the eighteenth century, many were younger sons of good Whig families and the bishop was caricatured as an idle port-drinking grandee. On the other hand, we find the extraordinary energy of the Welsh non-conformist chapel, the scholarship in Old Testament Scripture, the domination of Welsh culture by the minister knowing every individual in his flock and providing education in the Sunday school; all, of course, in the Welsh language. Gladstone recognised this. He carried Irish disestablishment and favoured it in Scotland (where he himself, as an Episcopalian, was a nonconformist), and in principle he came to favour it in Wales. But he did not think the question 'ripe', any more than he thought home rule 'ripe' either in Scotland or in Wales.

One excuse in the case of Wales was that it would be very complicated because the dioceses were within the Province of Canterbury.

Gladstone did not pay much attention either to Welsh nationalism or to disestablishment until Wales as a Liberal stronghold became politically essential to the majorities voting for his later Governments. But this is not to say that he was unsympathetic in principle either to some form of 'home rule' or to disestablishment of the Church. In fact, he favoured both. Disestablishment in Wales would have meant the end of compulsory payment in support of the Church, notably church rates or tithes or their residue in the form of commutations. But any such taxes could have been abolished by a simple Act of Parliament. The nonconformist motivation favouring disestablishment was, no doubt, not only resentment about finance but also to remove the principle that the

Anglican Church was the 'official' Church of the country. The disestablishment of the Church of Ireland had, however, also involved the more or less arbitrary removal of most of the ancient endowments which had been piously donated by past generations for its support, and the even more arbitrary act of allowing the councils of local government to dispose of the income as they thought fit in the support of 'good causes'. It does not appear that nonconformists in Wales had their eyes on this golden egg, to be provided by a process of legalised theft. Gladstone had convinced himself that these endowments were being misapplied, and were likely to be correctly applied under a different regime. He had his eye on other ancient endowments, too, those of schools, and he proposed to redistribute them by his Endowed Schools Act, which was to be administered by a commission with three non-expert members with inadequate administrative support. It achieved almost nothing; the old endowments, mostly very modest, remained where they were instead of being aimlessly whittled away by well-meaning local authorities.

In June 1887 Gladstone accepted the latest of several invitations from Sir Hussey Vivian, soon to be Lord Swansea, to visit Swansea on his return from Hawarden to London for the new session of Parliament. Gladstone's motive was to consolidate the support of Welsh Liberals, in particular for Home Rule for Ireland. Thirty of the thirty-four Welsh MPs were Liberals, some with small majorities, the only notable opposition coming from Cardiff where the corporation was adamantly Unionist. Gladstone needed to convince his supporters that 'the cause of Ireland is the cause of Wales': he was largely addressing the converted. His journey to Swansea was to be used to marshal his forces, and in spite of the inconvenience he was persuaded to travel by the Cambrian and Mid-Wales railways rather than the Great Western. There was plenty of jockeying to get in on the act.

The train ran from Saltney to Wrexham, a familiar stamping-ground, where it seems however that it was Gladstone rather than his supposed audience who got a talking-to, with a strong lecture from the Liberal Association on the right of Wales to be recognised as a nation capable of running its own affairs. The schedule had not included a stop at Newtown; but the MP, Rendel, (one of Gladstone's closest personal supporters whose daughter was to marry Harry Gladstone), with the aid of Arthur Humphreys-Owen (who was to succeed him as MP and who was a director of the Cambrian Railway), soon changed

[179]

that. Not only was a stop arranged at Newtown, but a special platform was erected for the occasion and a crowd of 3,000 sang 'See the conquering hero comes'. So Llanidloes had to have a special platform too; and let off some fog signals in celebration. Then came Talyllyn with an arch of white lilacs; then Merthyr, 'the Jerusalem of Welsh Radicalism', the site of the famous riots of 1841. 'You know what a Welsh crowd is,' said Humphreys-Owen; and 'excited men literally stormed the platform'. Gladstone bowed for ten minutes to the cheering crowd. At Neath, again, there was 'See the conquering hero' and eventually, with Gladstone hoarse and exhausted, the train reached Swansea High Street Station. After a roaring welcome the Gladstones were taken to Vivian's seat at Singleton Abbey in his carriage. The only opposition to be recorded that day was an attempt to part the horses from the vehicle: it was prevented by the police. Friday was a day of rest, with a little tourism, in preparation for Saturday 4 June.

All the coal mines and tin-plate works were closed for a public holiday and sixty special trains delivered Liberals from all over Wales, and even some from Ireland. A procession estimated at between 49,000 and 60,000, marching six deep, took 4 hours and 25 minutes to pass Gladstone, who was wearing a leek in his buttonhole. Then he addressed them for nearly an hour. A deputation consisting of the ex-officers of the Cardiff Liberal Association (who evidently had much support from commercial interests) delivered an address, for which they subsequently received a sharp rap over the knuckles from those of the local press who took the Unionist view. The rivalry between Cardiff and Swansea, the older corporation, which regarded the new capital as an upstart, was intense. However, Gladstone was well received in Cardiff after leaving Swansea, and spoke there to an audience of 3,000 for about an hour.

After the great Swansea procession there was dinner at Singleton for 100 guests, where Gladstone spoke for almost another hour: 'Got through a most difficult business as well as I could expect.' He explained his Home Rule Bill, defeated the previous year, emphasising the flexibility of his current approach to details and making it clear that his main concern was to achieve what the Irish wished. This seems to have been the first time he spoke in public about reversing his proposals of 1886 by including Irish MPs at Westminster, as he was to do in 1893. It was not truly a volte-face, since it was what he had originally suggested.

On Monday Gladstone opened the Free Library – the official

purpose of his visit – and received the Freedom of Swansea, and on Tuesday morning the Gladstones set off for London. After Cardiff there was a succession of processions, hustles and speeches, that at Newport 'in the worst atmosphere known since the Black Hole': crowds impeded the progress of the train. He spoke too at Gloucester and Swindon and arrived at Carlton House Terrace at 6.20: 'It really has been a progress, and an extraordinary one.' This was true; the whole expedition had, indeed, been a triumphal progress: Gladstone's problem was to avoid getting drawn into discussions about his future policy, and above all, to avoid making promises about future legislation – except in general terms for a further attempt to achieve Home Rule for Ireland.

Gladstone remained an indefatigable traveller and speaker after 1887. He spoke (to a crowd of 18,000) in Birmingham in 1888, in Plymouth and the West Country in 1889, with eighteen speeches in Edinburgh and Dundee in 1890, on Clapham Common in 1892 and that year, in his election campaign, in London, Glasgow and Edinburgh. Becoming Prime Minister for the fourth time in August 1892, he toured North Wales in September and made a long-remembered speech on the slopes of Snowdon. The invitation came from Sir Edward Watkin, who had built a large chalet of corrugated iron there as a holiday home, and the tour was orchestrated by Herbert Gladstone and by Tom Ellis, MP for Merioneth, who had campaigned for Home Rule in 1886. Since then the number of Welsh Liberal MPs had increased from 30 to 31 out of 34.

Watkin was a railway entrepreneur who had completed the line to Liverpool from Chester and Wrexham, via Hawarden Bridge and the Mersey Tunnel. Catherine Gladstone had opened the bridge in 1889 and now Watkin was promoting the Channel Tunnel, for which he required Gladstone's support; but when he mentioned the project at his chalet, Gladstone replied with a panegyric on the virtues of the French people. This was appropriate since Watkin, seeking to promote the Tunnel project, had also sponsored Gladstone's visit to Paris in 1889 for the celebrations marking the centenary of the French Revolution. Salisbury's Conservative Government had refused to give the centenary official recognition, so Gladstone as leader of the Opposition went instead. He was anyway recognised as the leading British statesman, and so was accorded official status in France. When he entered the Hippodrome, the performance was stopped and the national anthem played. At the Opera he used the President's box. He went up the Eiffel Tower, attended the exhibitions and spoke when required. He even gave a lecture in French 'after doubting to the last moment' to the Society of Political Economy.

The Snowdon tour began with a special train from Hawarden to Caernarfon on the London and North Western Railway. There Gladstone was greeted by David Lloyd George, who had been elected MP in 1890 and was now twenty-nine years old. Lloyd George had already irritated Gladstone during an excursion to Hawarden with a Methodist party in May 1890. On that occasion he had brashly attempted to wring a promise from Gladstone to disestablish the Church in Wales. When he refused, to the evident annoyance of Catherine, their hostess, to accept Gladstone's response that prudence, moderation and unanimity were requisite, Gladstone put him down in no uncertain terms by pointing out that, contrary to Lloyd George's attempt to enlist history on his side, non-conformity was a comparatively recent phenomenon. 'Since you set yourself up as the champion of Welsh non-conformity, perhaps you can tell me how many non-conformist chapels there were in Wales in 1742?' Lloyd George was obliged to admit that he did not know. 'Well, I do,' said Gladstone. The young member for Caernarfon was silenced; but this did not prevent the address presented to Gladstone in Caernarvon two years later from requesting disestablishment. Here Lloyd George obliged Gladstone to make two speeches, 'by which I was cheated of the castle', before the train set off on the narrow gauge Highland Railway to Rhyd-ddu. The observation car in which Gladstone travelled has been recently restored and renamed after him. The party completed the journey to the chalet by horse-drawn carriage.

The avowed purpose of the visit was for the Prime Minister to open the Watkin path. But there is no mention of this in the press accounts of the expedition that recorded Gladstone's speech the next day from a specially erected platform on a great rock, ever since known as the 'Gladstone Rock', and furnished with a plaque recording the occasion. The script for the plaque was handed by Watkin to Tom Ellis who translated it into Welsh and placed the Welsh version above the English, thus ensuring its survival to this day. The holes for the bolts securing the platform can still be found by the connoisseur. It appears that Gladstone had not been forewarned that he would be obliged to make a political speech: 'I had to address 2,000 *malgré moi*,' he wrote. He spoke of the nationhood of Wales, and although he was also obliged to touch on 'the land question', meaning the agricultural depression, he managed to satisfy his audience well enough. Welsh farmers, concentrating on livestock, were not suffering as badly as English ones from imports of cheap prairie wheat.

A photograph shows a sea of bowler hats; not a single cloth cap is to be seen. At the big Hawarden gatherings the numbers were about equal; but one could get there on an excursion train for a few pence. It was perhaps therefore not entirely easy to satisfy those present with generalisations and platitudes. Gladstone seems to have succeeded in doing so, but William George, David's brother, shrewdly noted that 'he managed to say very little of what we expected him to say'. The hymn singing, before and after, was warmly reported, not least by Gladstone himself: 'I heard *noble* music.'

David Lloyd George hesitated before joining the carefully posed group photograph taken outside the chalet. Perhaps not invited by Watkin but urged by the photographer, he stood about a yard apart on the right (the left in the photograph), wearing a homburg hat. He was then brushed out of the photograph, perhaps at the instance of the press editor, but his hat defeated the photographer's skill and can still be seen. The next stage, in providing the photograph for the fine album of the tour, of which a copy was presented to Gladstone, was to cut out Lloyd George altogether and to enlarge the remainder of the print to the appropriate size. The camera never lies, but the editor's task is to edit.

The following day the party from the chalet ascended the Watkin path. Gladstone went some of the way on a pony and then climbed about 1,000 ft on foot. The next day the Gladstones enjoyed a 'lovely drive to Port Madoc' and then went to Barmouth by special train ('there seized for a speech, say 20m') to stay for a week at the Marine Hotel.

It may seem strange that the octogenarian Premier could take a holiday the month after he had taken office, but the Gladstones no doubt wished to 'fortify themselves against the winter' by means of a Welsh seaside holiday. In fact Gladstone wrote a number of memoranda to his new Cabinet, some of them quite elaborate: to Kimberley, Indian Secretary, about the need for a professional financier on the Viceroy's Council; to Ripon, Colonial Secretary, about the Governor-Generalship of Canada; to Rosebery, Foreign Secretary, briefly on Egypt and three times in detail on Uganda (he had no map in Barmouth: was it ninety days, or seventy, or even sixty, from Mombasa to Uganda?); and on 'zones of influence' and the need for Rosebery to look up the history. Gladstone recollected the occasion when the Czar had conceded a point on some region ('Was it Badakshan?' he asked) on the grounds that the British had a better idea of where it was than he did. There was a short memorandum to Asquith, Home Secretary, about the Queen striking out a number of names from Gladstone's list of knighthoods; one to Morley (Irish Secretary) about the most appropriate legal forum for evicted tenants, and one to Harcourt, Chancellor of the Exchequer, on the cost of the Uganda evacuation and the arguments for a silver standard rather than a gold standard. There was a memorandum to Sir C. Russell, Attorney-General, about Church patronage and the Parnell case, and one to a civil servant, Rivers-Wilson, comptroller of the National Debt Office, about the management of the debt. Finally, there is a letter to Andrew Carnegie, a great admirer, thanking him for his congratulations on the Premiership and praising him for his good example on the proper use of wealth: wealth, says Gladstone, is 'at present like a monster threatening to swallow up the moral life of man'. So the week at Barmouth was not wholly recreational. In October, after much preparation, he delivered the inaugural Romanes Lecture at Oxford on Medieval Universities; thus, as at Barmouth, he was still not entirely preoccupied by Prime Ministerial duties. The Snowdonia tour was, however, the last programme of its kind that he undertook. His public appearances in Wales thereafter were on his home ground at Hawarden, and were non-political in character.

Index

between him and WEG, reconciled in 1874, 114

Gladstone, Thomas, WEG's grandfather, 21, 113

Gladstone, William Ewart, author's introductory appraisal, 9–10; and biographer John Morley (q.v.), 10–11; diaries, 11–12, 25, 32, 58, 60, 68; chronology of life, 13–19; and Homer, 28, 128–34; Liverpool connections, 21–4; at Eton, 25–9; at Oxford: undergraduate at Christ Church, 30–3, MP for University of Oxford, 33–4, 35, elected again 1848, 71; and classics, 28, 30–1, 33; portraits of, 37–8; travels in Europe, 39; maiden speech, 40; Under-Secretary for War and the Colonies, 40; speech on West Indies plantations, 40–1; and Sir Robert Peel, 42–52; and railways, 46–8; Bank Charter Act, 48; Companies Act of 1862, 49–50; and Disraeli's 1852 Budget, 54–8; Budget of 1853, 59–65, Budget of 1854, 67–9; emergence as 'The People's William' 1859, 70, 166; visits to Italy, 71, 95; Corfu, 72; work with prostitutes, 72–3; and Hawarden, 75–83; physical exertions, 78–9; voracious reader and prolific author, 79–80; and St Deiniol's Library, 82–3; Budgets of the 1860s, 84–91; 'What Did Mr Gladstone Say in 1864?', 91–4; his visits to Italy, 71, 95; and Garibaldi, 97–100; first ministry, 101–12; Disestablishment Act, 103; Land Act, 103–5; at Balmoral 1869, 105; attitude to nonconformists, 108; enjoyment of wine, 109; reluctance to trim sails, 109; agrees to pay damages in *Alabama* case, 111; defeated over Irish University Bill, resigns, 112; and Fasque, 113, 114; political differences with brother Tom, 114; and foundation of Glenalmond College, 114; and visits to Scotland, 115–16; pamphlet on Bulgaria, 116; Rector of Glasgow University, 116, 117–18; political campaigning, 116–18; religious convictions, 120–7; and Lyon Playfair, 124–5; and Eastern Question, 135–41; *Bulgarian Horrors* pamphlet quoted, 137–8; wins election of 1880, 142; and Ireland, 142–54; Prime Minister for third time, 150; his political inclinations evaluated, 155–74; his four 'doctors', 156; guest on *Tantallon Castle*, intimations of war with Kaiser's Germany, 165; how radical?, 166–8; relationship with Queen Victoria, 169–74; and Wales, first visits at age of fifteen, 175; Penmaenmawr holidays, 175–7; sea-bathing, 176; speech-making tour, 179–81; visit to Paris, 181–2; Snowdon tour, 182–3; memoranda to new Cabinet members, 183–4

Gladstone, William (Willy), WEG's eldest son, 77, 80, 175, 176; death of, 81

Glasgow University, 116, 117–18